Love and the Postmodern
Predicament

VERITAS
Series Introduction

"... the truth will set you free" (John 8:32)

In much contemporary discourse, Pilate's question has been taken to mark the absolute boundary of human thought. Beyond this boundary, it is often suggested, is an intellectual hinterland into which we must not venture. This terrain is an agnosticism of thought: because truth cannot be possessed, it must not be spoken. Thus, it is argued that the defenders of "truth" in our day are often traffickers in ideology, merchants of counterfeits, or anti-liberal. They are, because it is somewhat taken for granted that Nietzsche's word is final: truth is the domain of tyranny.

Is this indeed the case, or might another vision of truth offer itself? The ancient Greeks named the love of wisdom as *philia*, or friendship. The one who would become wise, they argued, would be a "friend of truth." For both philosophy and theology might be conceived as schools in the friendship of truth, as a kind of relation. For like friendship, truth is as much discovered as it is made. If truth is then so elusive, if its domain is *terra incognita*, perhaps this is because it arrives to us—unannounced—as gift, as a person, and not some thing.

The aim of the Veritas book series is to publish incisive and original current scholarly work that inhabits "the between" and "the beyond" of theology and philosophy. These volumes will all share a common aspiration to transcend the institutional divorce in which these two disciplines often find themselves, and to engage questions of pressing concern to both philosophers and theologians in such a way as to reinvigorate both disciplines with a kind of interdisciplinary desire, often so absent in contemporary academe. In a word, these volumes represent collective efforts in the befriending of truth, doing so beyond the simulacra of pretend tolerance, the violent, yet insipid reasoning of liberalism that asks with Pilate, "What is truth?"—expecting a consensus of non-commitment; one that encourages the commodification of the mind, now sedated by the civil service of career, ministered by the frightened patrons of position.

The series will therefore consist of two "wings": (1) original monographs; and (2) essay collections on a range of topics in theology and philosophy. The latter will principally be the products of the annual conferences of the Centre of Theology and Philosophy (www.theologyphilosophycentre .co.uk).

Conor Cunningham and Eric Austin Lee, *Series editors*

Love and the Postmodern Predicament

Rediscovering the Real in Beauty, Goodness, and Truth

D. C. SCHINDLER

CASCADE *Books* · Eugene, Oregon

LOVE AND THE POSTMODERN PREDICAMENT
Rediscovering the Real in Beauty, Goodness, and Truth

Veritas 28

Cascade Books
An Imprint of Wipf and Stock Publishers
199 W. 8th Ave., Suite 3
Eugene, OR 97401

www.wipfandstock.com

PAPERBACK ISBN: 978-1-5326-4873-1
HARDCOVER ISBN: 978-1-5326-4874-8
EBOOK ISBN: 978-1-5326-4875-5

Cataloguing-in-Publication data:

Names: Schindler, D. C.
Title: Love and the postmodern predicament : rediscovering the real in beauty, goodness, and truth / D. C. Schindler.
Description: Eugene, OR: Cascade Books, 2018 | Veritas 28 | Includes bibliographical references and index.
Identifiers: ISBN 978-1-5326-4873-1 (paperback) | ISBN 978-1-5326-4874-8 (hardcover) | ISBN 978-1-5326-4875-5 (ebook)
Subjects: LCSH: Metaphysics | Good and evil | Truth | Reason | Aesthetics—Religious aspects | Philosophical theology | God | Postmodernism | Philosophical anthropology | Love—Religious aspects—Christianity
Classification: B171 S35 2018 (print) | B171 (ebook)

05/08/18

Contents

Preface

The present book offers the outlines for a basic philosophical anthropology, drawn from themes in classical metaphysics, which are retrieved in response to what is evidently a crisis in contemporary existence. The crisis can be described in simple terms as a loss of a sense of reality, which inevitably entails as its counterpart a dissolution of the self. If it is true, as Robert Spaemann has argued so beautifully in *Happiness and Benevolence*, that love is an awakening to the reality of both the other and the self at once, then love promises to offer a way beyond our "postmodern predicament." In contrast to the typical reduction of love to a mere emotion, or an act of the will, or perhaps just a biological function, the book aims to rethink love in relation to beauty, goodness, and truth, understood as "transcendental properties" of being. A secondary purpose of the book is, thus, to offer an apologia for the continuing importance of philosophy (and especially metaphysics) in the face of the anti-intellectual currents of modernity.

Though it assumes an interest in philosophy, and a general familiarity especially with the classical tradition, the book is not addressed first of all to professional academics, but hopes to reach a wider audience. It should be pointed out, nevertheless, that Part II of this book (chapters 5 and 6) enters into more sophisticated areas, which was necessary in order to deepen the philosophical background of the matters presented in Part I. The discussion there thus presupposes more technical knowledge, but I have attempted to present the material as clearly and as simply as I could. There is also a glossary of Latin terms at the back of the book for those unfamiliar with Latin. The general hope is to invite readers more deeply *into* the tradition.

Four of this book's chapters first entered existence as part of two miniseries of lectures, which I was honored to have been invited to deliver at Geneva College (chapters 3 and 4) on March 25–26 of 2015, and at Hillsdale College (chapters 2 and 7) on March 2–3 of 2016. I wish to express my gratitude to Esther Lightcap Meek and Robert M. Frazier for organizing the "Bitar Lectures" at Geneva (and to the Bitar family for making the series possible), and to Lee Cole for inviting me and arranging my visit to Hillsdale. Discussions with them, and their colleagues (let me mention in particular Matthew Gaetano, Dwight Lindley, Jeffrey Lehman, Jordan Wales, and President Larry P. Arnn, at Hillsdale), have contributed greatly to my understanding of the ideas contained in this book. I wish especially to acknowledge the helpful comments from J. J. Sanford, who was invited to respond to my lectures at Geneva. The invitation enabled J. J. and me to pick up a philosophical conversation that had lain dormant for more than twenty-five years. As we balanced precariously on scaffolding painting houses for summer employment, J. J. and I discussed at length the endlessly fascinating figure of Socrates. Neither of us knew then that we were talking about what would become our life's work. As, in part, an apologia for the importance of philosophy, this book may be seen as a very distant fruit of those youthful meditations. Chapter 7 appeared originally in *Communio* as "'Unless You Become a Philosopher . . .': On God, Being, and Reason's Role in Faith," *Communio* 43.1 (2016) 83–103. Finally, I would like to thank the staff at Wipf and Stock for their gracious help in bringing this book to publication. Editor Robin A. Parry was especially generous with his time and expertise through the many stages of production.

Abbreviations

I Sent.	Aquinas, *Scriptum super Sententiis*. Volume 1
III Sent.	Aquinas, *Scriptum super Sententiis*. Volume 3
De caritate	Aquinas, *Quaestiones disputatae De virtutibus*
De malo	Aquinas, *Quaestiones disputate De malo*
De pot.	Aquinas, *Quaestiones disputatae De potentia*
De ver.	Aquinas, *Quaestiones disputate De veritate*
In Boeth. de Hebdom.	Aquinas, *Exposito Libri Boetii De hebdomadibus*
In. div. nom.	Aquinas, *Super Librum Dionysii De divinis nominibus*
NE	Aristotle, *Nichomachean Ethics*
SCG	Aquinas, *Summa Contra Gentiles*
ST	Aquinas, *Summa Theologiae*

Introduction

Renewing the Tradition

Aristotle begins his *Metaphysics* with a sentence that is as familiar as any in philosophy: "All men by nature desire to know." It is so familiar, no doubt, because people for generation after generation have reaffirmed it as formulating something both true and of fundamental importance. The desire to know is perhaps man's most distinctively human desire—and so the cultivation of this desire is one of our most crucial cultural tasks.

The evidence that Aristotle offers for his statement is the delight we take in our senses. It is not immediately obvious, however, why this delight should serve to show that we possess a native desire for knowledge. What does the enjoyment of a certain bright yellow, or the smooth, cool feel of silk, for instance, have to do with our understanding of things? If we wanted knowledge in this case, someone might observe, we would attempt to explain *why* we experience color the way we do, or how our nerves communicate the contact that occurs between our skin and the fabric to a controlling center of our brain, but none of this would seem to have anything to do with the actual sensation itself, much less any delight in it. This observation, however, betrays a concept of knowledge profoundly different from the one Aristotle takes for granted, a difference it will be one of the aims of this present book to explore. To get a sense of his conception of knowledge, we ought to reflect for a moment on the word just used to describe the event that occasioned the sense of touch: *contact*. Whatever the physiological mechanisms might be through which sense experience occurs, what it *is*, most fundamentally, is a direct encounter with things in the world we inhabit. In sense experience, *we make contact with reality*. To put the matter more poetically, perhaps, we might say that the senses are the five gateways through which reality enters into one's soul. For Aristotle, we can draw an inference about why we know from our experience of sensation because both knowing and sensing are forms of contact with the real.

To observe, then, that we take not just pleasure but *delight* in sense experience is to indicate that we enjoy this contact *in itself, for its own sake,* and not merely for the various benefits it may bring. If it is indeed the case that the senses are the gateway of the real, this delight means that there is something fundamentally good about this encounter with the world, about the mere fact of our coming face-to-face, so to speak, with things that are "other," things that are different from us. In this sense, the desire for knowledge is at root a desire for this intimacy with the world. To say, moreover, that this desire arises from our nature, to say, that is, that this desire is a fundamental part of what makes us human, is to say that we are made for this contact: encountering reality is a basic part of the meaning of human existence.

One of the things that specifies modern culture, however, and distinguishes it from the traditional cultures of the world, is the effort to buffer this encounter. Modern culture is largely a conspiracy to protect us from the real. Though it has opened up horizons in all sorts of ways that would have been utterly inconceivable to the pre-modern world, it does so only under controlled conditions. We do not at all deny the delight we take in our senses—in fact, we indulge them—but we try as far as possible to *isolate* these experiences, to make them *mere* sensations and precisely *not* gateways to the real. The ideal, perhaps aimed at asymptotically, is "virtual reality," having the sensation without any contact with the real at all, and so without genuine involvement or responsibility for implications. We mediate our encounter with the world as far as possible through technology, which is said to "enhance" it in various ways, but technology in fact always sets the terms for our encounter, and so in subtle but profound ways determines what we can experience. It gives our experiences a particular shape and character. Our experiences are thus largely "pre-planned" affairs, moderated in a manner that gives us some control over possible consequences. And for those consequences that we cannot possibly anticipate, we take out insurance policies. Or, if these are unavailable, we can take some consolation in the notion that we have the power, in principle, to sue.[1] We encourage, more than any other culture in history no doubt, a stepping out of our "comfort zone," an exploration of other cultures and ways of thinking different from our own. But all of this falls under the wholly modern category of "diversity," a category that, in its complete relativizing of all identities, and therefore all differences, simply would not make sense to any culture outside of the

---

1. We witness this phenomenon in the tendency to blame the government above all for natural disasters. The presupposition is that the whole point of civilization is to make us *safe,* and that this project is somehow under the deliberate control of particular individuals.

modern West. "Diversity" is like a guided-tour package for the realm beyond our "comfort zone." In short, the energies of the modern world are
largely devoted to keeping reality at bay, monitoring any encounter with
what is genuinely other than ourselves, and protecting us from possible
consequences, intended or otherwise.

If all men by nature desire to know, however, then this project is radically anti-human. The purpose of the present book, in the face of this project, which we are increasingly taking for granted as something altogether
normal, is to recall a pre-modern vision of man as ordered to communion
with reality. To the Greek insight that man is made to know, we ought to
add the biblical claim that man is created to till the garden, and to "be fruitful and multiply": our purpose is not only to know reality, but to involve
ourselves in cultivating and caring for it, to encounter the world, and indeed
each other, in a way that bears—always in some respects unexpected—fruit.

We pursue the aim of recollecting this pre-modern vision of man here
principally through an exploration of three of the traditional "transcendental properties of being," namely, beauty, goodness, and truth, each of which
we interpret as characterizing a special form of man's encounter with reality.[2] In beauty, reality first presents itself to man in a way that awakens his
desire and intellectual capacities; the delight we have in our senses, which
manifests our desire to know, is in fact a description of the experience of
beauty. In goodness, man pursues the real, engaging in the free action that
is inescapably a kind of gift of self, an involvement of his person with what
is other than himself. In truth, he "becomes what he knows"; he identifies
himself, in a certain respect, with what he comes to understand, taking it
into his very being. All of this, the book will try to show, is best understood
as an expression of love, which is interpreted as a kind of unity we share
with all things by virtue of creation, a "given" relationship that precedes
our deliberate acts of intellect and will in such a way as to give these acts
substance, or genuine ontological depth. The book begins and ends with an
apologia for philosophy, interpreted here precisely as *an all-encompassing
love of the real*, a love that is only deepened by Christian faith.

Though this book is meant to be most basically a recollection of the
classical tradition regarding the meaning of man, it is worth pointing out
two dimensions of the argument that represent relative novelties with
respect to that tradition, or at least apparent ones. First, the order of the

2. In *De ver.* 1.1., where Aquinas unfolds the different transcendental properties
and explains their relation to each other, he presents truth and goodness as the properties that being has specifically in its relation to the human soul. Beauty is typically
grouped with these two, though, for reasons we will discuss later, Aquinas does not
himself include it in this particular exposition.

4 Love and the Postmodern Predicament

transcendentals. In the Thomistic tradition, it is understood that the appetite always follows upon apprehension, which means that, for man specifically, the will is always subordinate to the intellect in its activity. Thus, in discussions of the transcendentals in this tradition, goodness, the object of the will, typically comes after the truth, which is the object of the intellect. We, however, present goodness before truth, both of which are preceded by the beautiful (which, if it is addressed in the Thomistic tradition, usually comes last, as a sort of "crowning" of the whole). We do so, however, not in the least to privilege a kind of "Franciscan" voluntarism over against Thomistic intellectualism.[3] In fact, we reverse the typical sequence precisely in order to avoid any voluntarism. It is not possible, here, to lay out a full argument on this matter, but we observe that one cannot place truth before goodness without placing goodness after truth—which has the tendency, however unintended, to instrumentalize knowledge to action, or in other words, to promote an essentially pragmatic conception of truth. This tendency is exacerbated in the contemporary culture, which permits understanding only to the extent that it produces practical results: the important thing is not in the end what we know but what we *do* with our knowledge. In the following, we offer beauty as a cognitive grasp, an apprehension, that precedes and so in a basic sense guides, informs, and governs appetite, which is the role traditional Thomism gives to the intellectual grasp of the truth. Because we have thus already affirmed an apprehension prior to appetite, we are free to *end* with truth, with an understanding of reality as the final fruit of our genuine involvement with it. Thus, if we appear to invert the more classical order of the transcendentals, it is only in order more fundamentally to secure the *ultimacy of contemplation* that lies at the core of the classical conception of man.

Second, and closely related to the first point, in the interpretation of human nature we offer here, we give an absolute priority to *love*. This seems to run counter to the classical conception of man as, above all, a creature of *reason*: man, according to this conception, is the ζῷον λογικόν, the animal with "logos," and the soul that constitutes human nature is essentially intellectual.[4] To emphasize love would seem to elevate the will above reason, and just so far to depart from the classical tradition, though some might think such a departure is in any event demanded by the novelty introduced by

3. Voluntarism is a school of thought that gives priority to the will in human psychology over intellect or desire, that is, over anything that might ground the will in reason or purpose. In its extreme forms, voluntarism thus tends to conceive the will and its freedom in purely arbitrary and irrational terms.

4. Aristotle describes man as possessing reason of his essence in *NE* I.13; Aquinas defines the human soul as an essentially *intellectual* principle in *ST* 1.75.2.

Christian revelation, a novelty that the Catholic tradition has not always sufficiently recognized.[5] The argument of this book, however, is that the classical tradition is central to Christianity and that the faith entails not a relativizing of that tradition but a more radical reception of it. As we will explain, love is best understood not merely as an act of will, in contrast to the act of the intellect, but rather as an ontological unity, *within which* we properly will and understand. From this perspective, the operation of *both* the will and the intellect can be understood in different ways as acts of love. The privileging of love, in this case, will turn out to be a way of preserving the full integrity of the orders of goodness and truth, as different modes of the revelation of being. There is thus no voluntarism or emotivism implied by the fundamental importance given to love in these pages. On the contrary, the point is to acknowledge the significance of reason more than we are accustomed to do in the modern world.

In a word, this book takes as a guiding presupposition that Christians are called in a special way to be guardians of the classical tradition. As the monks did in the chaos of the barbarian invasions of the "dark ages," so too must we hold on to the things that make us human in the face of the various forces that seek, if not to destroy them, at least to bury them. What is different now is that the barbarians have become the regulators of society, not threats to the common culture, but the very purveyors of it. Because this invasion is an apparently more peaceful one on the surface, because it is more insipid and more penetrating, our fidelity to the call to guardianship, the call to be true to our human nature, requires a more conscious and vigilant formation. In this respect, philosophy, the cultivation of our natural desire *really* to know, is perhaps more important now than it ever has been.

---

5. In what has come to be known as the "Regensburg Address," Pope Benedict XVI explained the importance of the encounter between biblical faith and Greek philosophy, and described the subsequent misguided movements in Christianity to "purify" the faith by attempting to remove the influence of philosophy: "Faith, Reason and the University: Memories and Reflections," 12 September 2006.

PART I

Reality and the Transcendentals

1

Philosophy, the Transcendentals, and Reality

1. The Impossible Grass, and Our Bourgeois Metaphysics

At the end of his collection of essays entitled *Heretics*, G. K. Chesterton prophesies that the most common sense truths will turn into creeds requiring the fidelity and courage of martyrs to proclaim in the face of the "great march of mental destruction" that is modernity.[1] In the concluding paragraph, his tone climbs to an almost fevered pitch, so that one might worry he is overstating his case, even as one admires his genius:

> Fires will be kindled to testify that two and two make four. Swords will be drawn to prove that leaves are green in summer. We shall be left defending, not only the incredible virtues and sanities of human life, but something more incredible still, this huge impossible universe which stares us in the face. We shall fight for visible prodigies as if they were invisible. We shall look on the impossible grass and the skies with a strange courage. We shall be of those who have seen and yet have believed.[2]

Blessed are those who believe *even though* they have seen with their very own eyes! A century ago, such a declaration would no doubt have appeared as a comical exaggeration, cleverly employed to make a point. Today, however, we read this passage with a dawning suspicion that Chesterton may have been entirely serious. For a host of reasons we will be exploring, we have been learning to deny the obvious as a matter of course.[3] It is not

1. G. K. Chesterton, *Heretics*, 305.

2. Ibid.

3. As a mini social experiment, a Caucasian man, of average height, ventured onto a college campus in order to ask some students at random how they would respond if he told them he was a Chinese woman, six-foot-five, and seven years old. The results are both astonishing, and altogether predictable: https://www.youtube.com/

only that we have become accustomed to deny in public—for the camera, as it were—things that we know to be true, which is evident enough. But we have begun not even to recognize that we know them as true; the camera has become our most intimate conscience, which is to say that it has insinuated itself not only between us and the world, but between us and ourselves. The "Father who sees in secret" has not only been replaced by "Big Brother," with his extensive system of surveillance, but even "Big Brother" has ceded his place, in trusting confidence, to each person's super ego. We feel that we are betraying something if we admit to certain straightforward truths that are simply there for anyone to behold.

There is no need to offer examples of this self-policing in the matters that revolve around the extremely charged theme of identity politics, and especially at the moment that which concerns gender. But Chesterton's text suggests that this controversy, however abruptly it may have entered the scene just yesterday, is not a strange novelty. Rather, it is arguably the implication of a disposition, the inexorable working out of a logic that has deep roots. Chesterton identifies this logic as modern skepticism, a general reluctance to admit anything as definitively true. Skepticism itself is, of course, not an exclusively modern phenomenon; the ancient Greek world was well acquainted with eccentric individuals who sought to break radically with conventional beliefs, and through rigorous training to learn to suspend any and every judgment so as to achieve a perfectly undisturbed tranquility of mind, or absolute equanimity. It is just this point, however, that sets into relief what is distinctive about *modern* skepticism: this more recent version tends not to be the result of rigorous training, unless we would use that phrase to characterize the normal program of public education, and it is not so much a break with conventional belief as a standard expression of it. The modern skeptic is not the heroic individual, but the everyday "person in the street." The skeptical "suspension of judgment" is not an extraordinary judgment, the fruit of long ascetic discipline, but has become the "default" frame of mind of contemporary people.

Now, Chesterton is quick to point out the deep inconsistencies in this frame of mind. Though it evinces a reluctance to affirm any definitive truth, it is quite definitive about *its own* truth, so much so that we have to recognize modern skepticism as *dogmatic* in spite of itself, since it rules out any opposing view *a priori*: "It is the vague modern who is not at all certain what is right who is most certain that Dante was wrong."[4] There is a humorous self-contradiction in this, but it is important to recognize that this is not

watch?v=xfO1veFs6Ho.

4. Ibid., 295.

a typical one, the simultaneous assertion and denial of a particular claim. Instead, it is a contradiction that goes to the core of what it means to be human; if man is defined as the animal with logos (speech or reason), then this confusion represents man's contradiction of his very humanity, which is why Plato, for example, characterized this loss of faith in reason—which he called "misology" (literally, the "contempt for reason")—the worst thing that can befall a human being.[5] But any denial of reason never gets rid of the contradiction, since we cannot help but affirm reason at the same time. As Chesterton goes on to show, quite irrefutably, it is simply impossible to be a human being, to put any two thoughts together, to express any preference for anything at all, without presupposing a philosophical vision about the nature of reality, the nature, therefore, of the Creator of reality, and so in inevitably quite concrete ways what it means to be a human being: "Every man in the street must hold a metaphysical system, and hold it firmly."[6] Even if one hates reason, one will always do so as "an animal with logos," and one cannot be such an animal without "holding a metaphysical system," however unconsciously or unwillingly. It is therefore in the end never a question of *whether* one has a metaphysics, but only whether one's metaphysics is *adequate*.

Adequate *to what?* This is, of course, the decisive question, but we will leave it to the side for the moment. In order to say anything meaningful in response, beyond what might seem a facile truism—"adequate to *reality*"—we need to reflect in more depth on the problem that Chesterton is presenting here. The problem turns out to be, in fact, much more subtle and profound than it initially appears. One might get the impression that the traditional quarrel between the ancients and the moderns that Chesterton invokes here by criticizing "the modern" is a contest between two metaphysical systems, the claims of which might in principle be placed side by side and compared, so that a judgment could be reached about which is the right one. While it is certainly true that there are different metaphysical systems at issue, the contest is a very peculiar one in this case, because the difference is so radical: it is sort of like a contest—if such a thing could even be imagined—between an American football team and a British football team. Not only are the rules governing the two teams incommensurate, and not only is the ground under their feet different, but the very projectile around which the game turns is an equivocation. How would one determine, in such a contest, which is the better team? In the contest between the ancients

5. Plato, *Phaedo* 89d. It is interesting to note that, in this dialogue, Socrates also presents an argument against suicide (see 62aff.). Misology might be seen as the suicide of human nature, and not just a particular man.

6. Chesterton, *Heretics*, 301.

and the moderns, a metaphysics has been challenged by a *non*-metaphysics, or rather, since there can be no challenge where there is no common playing field at all, as it were, we have to say instead that the pre-modern metaphysics has simply been *supplanted*, in the etymological sense of the word: the ground has been taken out from under it, so that it is left in a sense floating in the air. In this respect, it has been effectively neutralized, and so there ceases to be any need to challenge it, much less replace it by another metaphysics.

This point requires more explanation. Chesterton said that "swords will be drawn to prove that leaves are green." One might object, in response, that this is ridiculous: no one denies that leaves are green. If anyone denies some other traditional "truth"—for example, that one's sex determines one's gender and whom one is capable of taking in marriage—it is because he believes there is something real at stake here, namely, the possible happiness of many concrete individual human beings. But there is nothing comparable at stake in the question of the color of leaves. So there is no one who cares to deny it.

This is a revealing objection: note that the reason offered here for the willingness to accept that leaves are green is that it does not really matter one way or the other, which is to say that it (apparently) does not immediately bear on the desires of concrete individuals. In other words, we may be willing to admit the truth that leaves are green, *but not strictly because it is true.* In fact, were we pressed on this point, we would very quickly grow uncomfortable. To say that this claim is "true" sounds "absolutist." If we were presented with another person who passionately declared that it is *not* true, even if it "seemed" so to us, we would be inclined to recognize the right of others to think otherwise: How in the world can we know, after all, what color leaves might seem to someone else, perhaps from a radically different background from our own? How do we know that we don't all perceive different colors, but have just learned to use the same name for these different perceptions? In making this concession, we ask only in return that these others, who see things differently, recognize our "right" to perceive leaves as green. This is what was meant earlier by saying the old metaphysics is left suspended in the air: we moderns continue to say, perhaps, that it is "true" that leaves are green, just as the ancients did, but everything is now different. The meaning of "true" is no longer the same—not to mention the meaning of "leaves" and of "green." In fact, the very nature of words has been transformed, since they no longer serve to make manifest what is, but instead have become mere instruments for the expression of subjective judgments, the personal content of individual minds. In short, "meaning" now *means* something different, and the very act by which it means this different thing is not the same. We are thus talking about as radical a change as can be imagined.

To be sure, the reasons one might offer to justify doubt regarding the truth *qua truth* of the greenness of leaves are not without some purchase. The ultimately rhetorical worry that we have just learned to use the same word for what is a different experience for every individual may have something Alice-in-Wonderlandish about it, but there are more "scientific" possibilities.[7] One could, for example, point to the physical components of the event of perception, the reflection and absorption of certain frequencies of light waves, the stimulation of retinal nerves, and so forth, and say that *these* are the reality of which the subjective seeing of green is simply an epiphenomenon. One might ask, then, what it actually means in fact to call the perception of green *true*, and indeed what it means, really, in the end to call anything "True," with quotation marks and a capital T. What is gained by putting this additional "label" on a generally recognized fact, especially if there is no one intent on challenging it?

Whether there might be a genuinely serious question in any of this is not our concern at the moment. We will return to this issue when we discuss truth in chapter 4. The principal point here is that these sorts of questions are rarely raised in a serious manner—that is, as questions to which there may in fact be a real response, questions that ought to be studied, given the real dignity of a careful discernment and final judgment. Instead, in most instances, they are raised principally to *deflect* the question of truth, or in any event *to deflate* it, in a manner that is similar to the therapy proposed by the ancient Hedonists: Epicurus offered a variety of possible scientific theories to explain certain meteorological events that had a tendency to instill awe and fear of the gods in the common man, not in order to come to any insight into the truth, but simply to relieve the anxiety that seems inevitably to be entailed by a belief in the gods. There was no effort to test any particular theory; the point was simply to offer sufficiently plausible alternatives to conventional belief to relax the gods' hold on the mind. If

7. It is nevertheless disturbing how common these sorts of proposals are becoming in high-level physics: we are all just characters in a cosmic video game, and so forth. It seems as if we have learned to take for granted that "theoretical" physics needs to have no correspondence whatsoever with our normal experience of the world and have, perhaps for that very reason, come to give it a certain untouchable license to pronounce on the nature of things. The actuality of the real seems to have lost all spontaneous authority, so that any model, no matter how preposterous, is equally plausible, as long as it can demonstrate mathematical consistency. In this, we hear an echo of late medieval nominalism, which detached possibility from any intrinsic relation to actuality, and therefore accepted only the most formal limitation: anything is possible that is not logically self-contradictory.

a child is frightened by a noise in the closet that he thinks was caused by a ghost, we calm him down by proposing a number of other, perfectly reasonable explanations. Our aim is not principally to discover the actual truth of the matter, but simply to relieve his fears. Similarly, doubts about the content of a particular truth claim, no matter what the claim might happen to be, are often raised not to open up a genuine line of inquiry but simply to neutralize the truth-quality of the claim. If a person asks in an argument, "How are we supposed to know what's true?" he would be astonished to receive in response a detailed description of the way the mind achieves knowledge, because questions such as these are not meant as invitations for reflection and considered response. Typically, these questions are raised instead *just enough* to force one's "grip" open, just enough to undermine strong conviction, just enough to persuade one to leave off wondering and worrying about whether the claim might be true.

Why might this neutralizing of truth claims be desirable? The point seems to be, above all, not to *deny* any particular truth claim outright, in the sense of taking a definitive position on the matter ("It is *absolutely not the case* that leaves are green, and anyone who says that they are is therefore wrong."), but, just the opposite, to avoid taking an inflexible stand on one side of the question or the other. We want to allow a particular claim to be true, but only "as far as it goes," and as long as this does not exclude the possibility of someone else taking a different view of the matter.[8] Gianni Vattimo, the Italian philosopher-cum-politician, has advocated *irony* as the proper stance of citizens in the modern world: democracy works, he believes (ironically?), if we are sufficiently detached from our convictions to be capable of genuine tolerance of others, whose convictions may be different from our own.[9] Such a stance is what Charles Péguy took a century ago to be the essence of modernity. According to him, to be modern means "not to believe what one believes."[10] Along these lines, we might think of the status of truth claims in terms of the so-called "right to privacy," as analogous, that

8. Just a few days ago, the head of the FBI explained the Bureau's decision that no crime was committed in Hillary Clinton's use of a private email account to conduct official business. He said in response to a question at the congressional hearing, "That's just the way it is. Folks can disagree about it." What a bizarre statement! These two claims contradict each other, and yet they tend not to strike anyone that way: to say "that's just the way it is" means that this is a true fact, regardless of what anyone might think. To say "folks can disagree about it" means that whether it is true or not is debatable. He is thus "pretending" to allow people to form their own opinions on the matter, regardless of what those opinions happen to be, and at the very same time making that allowance only by eliminating any possible significance the opinion might have.

9. See Vattimo, *Nihilism and Emancipation*, xxv–xxx and 49–59.

10. Péguy, "L'Argent," 821.

is, to *private opinions*. A thing is permitted to be true, as true as it wants to be, as long as that truth does not impose itself on others. Its truth is its own, as it were, and may not bear on anything beyond itself, may not transgress its particular boundaries. It is a self-contained truth, and, so contained, it is free to be perfectly "absolute."

Let us call this a "bourgeois metaphysics."[11] "Bourgeois" is an adjective meant to describe any form of existence, pattern of life, set of "values," and so forth, that is founded on the principle of self-interest, which is posited as most basic. To speak of a "bourgeois metaphysics" is to observe that such an interest, such forms, patterns, and values, are themselves an expression of an underlying vision of the nature of reality, namely, a view that absolutizes individuals, that holds that things "mean only themselves"; it does not recognize things as belonging in some essential manner to something greater, as being members of some encompassing whole, and thus pointing beyond themselves in their being to what is other, but instead considers them first and foremost discrete realities. On the basis of such metaphysics, it is perfectly natural to make self-interest the basic reference point for meaning, the primary principle of social organization.[12] In fact, given such a view of the nature of reality, nothing else would make any sense. This principle of social organization does not in the least exclude the possibility of what is called "altruism."[13] Quite to the contrary, we just articulated an expression of the "bourgeois metaphysics" precisely as a kind of concern for others: we are willing to affirm something as true only on the condition that we leave open the possibility for others to take a different position. We thus seek to give others a special respect. Toleration is, at least in our postmodern era, essential to this view of reality. In a certain respect, then, there is nothing

---

11. The phrase is inspired by Robert Spaemann, who described the moral thinking dominant in the eighteenth century as a "bourgeois ethics and non-teleological ontology": see the essay of that name in Spaemann, *Philosophical Essays on Nature, God, and the Human Person*, 45–59.

12. One of the best ways to characterize this metaphysics in technical terms is as the loss of an *analogical* sense of being, which entails self-preservation (positivistically conceived) as the fundamental energy of nature. One of the first systematic articulations of this vision in the modern era is Spinoza, who expressed this principle as the *conatus essendi*. An excellent presentation of the transformation of the notion of nature in modernity can be found in Robert Spaemann, "Nature," in *Philosophical Essays on Nature, God, and the Human Person*, 22–36.

13. It is significant that the term was coined by Auguste Comte (1798–1857), the founder of "positivism," who also rejected metaphysics and so aided the replacement of philosophy ultimately by "sociology" (another term he coined, at least in the now-typical sense). Altruism was meant to overcome egoism, through the development of a scientifically planned society.

preventing our judging that the "bourgeois metaphysics" is radically altruistic or other-centered.

Nevertheless, this judgment demands two qualifications. First, insofar as it is founded on a "bourgeois metaphysics," it follows necessarily that any altruistic act will be equally explicable in purely self-centered terms. In this case, altruism will always be vulnerable to the "hermeneutics of suspicion," such as we find, for example, in Friedrich Nietzsche: there can be no rational disputing the charge that what appears to be done for altruistic reasons is "really" motivated by the prospect of selfish gain.[14] Second, the affirmation of the other inside of a "bourgeois metaphysics" is inevitably an affirmation of the other specifically as a self-interested individual. Altruism is not in the least an "overcoming" of egoism, but rather the multiplication of it. This is the essence of toleration: "live and let live" means, "let us agree to be self-centered individuals; we will give space to each other so that each may do and be what he likes, and will transgress our separateness only to confirm each other in our own individuality, that is, to reinforce each other's selfishness." One thinks here of Rilke's famous definition of love, which may indeed have a deep meaning in itself, but not so much when it appears on a refrigerator magnet: "Love consists in the mutual guarding, bordering, and saluting of two solitudes."[15]

One thus discovers a basic gesture of self-protection in the "bourgeois metaphysics," even in its altruistic expressions. I affirm some truth, but only in the liberal-mindedness that allows anyone else the "freedom" to deny it, and this altruistic sentiment happens to have—or indeed cannot but have, regardless of anyone's conscious intentions—the not-insignificant benefit of relieving *me* of the burden normally carried in truth. Specifically, it eliminates any need I might otherwise encounter to justify the truth claim I make in some serious way, and thus of any need to take responsibility for it or be in any sense accountable to it. In other words, it eliminates any genuinely *social* quality of truth, any sense that it is the nature of truth to be held in common. The absence of any social quality in truth leads to a peculiar dialectic in our relationship to our convictions. On the one hand, we affirm them with an odd detachment, a "self-irony," such as Vattimo advocates, and which may not even be conscious. We don't really believe *anything*. On the other hand, whatever attachment we do have becomes absolute, because it is

---

14. Thus, one hears students explain that even the mother who throws herself in front of the speeding car to save her child does so simply because of a selfish desire for the child. This is a perfectly correct explanation inside of the terms set by a "bourgeois metaphysics," and does not exclude our calling the act, from another perspective, perfectly altruistic.

15. Rilke, *Letters to a Young Poet*, 428.

unreflected and *immediate*, i.e., not mediated by reason. In this respect, the conviction has the essential form of fanaticism, an emotional attachment that is immune to all reasoning. There is thus no incompatibility between half-hearted irony and fanatical conviction; these can reinforce each other, produce each other in an escalating way, turn immediately into each other, and even in some sense exist at once in the same mind. The tolerance that is expressly embraced as an ideal by the modern West therefore fosters at the same time an ethos of irrational violence. This ethos strangely increases at the very same time that any apparent "conflict" is neutralized: no one is denying you the right to hold it as true that leaves are green, and even to declare this publicly—under certain conditions: as long as, when you say, "true," you do not mean that anyone else would have any obligation to accept it against his arbitrary will. You can only offer it to others as something they may choose, as their own private convictions. Obviously, this is not in fact an elimination of the conflict between the ancients and the moderns, but a "rigging" of it, so that only one side can possibly triumph. The challenge to meaning that modernity poses is far, far deeper than we typically think.

2. The Beauty, Goodness, and Truth of Being

It is important to realize that we have been using the phrase "bourgeois metaphysics" somewhat tentatively: hence the quotation marks. By using the phrase, we do not mean to imply a retraction of the earlier point, namely, that, in a certain respect, the quarrel between the ancients and the moderns is in a certain sense not a contest between two metaphysics, which might be measured against a common standard. In fact, the phrase "bourgeois metaphysics," strictly speaking, is an oxymoron for several reasons. First of all, metaphysics is essentially non-bourgeois, as indicated already in its very name.[16] "Meta-physics" means "beyond nature"; it is a study of reality beyond its manifestation at the level of natural being, which is generally bound up in some sense with the individuality of specifically *physical* existence. As occupied with what lies beyond the natural, and so physical, its interest does not lie in individuality, in the sense of being restricted to the

16. There is a controversy over the question whether the word "metaphysics," which Aristotle himself did not use but was added by an editor, was meant to characterize the first philosophy, or simply (and more likely) designated the place of this science in Aristotle's collected works ("after the *Physics*"). Whatever the original intent, the name has been embraced as indicating something essential to this science.

individual as such.[17] One cannot do metaphysics *as* a self-interested individual. By contrast, as we saw above, this restriction is just what defines the bourgeois. Second, metaphysics is defined, in the classical tradition, as "the study of being qua being"—that is, an investigation of what it means *to be* at all, the nature of being, its principal characteristics and its essential causes.[18] Metaphysics is therefore aimed, we might say, not just at truth, and not just at *universal* truth (which is in fact redundant), but at the most universal truth possible, that truth beyond which nothing more universal can be thought. It is an investigation into being, and so into what holds for all time and for all people. No one, therefore, can shield himself from metaphysics; it allows no gesture of self-protection; it has no room for merely "private" conviction. A bourgeois spirit is therefore incompatible with such a study. We can imagine that a bourgeois age will not often take up such a science, or even recognize its legitimacy.[19]

Finally, as we will elaborate in just a moment, the study of being qua being implies an investigation into the essential properties of being that became known as the "transcendentals." This theme emerged, not incidentally, most explicitly in the Middle Ages, and the special attention it received in this period is no doubt because the transcendentals stand out especially in the light of *God's creation*. The transcendentals are properties of being as such and so features of *any* and *every* particular thing precisely insofar as it exists. We will be focusing in the chapters that follow on the transcendental properties of beauty, goodness, and truth, but it is important to note that these are not the only ones.[20] The point here is the very notion of a "tran-

17. To say this is not to dismiss the significance of individuality, as people often assume. Instead, as we will suggest below, metaphysics, precisely in transcending the limitations of what is individual *qua* individual in fact *deepens* its significance, since it reveals it to disclose a universal significance, a meaning that transcends any restriction.

18. By simply stating the subject matter of metaphysics, here, we do not mean to suggest that it is straightforward and obvious. In fact, it is full of paradox and mystery, which demands careful thought and meditation to be understood properly.

19. In fact, the repudiation of traditional metaphysics has been one of the most common themes of twentieth-century philosophy; the main currents of "Continental" philosophy have been explicitly anti-metaphysical; in "Analytic" thought, language has in a certain sense replaced being as determining first philosophy, and so metaphysics, when it appears at all, does so as a particular science ("ontology"). A certain kind of metaphysics has been returning in the twentieth century (e.g., "speculative realism"), but it tends to reject the distinctiveness of the human soul (which, among other things, is a fundamental axiom in the metaphysical theme of the transcendentals), and so represents a significant departure from metaphysics in the traditional sense.

20. There is no single "official" list of the transcendentals, and even Aquinas's most detailed presentation (*De ver*. 1.1) may not be intended as an exhaustive list. In that list, the transcendentals that characterize being in its positive relation to the human soul

scendental": the word indicates that which *transcends*, or goes beyond, any particular restriction or determinate limitation. Some properties belong to certain kinds of being insofar as they are *that* kind of being—for example, extension in time and space belongs to being only insofar as it is physical, and so does not apply to immaterial being such as numbers, mind, abstract universals, and so forth. The transcendentals, by contrast, are precisely unbounded. They are so "unbounded," in fact, that they transcend even the borders of creation itself; they describe not only the being of all creation, but also the being of God, which is *infinitely different* from created being. If, in a "bourgeois metaphysics," things "mean only themselves," in classical metaphysics, to speak of the transcendentals is to indicate that the property exhibited by the individual thing that happens to face me in this particular moment is a reflection of something held in common by the entire universe; it is a unique participation in something altogether universal, which belongs not only to all things actual, but even to all things possible. Indeed, the property is in a privileged sense an image of the very being of God.

Let us dwell for a moment on this last point, since it leads us into the subject matter with which this book will be most basically concerned. One of the principal things we wish to propose in the present chapter is that in the transcendentals there is an inseparable connection between the particular and the universal, which is to say that it is ultimately not possible to affirm (or indeed: to deny) that any particular thing is beautiful, good, or true in a proper sense without implicitly affirming (or denying) that the property belongs to the nature of reality as such. Chesterton put his finger on just this point with his characteristic wit:

> We have a general view of existence, whether we like it or not; it alters, or, to speak more accurately, it creates and involves everything we say or do, whether we like it or not. If we regard the Cosmos as a dream, we regard the Fiscal Question as a dream. If we regard the Cosmos as a joke, we regard St. Paul's Cathedral as a joke. If everything is bad, then we must believe (if such a thing is possible) beer is bad; if everything be good, we are forced to

---

(truth and goodness) are preceded by a number of others: most basically *ens*, being itself, but also *res* (thing), *unum* (unity), and *aliquid* (some [other] thing, i.e., distinction). The origin of the notion of the transcendentals is typically attributed to Aristotle, though it is not hard to find anticipations in Plato, and the theme is an evident part of the Neoplatonic tradition generally. In the Middle Ages, the theme of the transcendentals was often investigated under the heading of the "Divine Names," especially in the wake of (Pseudo-)Dionysius the Areopagite, who wrote a massively influential book under that title around 500. Calling the transcendentals "Divine Names" indicates that their proper sense lies in God.

the rather fantastical conclusion that scientific philanthropy is good.[21]

In this passage, Chesterton is saying that one cannot avoid making some assumption about the nature of reality in general, specifically about its truth and goodness, and this assumption cannot but bear on every single particular thing we encounter insofar as it is real. He is thus appealing implicitly to the traditional doctrine of the transcendentals just mentioned.

But we can also make a correlative point with respect to this passage, a bit more subtle but no less significant: we cannot recognize any particular thing as beautiful, good, or true *in a profound sense* without affirming these attributes of the cosmos as a whole. By "profound sense," I mean in a way that concerns their very being, as a property that belongs to their innermost reality. A thing can be good in its being only if being as such is good. Note, we are not committing a logical fallacy in making this claim, invalidly deducing a universal from a particular. Rather, what we mean to say is that, in judging the particular, we are implicitly making a determination regarding the universal, in the light of which we decide about the particular. It is necessary to spell this out: if I take a particular thing to be good, I might recognize that goodness as merely an accidental quality, like the "tallness" of a particular man: this man happens to be good just as he happens to be tall, but there are plenty of things in the world that are neither tall nor good. Or, I might consider it a "proper accident," like the power of reason that all human beings have insofar as they are human:[22] this man is good *because* he is a man, but there are all sorts of other natures, i.e., "types," of things that are not good, just as there are things without the capacity to reason. Clearly, this kind of goodness is more profound than the first, which is a merely accidental accident, so to speak, but it is nonetheless not yet fundamental. I may, finally, recognize that a man is good *in his very being*. I can affirm him as good insofar as he *is*; in other words, I can take the goodness I perceive in him to be an expression of his innermost reality itself. But this is possible only if I recognize *being as such* as good. What I am doing in making this judgment is acknowledging something about the nature of reality in general, and interpreting this man in light of this recognition. I cannot deny that · being qua being is good and affirm that this man is good precisely insofar as he shares in being. At best, I can affirm an accidental coincidence, but this is just to fail to acknowledge the goodness of his being as such.

---

21. Chesterton, *Heretics*, 301.

22. To say this does not imply that only those beings capable of *exercising* their power of reason are human.

It is worth pondering the question whether such a failure would ulti-mately entail the collapse of beauty, goodness, and truth into merely "private conviction," but, however that may be—and we will be considering various aspects of this question throughout the present book—the more immedi-ate point of this reflection is twofold: first, to see that there is a connection between intensity and extensity, i.e., between inner depth and universal significance, so that precisely what is most unique about an individual is *re-velatory* of the meaning of reality more generally; and second, to recognize, therefore, that every time we engage with a particular thing in a meaningful way, the meaning of the entire cosmos, and indeed of God himself, is at stake. This may seem to be overly dramatic, but it is strictly true. When-ever we take a position with respect to the beauty, goodness, and truth of a *particular* thing, we are, as it were, pronouncing judgment on *reality as a whole*, and so implying a response of consent or refusal to the Creator of reality. There can hardly be anything more anti-bourgeois than this. We cannot even be genuinely *self*-interested except by being in some sense in-terested in *everything there is* in a certain respect. If we reject the notion that the universe is true, good, and beautiful in its very being, we cannot affirm ourselves in an ultimate way; we cannot enjoy ourselves, or in other words, take pleasure in our very being, which is, according to Aristotle, the basis for genuine friendship with others.[23] Indeed, the more *truly* personally held a conviction is—if we understand "personally" to mean: in the ontological depths of the person—the more it is a matter of universal significance.

Now, we began our discussion by considering the implication of truth claims, but our reflection on metaphysics and the transcendental properties of being has broadened that consideration. We are beginning to see that what is at issue in "bourgeois metaphysics" is not merely a question of what we can or cannot know for certain, but at the same time our basic attitude, our disposition toward the world and everything in it, the way we interact with the various things we encounter in our day-to-day living, and indeed in a subtle but profound way the quality of our experience—our experi-ence of absolutely anything and everything. Every genuine encounter with beauty, truth, or goodness is a "reality check," a confrontation with a mean-ing greater than ourselves and so at the same time a call to make a judg-ment about reality as a whole. As we are going to see in later chapters, the doctrine of the transcendentals involves not only our conscious thoughts and attitudes, but concerns relations that lie deeper than the explicit content of our intellect and will. Because we inevitably make a judgment, whether

23. Aristotle, *NE*, IX.4. As we will elaborate in chapter 6, this is just because the being that is most intimate to us (*"magis intimum cuilibet"* [*ST* 1.8.1]) is also most com-mon (*"communissimum"* [*De pot.* 3.7]), as Aquinas explains.

implicitly or explicitly, about the whole in the encounter with any part and about all of the parts in our consideration of the whole, we see that the reality of the transcendentals is in play in everything we say and do, at every moment.

The transcendentals characterize our basic relation to things; they reveal the nature of our very being in the world, as we will elaborate in the chapters below. We either take the world to be most fundamentally beautiful, in which case we receive it as a gift, in a spirit of gratitude and affirmation, or we do not take the world to be most fundamentally beautiful. In this case, gratitude is not precisely a way of *being*; it is not a matter of our deepest disposition, which is evoked by the simple existence of things, but is instead an occasional feeling produced in certain circumstances and often merely subjectively contrived, as it were, because it lacks an ontological basis. Similarly, we either respond to the world as ultimately good—as being desirable *in itself*, and not only in relation to us who happen to desire, or happen not to—or we stand first indifferently, outside of the world's appeal. If being is desirable in itself, beyond all our actual desiring, it means that our desiring has, as it were, an unshakable and inexhaustible foundation. A *radically* good world calls us out of ourselves and into itself by its very nature, and thus our interaction involves our very selves in response. To deny the ultimate goodness of things as such is to open at the foundation of the world and the foundation of our relation to it, our experience of it, a passageway to the "specter of nihilism" that waits at the door, which Nietzsche described so poignantly at the end of the nineteenth century. Finally, we either recognize things as *true* in their very being, or we ascribe truth simply to our knowledge according to its "correctness" in particular circumstances. In the former case, we come to see that knowing is not just an intellectual act, but involves the *whole* of us in response to reality *as a whole;* in the latter case, our intelligence will find itself increasingly enslaved to ultimately mundane projects and pragmatic concerns. "Truth" will become a bourgeois affair.

What is at issue in the transcendentals, in short, is the most basic meaning of things and so man's fundamental relationship with the world, with himself and others, and with God. It is for this reason that we are endeavoring to sketch in broad strokes a philosophical anthropology on the basis of the transcendentals in this book: to consider the basic "shape" of man's relating to the world in his perception, action, knowledge, and love, setting these in relief by contrasting them with how such "powers of the soul" appear in the absence of the transcendentals.

3. The "Forgetfulness" of Philosophy

Ours is a decidedly non-philosophical, even anti-philosophical, age. This is not to say that we lack "philosophers," of a certain sort; indeed, we have only too many. There is probably no age in history that has as many "professional philosophers" as we do, with scores of new PhDs waiting to compete for every slot that opens in the philosophy departments of scores upon scores of colleges and universities.[24] Outside of the academy, we have an even greater array of "professional thinkers" of every sort. There is the novel phenomenon of the "think tank," an institution whose employees are not paid to *produce* any tangible goods, but simply . . . to think. There is the rapidly growing sector of "white collar" labor, made up of those who work with their minds rather than with their hands, as do the "blue collar" workers. This sector includes, not only those whose thinking remains tied to industry in some respect—advertisement, management, and so forth—but those in more "liberal" fields, such as journalism, the aim of which is simply to communicate "what is going on in the world" and perhaps offering opinions on it, and the creative, exploratory work in science, computing, and technology. Moreover, the internet has opened up space for amateur, and not just professional, thinkers, and this space has been filled, in the blink of an eye, by an almost limitless number of "blogs," covering any topic imaginable, or simply recording daily events or impressions. Indeed, our privileging of the conceptual and intellectual is manifest, moreover, in our obsession with childhood development and preparation for success in schools, not to mention the vast sums of money our government spends annually on education. All of this would seem to indicate that we have an unprecedented love of intelligence. Nevertheless, while it may be the case that our age is more cerebral, more abstract, more preoccupied with brain power, with intellectual capacities and skills, than any other age in history, it remains true that we are *not* philosophical. Indeed, our very abstraction and preoccupation with intelligence is a sign of the "forgetfulness" of philosophy. What do I mean by this?

The preceding discussion of the transcendentals as a revelation of our most basic way of being in the world can shed some light on the problem. What is at issue here is summed up in an observation that Yves Congar made in his classic book on the special role of the laity.[25] As he put it, in

---

24. It is said that Aquinas had read, and indeed internalized, every book in the world in philosophy and theology that was available in Latin at the time in which he lived. Today, one could devote one's entire life to reading and not manage to make it through the material produced in a single year, much less internalize any of it.

25. Congar, *Lay People in the Church*.

modernity we find "a loss of respect for the true inwardness of things,"[26] or in other words, the loss of an intrinsic interest in things, an attentiveness to their reality in itself. This loss of an intrinsic interest in things is another way of expressing the absence of philosophy. To see the connection, we must hear this phrase in two senses at once; we must understand the adjective "intrinsic" to be describing both the nature of our interest, and also the *object* of our interest. In other words, what we have generally lost is an intrinsic interest in things, as opposed to an instrumentalizing interest (i.e., an interest in things merely as means to further ends), and an interest in the *intrinsic meaning* of things, *what things are in themselves*, as distinct from their possible implications or consequences.

It is here that we begin to see why this "intrinsic interest" just *is* philosophy. Plato revered Socrates as the quintessential philosopher because he *relentlessly* posed the "what is . . . ?" question ("τί ἔστι . . . ;")—"What is piety? What is justice? What is love? What is beauty?"—and elevated the importance of this particular question above all others. Socrates showed that this question, understood properly, differs from other sorts of questions, since it seeks after not just some information that can be made to serve a pressing need but the *intrinsic meaning* of things.[27] It is a question of a different order. To ask this question requires a certain change of heart, a capacity to set aside contingent interest, to look beyond implications, and simply to focus the mind on the essence of a matter: to enter, we might say, respectfully into "the true inwardness of things." If Plato left the "what is . . . ?" question in some sense without a conclusive answer in so many of his dialogues, it is not because of a radical skepticism or a "relativistic" desire to allow people to supply their own answers to the question, whatever they happen to be.[28] Instead, it is because the question itself has a certain absoluteness to it. Its value, in other words, is not simply relative to the particular answer it is able to produce as its result, an answer that would in turn be justified by the practical consequences it might entail, the particular achievements it enables. Instead, raising this question properly orients the mind to the world—specifically, it opens the soul to the heart of things, as it were—and this orientation is a good in itself, and does not need to justify itself by "producing." Indeed, we could confidently say that this openness to

---

26. Ibid., 20.

27. It is important to observe here that the point is *not* to dismiss usefulness, but only to relativize benefit to the intrinsic meaning of things. Arguably, things reveal even greater benefits on this basis, and it is altogether good that they do so.

28. For a more thorough argument on behalf of this interpretation, see my book: *Plato's Critique of Impure Reason.*

the heart of things is, if not the highest human good *tout court*, then in any event an inseparable part of the highest human good.

This claim becomes particularly intelligible when we see the connection between the "what is . . . ?" question of philosophy and the transcendentals. It might seem, initially, that we raise the "what is . . . ?" question in order to get a discrete—and ultimately useful—response, as we just described. But if truth is nothing more than a correct bit of knowledge, it is not a *transcendental* properly speaking; it is not a revelation of being itself. The "what is . . . ?" question, properly understood, opens us to truth in a revelatory sense. If we do not pause—"pause" in the sense of coming to a joyful rest, a completion that does not need to justify itself by its causal output—in *this* particular question, which asks after the essence of a thing, then there is no question at all that is capable of giving us pause. Anything that would happen to catch our attention would do so only because of what it promises to bring about *in addition* to itself, and of course *that* thing in turn cannot hold us, but only push us further along. As we will explain at length in the final chapter, if we are not disposed to ask the "what is . . . ?" question, then even the great question of religion, the "God question," will turn out to evoke only an instrumental interest. In this case, we raise the "God question," if at all, only because of its moral implications, and we want to be moral only because of the question of what might happen to us after death. We cannot deny that we want to be happy, and indeed happy forever, if such a thing is possible. This answer is admittedly the last one, because there is no logically higher consideration to which this answer can be subordinated.[29] It is not possible to ask in a meaningful way why we want to be happy. But if we finally come to a stop with this question, it is only because we have to. If we are unable to ask the "what is . . . ?" question in a genuinely philosophical way, we will be unable to rid ourselves of the suspicion, or in fact the deep anxiety, that this final happiness will not finally be all that interesting. If we are accustomed only to the instrumental values of things that are "good *for x*," then the end of instrumentality can only be "good for *nothing*," which is to say, as far as we instinctively feel it, not good at all.

If we recognize, by contrast, that the "what is . . . ?" question is intended not principally to enable us to procure a useful answer, but *most basically* to open the soul to the heart of things, the significance of the transcendentals becomes evident. According to the traditional doctrine, the transcendentals are "convertible," which means that they coincide in any given subject: *omne ens est verum et bonum (et pulchrum)*: whatever *is*, is true, is good, and is

29. Plato makes just this point in *Symposium* 204d–205a; see also Aristotle, *NE* I.4.1095a13–22.

beautiful, insofar as it is.[30] We wish to propose that their convergence in reality is essential for the proper existence of philosophy; when the transcendentals are denied, whether implicitly or explicitly, philosophy won't long remain. To inquire into the essence of things requires us to give them attention, to show them a special kind of interest, namely, an *intrinsic* interest in their *intrinsic meaning*, as we said above. If *that* interest is eclipsed by an instrumental interest, the very quality of our attention cannot help but be transformed; we will want to know them, in this case, just to the point that they reveal how they can serve that ulterior purpose. As the early modern thinker Thomas Hobbes put it, to know something means to be able to imagine "what we can do with it, once wee have it."[31] This implies that our attention *to* them is directed immediately to something else. Anything that resists this instrumental interest is "gratuitous," and if there is no room for gratuity in one's vision of the world, if gratuity has no substantial basis, no meaning, then the point of inquiring any further, beyond a thing's promised effects, will be undercut. But "gratuity" is the very point of the transcendentals: things are beautiful in their being, which is to say that it is good, *tout court*, that they exist. Their goodness, in other words, has an absolute quality; it is not merely relative to their capacity to fulfill some purpose or desire, even though of course it is just this gratuity that makes them supremely beneficial and fulfilling. Their goodness attracts us, drawing us spontaneously to themselves, which is why our attention to them has a real, objective basis, and why it can be in fact genuinely *intrinsic*. The "what is . . . ?" question implies a certain "care" for things—in all the senses of that term—and not only a curiosity. The truth of things, transcendentally speaking, is a display of their intrinsic meaning, which is to be affirmed for its own sake; it is not a mere set of facts,[32] a collection of data to be recorded in

30. The sentence is a classic formulation of Aquinas's teaching (with the addition of beauty), and indicates that the transcendentals coincide in the subject, which means they "*convertuntur.*"

31. Hobbes, *Leviathan*, 96.

32. Ludwig Wittgenstein, one of the founders of the analytic philosophy that dominates in the contemporary academy, not just in England and the US, but now all over the world, begins his first magnum opus with the following axioms: "The world is everything that is the case (1). The world is the totality of facts, not of things (1.1). The world is determined by the facts, and by these being *all* the facts (1.11)." In a profoundly interesting book that deserves to be "rediscovered," Henry Veatch has argued that what distinguishes the modern logic, which has its origins in Bertrand Russel (another founder of analytic philosophy) from the traditional Aristotelian logic is that the latter is based on the relation between a substance and its accidents, while the former is simply a system for relating abstract terms. This "relating-logic," as distinct from the traditional "what-logic," is ultimately *incapable of saying what anything is!* We might say that it is the very nature of modern logic to stifle an intrinsic interest in the intrinsic

relation to some project or other. Our most fundamental relation to a world as beautiful, good, and true is *love*—as we will explain in due course. To ask in a genuine and generous way *what* a thing is is therefore an expression of love; it presupposes love of a radical sort, and it is just such a love that inspires philosophy, the "love of wisdom." Whenever we ask such a question, the doctrine of the transcendentals is implicated in a direct way.

In the light of these reflections, it is instructive to pay attention to our public discourse, and indeed even to our own personal conversations about the world. If we do so, we will almost certainly see how rarely the "what is . . . ?" question arises, and if it does, how often it is relativized to concrete implications. At the highest intellectual level, we will discuss economic conditions, for example, and the focus will be on how to improve them, how to stimulate growth, how to make possible a more equitable distribution of wealth, and so forth. But we do not ask what an economy, after all, *is*, or what wealth *is*. We discuss education, its cost, its availability, its effectiveness, and so forth. But we do not ask: What *is* education? We discuss foreign policy, the question of immigration, of the just use of force, but we do not ask: What *is* a nation? What *is* a citizen? What does it mean to belong to a political community? What *is* justice? As we reflect on these neglected questions, it becomes evident to us how radically different the "what is . . . ?" questions are from the others, how they draw the mind spontaneously beyond the particularity of circumstances or practical needs, how they immediately evoke other sorts of questions that come to bear rather quickly on what it is to be a human being, the ultimate meaning of life, and indeed the beauty and truth of things. To ask the question "what is . . . ?" is to be philosophical, regardless of one's level of education and line of work. A carpenter who *loves* working with wood, who delights in the feel of the wood in his hands, who takes care to make things of value and not *simply* for a paycheck, is in this sense philosophical, and in subtle ways is affirming, in the attention he gives to *this particular* project, the beauty, goodness, and truth of the universe—and the love of its Creator. By contrast, the one who betrays a lack of an intrinsic interest in things, who fails to ask the question "what is . . . ?"—both in what he says and in what he does—and give it the care and attention it naturally calls for is *not* a philosopher, even if he earns his living in a philosophy department.

One could write a book on the particular problem that technology poses in this regard,[33] but in the present context we have room only to make

---

meaning of things. Veatch, *Two Logics: The Conflict between Classical and Neo-Analytic Philosophy.*

33. In fact, several such books have already been written: see, for example, Grant, *Technology and Justice*; Borgmann, *Technology and the Character of Contemporary Life.*

a general assertion. The more technology dominates our culture, the less philosophical we are capable of being, which is to say the more remote we become from the real.[34] Technology, of its essence, is about *means*, about instrumentality; as technology becomes a focus, or central concern, the object of our energies, our capacity to pay attention tends to atrophy. We become increasingly occupied with what is immediate, and so lose an intrinsic interest in the intrinsic meaning of things.[35] The mere "use" of technology mediates the world we experience, giving it shape, and so, as we will argue further below, changes our relationship in subtle but important ways. It may allow us access to things in a functional sense, but this tends to come with the obscuring of the presence that is part of an encounter with reality. If what we have been saying is true, a *focus* on technology is an implicit denial of the transcendentals. Truth, beauty, and goodness in this case will become increasingly impoverished and outdated notions. A culture that is obsessed with technology will, in spite of anyone's explicit intentions, cultivate habits of being that are anti-philosophical. We will find it increasingly difficult in such a culture to *love* in anything more than a merely subjective sense. What Balthasar says about the consequences of separating beauty from truth and goodness applies here: "We can be sure that whoever sneers at her name [i.e., the name of beauty] as if it were the ornament of a bourgeois past—whether he admits it or not—can no longer pray and soon will no longer be able to love."[36]

If we do not hear the question, "what is . . . ?" as one that in some sense imposes itself on us with all the weight of the beauty, truth, and goodness

---

34. "The digital technologies of autonomy, rather than inviting us into the world and encouraging us to develop new talents that enlarge our perceptions and expand our possibilities, often have the opposite effect. They're designed to be disinviting. They pull us away from the world" (Carr, *The Glass Cage*, 219).

35. To take an obvious example: we have all experienced that using a GPS tends to diminish our capacity to get around by ourselves without technological help, i.e., our awareness of where we in fact really are. There are many reasons one can offer to defend the use of this device, but they tend to be entirely *practical*. Resisting usage creates all sorts of burdens, but in the end would seem to have a single justification: because it is intrinsically good to get to know a place.

36. Balthasar, *The Glory of the Lord*, vol. I, 18. There is an argument to be made that the loss of beauty is a root cause for the disappearance of the transcendentals more generally. Balthasar goes on to say: "Thomas described Being (*das Sein*) as a 'sure light' for that which exists (*das Seiende*). Will this light not necessarily die out where the very language of light has been forgotten and the mystery of Being is no longer allowed to express itself? What remains is thus a mere lump of existence which, even if it claims for itself the freedom proper to spirits, nevertheless remains totally dark and incomprehensible even to itself. The witness borne by Being becomes untrustworthy for the person who can no longer read the language of beauty" (ibid., 19).

of the world, and indeed of the world's Creator, then it will reach us, if at all, only in some distorted form that in fact draws our attention away from the essence it is meant to reveal. Raising this question requires the proper conditions; in a sense, it is like the things Tolkien says can be spoken only in Elfin because they require an ancient language. Outside of proper conditions, the question will necessarily get drowned out by other, more immediate and obviously forceful noises, because it is the very nature of such a question to be unable to compete with these. As Plato so profoundly portrayed, such a question is by its very nature *untimely*; it cannot fit into any of the pressing designs that define the "mundane" business of existence. But there is no such thing as a truly *human* culture that does not have its roots in the "untimely," in what is essentially "timeless." If the timeless is not *most basic*, it is altogether absent, because it is oxymoronic to "carve out a little time" for it here and there. What is at issue in all of this is not simply the decisions and dispositions of various individuals, but the basic shape of a culture. Does our culture reflect and amplify the truth, beauty, and goodness of the world in such a way that the human beings who inhabit it may be said to live in reality?

We thus come back to Chesterton's prophecy: swords will be drawn to defend the truth that leaves are green. If we take this truth to be a mere "fact," a "data point," then it strikes us as silly: this bit of information will never evoke enough passion in anyone to defend it because there won't be anyone sufficiently passionate to attack it in the first place. But if we understand Chesterton to be referring here to the intrinsic meaning of reality, then we recognize that the battle is already afoot, and has been for some time. We as a culture have come to the point that we will explicitly deny the reality that "stares us in the face," and we will do so, not as socially deviant individuals, but precisely *as* a society. The denial has become institutional policy, conformity to which is enforced by the coercive power of law, and even more ruthlessly by the coercive power of social media. And since we cannot deny reality in any particular case without in fact denying it in *every* case, this social policy requires us to take a skeptical distance even from the simplest truths of reality, from the manifest evidence of nature, from the greenness of leaves. Nothing poses a greater threat to a culture that seeks to protect itself from the claims of the real than beauty, goodness, and truth, and so these must be neutralized, rendered "subjective" or merely functional at every turn. It may indeed come to the point that resisting such neutralization requires a willingness to sacrifice, if not one's life in the literal sense, at least one's career, one's "relevance," or one's standing in the world.

According to Aquinas, goodness and truth (and beauty) are properties of being, but specifically those properties that concern the relationship of being to the human soul. They are an encounter with reality, in other words, that concerns the meaning of being as such and the essence of man. Everything that exists is real, but man is the only creature in the physical universe that is capable of experiencing the real precisely as real. To experience reality is a great gift, but at the same time a daunting task, with a lot at stake. It is not too much to say that if man establishes as a basic cultural purpose to shield himself from reality so as to render the things of the world vulnerable *to him*, then reality will simply cease to be, no matter how much "stuff" might still be around. There is therefore no more *pressing business* than the untimely recollection of beauty, goodness, and truth.

2

Beauty: The Manifestation of Reality

1. Our Impoverished Experience

Beauty is notoriously elusive, and not simply because it is difficult finding agreement among people of different cultures, say, or even individuals in the same culture, about whether one thing or another is beautiful (*de gustibus non est disputandum*[1]). Even more fundamentally, it is because there does not seem to be any single widely accepted definition of what beauty *is* in the first place. The extent to which this impression is altogether true is a question we may leave aside for the moment. What I wish to observe here at the beginning is that a thoughtful survey of philosophical descriptions and accounts of beauty from the ancient, through the medieval, to the modern and even postmodern world, comes across something quite remarkable, though perhaps not often remarked on: namely, that, however different the accounts of beauty seem to be, they agree with a surprising regularity on presenting beauty, in some respect, as a *coincidentia oppositorum*, that is, an often quite paradoxical unity of extremes that would otherwise seem to stand in irreconcilable opposition.

In the Platonic tradition, beauty is an extraordinary coincidence of the transcendent and the immanent, of reason and the senses, spirit and matter, of unity and diversity.[2] For the Aristotelian/Thomistic tradition, beauty represents the strange intersection of both the "closed" perfection of order, or form, and the "open" in-breaking of a light from beyond the form

---

1. "In matters of taste, there can be no disputes."

2. Plato describes beauty as the transcendent form, beyond all sensibility, that is able to be perceived *even* by the eyes, and so is able to mediate between the intelligible and sensible realms (*Phaedrus* 250b–252b). On Plato's notion of beauty as a coincidence of opposites in the *Symposium*, see my essay, "Disclosing Beauty: On Order and Disorder in Plato's *Symposium*"; for Plotinus's account of beauty as the coincidence of unity and diversity (i.e., the manifestation of unity in what is diverse), see *Ennead* I.6.

(*claritas*), and it unites the logically opposed movements of the intellect and will.[3] In the modern era, it is especially the Germans who have reflected philosophically on the nature of beauty in this regard: for Kant, beauty is simultaneously subjective and universal, it involves reason but is not a matter of concepts, it is both free and yet necessary, it satisfies one's nature but is essentially disinterested;[4] for Schelling, beauty is the *finite* presentation of the *infinite*;[5] for Hegel, it is the *sensible* manifestation of *rational* truth, and so the essentially relative expression of what is essentially absolute;[6] and for Heidegger, beauty is the tension-filled encounter (the "strife") between *world* and *earth*[7]—or to put it in non-Heideggerian terms,[8] between the brightly intelligible realm of human culture and artifice and the darkly hidden depths of nature. Of all the philosophers of beauty, there has been perhaps none more alive to its astounding union of opposites than the turn-of-the-nineteenth-century polymath Friedrich Schiller. This poet cum dramatist cum historian cum philosopher saw a *coincidentia oppositorum* at every turn in beauty, which he characterized as the unity of ever-changing life and definitively fixed form, of freedom or reason and nature, of tension and calm, of action and passion, of creativity and receptivity, of universality and individuality, of seriousness and play, of the ideal and the real, of the eternal and the temporal.[9] And so on.

There is, on the other hand, one tradition in which beauty does not appear in any significant sense as a unity of opposites, and it happens that this is the tradition that has arguably come to dominate in contemporary American culture (not only with respect to aesthetics), and that is the tradition of British empiricism. This tradition tends to reduce beauty to its subjective dimension, whether that be the judgment of taste or the experience of pleasure. Now, it happens also to be the case, as we suggested in the first chapter, that our culture suffers today in a special way from a loss of a sense of what we might call the *reality* of reality: the density of things, their objective significance and value, their being "in themselves," beyond their immediate relevance to utility and ulterior interests. For the most part, we

3. See Aquinas, *ST* 1.39.8, and *In div. nom.* IV.5.

4. Kant, *Critique of Judgment*, part 1, division 1, book 1, 43–95.

5. Schelling, *System of Transcendental Idealism (1800)*, 225.

6. Hegel, *On Art, Religion, and the History of Philosophy*, 22–48, esp. 29–30.

7. Heidegger, "The Origin of the Work of Art," 139–212, esp. 174.

8. These terms simplify Heidegger's own, and are not meant to do justice to their full breadth and depth. Instead, their purpose is to bring into relief one aspect of Heidegger's meaning in a non-technical way.

9. See Schiller, "Kallias or Concerning Beauty: Letters to Gottfried Körner," 145–83, and *On the Aesthetic Education of Man*.

do not feel the weight of the *givenness* of the nature of things. We live in a world increasingly mediated by technology, by the contrivances of human artifice, which tends to set the terms for what things mean to us and how we experience and interpret them even when we are not directly occupied with a particular device. (We talk about "going off the grid" or living "unplugged": These privative expressions imply that the *default* position is "on"—i.e., that in taking the plug out we are departing from the norm or detaching ourselves from what has effectively become the "real world." We think of putting away cell phones or turning off the computer, as "escaping," and so forth.) The terms of technology and social media have come to prevail to such an extent that we, as a culture, are always just a hair's breadth away from despair regarding the intrinsic reality of the world "out there" beyond the steady flow of appearances delivered directly to our consciousness.

What I mean by this despair is not just the abstract skepticism that we play at in Intro to Philosophy classes, which strikes the average person as absurd and extravagant. Instead, I mean something far more pervasive, and for that reason less immediately present to consciousness: a certain "lightness of being" that affects all of us, even those who have not read Descartes or Hume in an Intro class. We perhaps allow that the affirmation of a real world existing beyond our consciousness is a kind of "leap of faith," but this does not trouble us significantly because we see no reason to resist making the jump. Nevertheless, if this admission is taken in fact to be a leap of faith, even one happily and spontaneously performed, it implies a dependence of reality on our subjective disposition (which may of course be a perfectly willing one, but that doesn't change the fact of dependence). Reality is in this case something related *to us*, and not something to which we ourselves are in turn related, something to which we need to conform, and for which we are accountable. Though this is not something we tend to think explicitly about, it remains a kind of unconscious assumption that gives our culture a general ethos of frivolity, just under the surface of which lies a quiet anxiety and perhaps even the first tremors of panic.

I would like to suggest that there is a profound connection between the impoverished state of our conception of beauty and our despair over the density of the world in its natural givenness, so that a recovery of beauty in its rich, ontological significance can help us restore our rootedness in the "real world." To justify this suggestion, we will first explore how the encounter between man and world gets distorted, and so both man and world are impoverished in their real being, to the extent that beauty gets reduced to mere subjectivity. And then we will draw on the philosophical tradition alluded to at the outset to argue that beauty alone establishes the horizon for a genuine human existence, one that allows an encounter between man and the world that brings forth each in their integral wholeness. Once we have set this horizon, we will be in the proper position to unfold the acts of will and intellect in subsequent chapters, before returning to beauty, once again, in chapter 5, to consider its specific relationship to love.

2. The Doors of Perception

Let us begin by inquiring into the connection between the loss of a sense of reality and the impoverishment of beauty. The classical definition, or at least essential description, of beauty is *"id quod visum placet,"* "that which, when perceived, pleases or gives delight."[10] As we can readily infer from this description, beauty is, and always has been, in some respect a matter of appearances.[11] What pleases us in beauty is not the reality of the thing that shows itself to us, but the *appearance* of the reality. The direct satisfaction in the reality itself belongs, according to the classical tradition, more specifically to the aspect of goodness, as distinct from beauty. We take delight, for example, in a still-life painting of a bowl of fruit, which offers an artfully rendered appearance of the fruit, their sensible image, to our perception, and we can enjoy this appearance in relative indifference to the fact that there is no real fruit immediately on hand to satisfy our appetite.[12] What pleases us in beauty is just that aspect of things that is offered to our perception—above all to our hearing and vision[13]—which is to say, once again, that what pleases us is their *appearance*, or sensible manifestation, the look or the sound of things.

Now, one might think that to admit that beauty is a matter of appearances is to doom it to triviality: doesn't this understanding make beauty superficial by definition, insofar as it locates beauty, so to speak, precisely on the surface (the *superficies*) of things? We all have learned, both in literature and in life experience, to take offence at those characters who are

10. This characterization first appears in Plato (*Greater Hippias,* 298a), seems to be alluded to by Aristotle (*Rhetoric,* 1.5.1361b10), and becomes standard in medieval thought: see Aquinas, *ST* 1.5.4 ad 1.

11. This does not mean exclusively *sensible* appearances, but also includes non-sensible analogies to such appearances.

12. Descartes claims that it is the *promise* of gratification that causes beauty, and he uses the only example in which this is *prima facie* plausible (though does not stand up to any scrutiny), namely, *erotic beauty.* See *Passions of the Soul,* article 90, 67–68. But his position is easily contradicted by experience: do we not find a sunset more beautiful than an apple?

13. This is a classic theme. See Plotinus, *Ennead* I.6.1; Aquinas, *ST* 1–2.27.1 ad 3; and Dietrich von Hildebrand, "Beauty in the Light of the Redemption."

more concerned about the way things look than the way they really are, or who self-indulgently surround themselves with what is "pretty," encasing themselves in a cocoon of cosmetic comfort, from which they never intend to emerge to face the sometimes cold light of reality. Aristotle articulates the commonsense truth that "it is better to aim at reality than at appearance," which would seem to indicate the superiority of intrinsic goodness or truth over beauty.[14] Too great a concern for beautiful appearance, we all say, is vanity. If beauty is a matter of mere physical appearances, it seems also to present a tool of manipulation, that by which we *use* one another, at best reciprocally. To love a person's beauty, it seems, is to love his or her skin, the body, rather than the soul. So, again we ask, is beauty essentially superficial, so that concern for beauty would be egotistical and self-indulgent?

That is precisely the question. If we believe that beauty's being a matter of appearances makes it irredeemably superficial, we are taking for granted that appearances are themselves superficial, and without meaning. But there is quite a bit at stake if we simply concede this.

At this point, I would like to propose a thesis, which will undergird the rest of our reflections in this chapter: namely, that *beauty offers a kind of paradigm of appearance and so perception*, which is to say that it represents appearance as perfected, isolated in its purity we might say. To put it another way, beauty captures the essence of both appearance and perception (it is "appearance-ness").

This is not an arbitrary thesis: the word that we tend to associate with beauty, and especially with the philosophy thereof, namely, "aesthetics," comes of course from the Greek word *aisthēsis*, which simply means "perception" in a rather generic sense. When the word was adopted in the mid-eighteenth century in the more modern connotation that associates it with beauty, it initially retained the general sense of "perception."[15] Thus, the philosophical study of beauty grew out of the study of what it means to perceive in general, which is in turn simply the subjective side of the study of what it means to appear: or, what is appearance. The reason it is important to recall the original sense of "aesthetics" becomes evident in what is an implication of the thesis stated above: the way we interpret beauty, and the disposition we adopt toward it, has a profound bearing on how we interpret

14. Aristotle, *Rhetoric*, 1.7.1365a35ff.

15. The original appropriation of this term can be found in Alexander Gottlieb Baumgarten's 1750 book, *Aesthetica*, in which the author presents sense perception, particularly in the form of beauty, as the *vague apprehension* of truth, which is then clarified by the mind. The shift in the meaning of "aesthetic" is witnessed in Kant's use of the term in the 1781 *Critique of Pure Reason* to indicate the realm of sense experience, and then in his 1790 *Critique of Judgment* to indicate judgments of taste.

appearance and perception generally. If we add to this the widely accepted belief that our primary, if not sole, access to reality comes through the windows or doors of our senses, it follows that the way we interpret beauty bears in a literally foundational way on our relationship to reality *simply*.

It is in light of this implication that we can see the connection between the impoverishment of the notion of beauty and the loss of a sense of reality. It is considered a truism, today, that "beauty is in the eye of the beholder." Behind this statement,[16] as I suggested earlier, lies a development in the philosophy of beauty that occurred in British thinkers of the eighteenth century, who represented what has come to be called the philosophy of empiricism, founded most directly by John Locke in his path-breaking work *The Essay concerning Human Understanding*. In this essay, Locke gave an account of the origin of our ideas in sense experience, which, inspired significantly by the new science of his time, he interpreted essentially as events occurring "in the brain," so to speak, as a result of external stimuli. Following along Locke's path, the British aestheticians came to interpret beauty in a way that departed radically from the classical tradition, which saw beauty as a transcendental property of being. For the empiricists, by contrast, beauty—to use David Hume's oft-quoted words—is "no quality in things themselves: it exists only in the mind that contemplates them."[17] In other words, beauty has *no objective reality*, but exists principally as *a sensation of pleasure that occurs in our perceiving apparatus*. The primary dispute among the British theorizers of aesthetics turns on the question of whether beauty occurs most basically in direct sensation, that is, in our immediate contact with external stimuli, or instead in the imagination, which is as it were a secondary sensation, derived from the first but just as materially grounded. But they virtually all agreed it is essentially something "subjective," even if they sought to determine more or less objective rules to provide a standard for the judgment of taste. When we call something beautiful, from this perspective, we

16. The statement seems to appear in this particular form first in the mid-nineteenth century, but it is in fact a variation on Hume's phrase, which we cite below. For his part, Hume refers to the sentiment expressed in the phrase already as a popular proverb.

17 Hume, "Of the Standard of Taste," 347. Hume actually uses these words to describe a position he takes as extreme. The quoted passage continues, "each mind perceiving a different beauty." What Hume objects to in this position is the implication that no objective rules can be determined as a standard of taste. He does not object to the fact that beauty is an "inner sense" rather than a real quality. In this, he represents the standard view of the empiricists on this point. Cf., the father of empirical aesthetes, Francis Hutcheson, who writes, "Beauty, like other Names of sensible Ideas, properly denotes the Perception of some Mind; so Cold, Hot, Sweet, Bitter, denote Sensations in our Minds, to which perhaps there is no resemblance in the Object, which excite these ideas in us, however we generally imagine that there is something in the Object just like our Perception" (*An Inquiry into the Original of Our Ideas of Beauty and Virtue*, 27).

are talking more basically about ourselves than about a reality in the world. It makes sense, in this case, that there would be both wide disagreements about what counts as beautiful, and also so much difficulty in finding any genuine criteria to make a determination that would have value beyond the individual who happens in a given case to be judging. This is one of the many problems that Kant inherited through David Hume, which Kant sought to solve, as he did the more generally epistemological problems, by an appeal not to any objective reality but to the *a priori* structures of the mind. Many people credit Kant, in this respect, with introducing the break with natural form that enabled the development of abstract art.

We will not pursue the question here about the adequacy of Kant's attempt at a solution or whether it is in fact possible to find some objective standard for judgments of taste once one has interpreted beauty essentially as an event in the brain. Indeed, if beauty is nothing more than a subjective feeling of pleasure, which occurs under certain conditions, then the question concerning objective standards loses any real urgency. It seems to me that, if the question was still posed with such zeal in the eighteenth and nineteenth centuries, it is due to a lingering sense that beauty is in fact something important, more than the mere turning of a screw in our mental machinery. If this is true, then the fact that people today seem less inclined to fight about judgments of taste, and show little interest in persuading others about what is beautiful, or learning to make good judgments, educating and forming their tastes, is something that should cause us great alarm. Our alarm ought to grow exponentially if it is in fact true that the way we experience and interpret beauty reveals an understanding of or disposition towards reality in general. In this case, to lose a sense of beauty's connection to reality is, I suggest, to lose a sense of the reality of reality *tout court*.

How exactly does this follow? We noted earlier that appearance is, so to speak, the flip-side of perception: in perception, a thing *presents itself* to our senses, which is to say that it *shows*, or *manifests*, itself; in beauty, reality "makes an appearance." Perception, in other words, is the *reception* of appearance, which means it is the reception of a thing precisely in its showing of itself. Here, the mode of perception includes in a certain respect a relatedness to the object that appears; what is perceived is not simply some abstracted content—a packet of information, so to speak—but, along with the content, the *co-presence of the origin*.[18] This co-presence will turn out

18. This is not altogether different from Walter Benjamin's notion of the "aura" in an authentic work of art, but the point here is a more general one regarding perception and appearance *tout court*, and the relation of the appearance to reality implied by beauty rather than the genesis of the particular work. Nevertheless, Benjamin's concerns about the effect on art of the technologies of mechanical reproduction certainly have a

to be especially significant in relation to our acts of will and intellect, as we will explain in subsequent chapters. If we interpret beauty as nothing more than a mental feeling, so to speak, then this has implications for the meaning of appearance more generally. Specifically, it implies an extrication of appearance from its source, a denial that appearance is the "self-showing" of an actually existing thing, that is, the *revelation* of a reality. By virtue of this separation, the experience of beauty becomes at best a mere sign, accidentally related to some cause in the world, which happens to trigger the experience, but otherwise has no intrinsic relationship to its content. The connection to the origin is in this case altogether severed; the reality no longer has any bearing whatsoever on the appearance, which means that the appearance becomes in some sense a reality in its own right,[19] without a meaningful relationship to anything else in its *form*.[20]

If beauty has no relationship to reality, what does this imply for our perception of the world more generally? The emptiness of perception, the lack of the co-presence of the origin, does not exclude the possibility of our taking the various events in our brain as communicating some *information* about the world, which turns out to be useful, or indeed indispensable, for our capacity to navigate things, to move around in the world, and to interact with one another. But there is nevertheless in this interpretation no *encounter* with the world, no *intimate contact*, no *real communication* between the self and its other—in either direction. It is precisely this emptiness, this sterility, that evokes the ethos of despair we discussed at the outset. Even if I unquestionably trust that when I move my foot forward and set it down it will land on the solid ground and advance me a step further, and even if I have no doubt at all that if I put my hand over the candle flame it will be only a second or two before I begin to feel a searing pain, nevertheless, if these are but physically effected signs referring with perhaps a causal necessity to certain future sensations, there is no encounter with the world occurring in this or in any other perception.[21] Such certainty, however unshakable it may

bearing on what we are describing as an impoverishment of the notion of beauty. See Benjamin, *The Work of Art in the Age of Mechanical Reproduction.*

19. See Spaemann, "What Does It Mean to Say that 'Art Imitates Nature'?" esp. 208.

20. The regular concern in modern art to create significance by delivering some kind of *message* may be interpreted as an attempt to compensate in content for the loss of significance in the form. It is not a coincidence that the increase in the "conceptual" or the "cerebral" qualities of modern art comes with a diminished interest in beauty.

21. Richard Dawkins attempts to explain consciousness along just these lines. He reduces the reality of consciousness to altogether functionalistic terms, and so describes "communication" ultimately as a specific form of *manipulation*, the capacity to influence the behavior of another being for one's own purposes. There is no "intimacy" here, obviously. Dawkins's description is illuminating precisely because it is a "popularized"

be, is perfectly compatible with a deep despair concerning the reality of the world. David Hume, who located beauty as we saw in the mind, said that "we never really advance a step beyond ourselves" (i.e., outside the confines of our subjectivity).[22] Beauty, also for Hume, turns out to present itself as the paradigm for what is generally true about our experience of the world, as we discover when we consider his description of that experience. According to the Scottish philosopher, "nothing can ever be present to the mind but an image or perception, and . . . the senses are only the inlets, through which these images are conveyed, without being able to produce any immediate intercourse between the mind and the object."[23] Indeed, it is already too much to say that images are conveyed through the senses, as Hume does, which would seem to imply at least some sort of communication. Instead, speaking more precisely, we would have to say that, in the view of empiricism, the images we receive in perception are only *occasioned* by external stimuli, but *generated* entirely immanently, from inside the brain. Here, there is a self-produced content that does not include implicitly within itself the presence of a source beyond consciousness. We are not in the world, and the world is not in us. In fact, there *is* no world in any meaningful sense.[24]

3. Beauty as a Place of Encounter

The anxiety of this floating unmoored in the empty space of subjectivity enhances, let us say, our interest in recovering the more robust understanding offered by the classical tradition. There is of course no space here to work out all of the arguments that would be required to explain and justify the nature of beauty and our experience of it, but there is something to be gained simply by sketching out some basic features, drawing rather freely on the thinkers in the broad philosophical tradition alluded to at the outset, without attempting to reconcile whatever differences there may be among them.[25] To reiterate the overarching claim: we are suggesting that beauty is an encounter between the human soul and reality, which takes place in the "meeting ground," so to speak, of appearance. Thus understood, beauty

---

account, and so reveals what might be considered the general imagination on such matters. See his *Selfish Gene*, chapter 4, especially 63.

22. Hume, *A Treatise of Human Nature*, 67.

23. Hume, *An Enquiry concerning Human Understanding*, 104.

24. For a fuller elucidation of this theme, see my chapter "The Iconoclasm of the Intellect in Early Modernity," in *The Catholicity of Reason*, 119–36.

25. It is worth pointing out that we do not intend to offer a complete definition of beauty; we are instead simply describing an essential feature.

turns out to function as the foundation for all of man's subsequent interaction with things in the world. It opens the horizon for there to be a world at all, and so is indispensable for proper human existence. The full meaning of this claim will become evident only over the course of the argument developed in this book, in particular when we come to see the relationship between beauty and love and between love and being. At this stage, however, we will focus simply on the experience of beauty, first considering the subjective side of the experience, and then the objective side.

By the "subjective side," I am referring to the recipient of beauty, the *perceiver* whom beauty pleases: namely, man himself. One of the most striking things our brief survey of the philosophical tradition brought to light is that beauty has an astonishingly *comprehensive* quality: rather than simply stimulating a reaction in our brain that produces a feeling, or appealing to only one dimension of human nature, perhaps to the relative exclusion of others, it appeals to the *whole* of us, no matter how opposed the aspects of our nature may appear to be. Indeed—and this is absolutely crucial—it appeals to all of these aspects *all at once*, it appeals to them as integral parts of a whole, a genuine unity. In this respect, beauty "gathers us up" into a whole, and thus forestalls, or heals, the tendency to fragmentation. Beauty engages our mind and our senses at once, enlisting them as it were in the common project of *perceiving* beauty; as they pursue this project, the highest and the lowest parts of our nature converge in a single point. Beauty thus involves our spirit and so our sense of transcendence, our sense of being *elevated* to something beyond ourselves—and at the very same time it appeals to our flesh, and so our most basic, natural instincts and drives. In this way, it reaches into the depths of our nature, touching what is most basic and what is most essential. (In this, beauty represents a remarkable source of hope: it is, so to speak, a transcendent call that can be heard by the most flesh-bound ears. For the same reason, it has a universal scope: there is no human being that is not capable of being moved in some respect by beauty, whereas it would be difficult to say the same thing about truth or goodness.) As Schiller especially makes clear, beauty fulfills our humanity in all of its irreducible complexity; however paradoxical it may seem, beauty satisfies our craving for movement, life, change, surprise, novelty, and at the same time our desire for stillness, for rest, for permanence, for what transcends all disturbance.

Any one of these aspects could be fruitfully explored further in a different context, but I wish to focus on a single dimension here, insofar as our particular interest is the encounter between man and reality that beauty makes possible. According to Aquinas, beauty represents a kind of hybrid, or intersection, between goodness and truth. Like goodness, beauty appeals to our appetite, but what distinguishes it from goodness is that, like truth, it includes an ordination to the intellect at the same time.[26] Because of its relation to appearance, beauty is especially a matter of sense experience, though this does not at all exclude an analogous extension to non-material realities. Sense experience by itself, on the other hand, is not enough for an experience of beauty, as we can see in the case of non-rational animals: only an intelligent creature—only man—can perceive it. If we accept the classical view that the intelligence is that by which we "enter into" the reality of things (*intus-legere*), this fact alone already suggests that beauty involves more than sensual stimulation producing a feeling of pleasure, which is something that any animal is capable of. But beauty is not just a "combination" of the truth that appeals to mind and the goodness that appeals to appetite, which would be more or less equal to their sum. Instead, it is a distinct reality in its own right, and in this context we can draw on some of the later philosophers of beauty to bring to light a particular feature of that distinctiveness. Beauty appeals to appetite, but unlike the good, it does not aim at gratification in the sense of a direct enjoyment of the reality of a thing. Kant spoke of a *disinterested* pleasure, by which he meant not a lack of desire or a dullness of feeling but only the absence of an inclination to relate the beautiful thing immediately to some need pertaining to my natural, individual existence. "Disinterested" means "not self-interested" or "not self-serving" in the reductive sense of the phrases. There is, in other words, a kind of "non-possessiveness" in the enjoyment of beauty, a "letting be" rather than a seizing, a use, a consumption.

It is precisely on this score that we begin to understand the significance of beauty being concerned with the appearance *as distinct from* the reality of things. Speaking somewhat metaphorically here, we could say that, whereas the desire for the good is a desire to have the reality itself,[27] beauty is a more gratuitous appetite that allows the reality simply *to be*, in itself, and accepts what the reality gives or shows of itself. Similarly, while beauty appeals to our intellect, it does not satisfy our desire for understanding, in the way that truth does. The desire for truth is ordered to a grasp of the essence of a thing, which, again, concerns the inner reality beyond mere appearance.[28] But our desire for beauty is an *intellectual* desire that rests *in the appearance* itself. Note that we are not saying *mere* appearance, here. It seems to me that to say *mere* appearance would be to blur any meaningful

26. Aquinas: "Thus it is evident that beauty adds to goodness a relation to the cognitive faculty" (*ST* 1.27.1 ad 3).

27. Aquinas: "a thing is desired as it exists in its own nature" (*ST* 1.78.1ad1).

28. Aquinas: "we do not judge of a thing by what is in it accidentally, but by what is in it essentially" (*ST* 1.16.1).

distinction between intellect and the senses.[29] The appearance to which the mind relates in beauty, classically understood, is not mere appearance in the sense that it positively excludes the reality, but is rather the appearance *of* a reality, of something meaningful, even if what is perceived is not rendered into distinct concepts of reason.[30] We might say that beauty is appearance understood as a distinctively human experience, under the aspect of revelation, as a disclosure of reality. It is significant that the senses to which beauty most commonly appeals are specifically the "intellectual" senses, that is, the senses that are capable of grasping meaningful signs, namely, vision and hearing. The point is that appearance, in this understanding, is not a self-generated feeling stimulated in the brain, but an image, a representation, that includes within itself, however inchoately, the co-presence of its origin, or the reality it communicates. Some reality is implicit in the appearance in which we delight as beautiful.

Now, to say that beauty appeals to both our intellect and our will, but does not directly satisfy either one, is not to say that beauty is somehow incomplete. Not at all. In fact, we all recognize the experience of beauty as profoundly fulfilling. We come to rest in the vision of beauty, though this rest is nothing like a passive slumber, the ceasing of all activity.

But why should we experience beauty as fulfilling if it neither sates our hunger nor instructs our mind? If it doesn't do either of these, what *does* it do? What, indeed, is the *point* of beauty? It is not difficult, if we stick with this line of questioning, to begin to appreciate the suspicion we spoke of earlier, that there is something self-indulgent in beauty, which seems to offer little more than titillation of the senses. But this suspicion is a temptation, and if we fall to it, we end up, in spite of ourselves, denigrating the world and losing the reality of reality. I would like to suggest that the reason we experience a profound sense of fulfillment in beauty is that we were made to perceive the appearance of things:[31] not just "all men by nature desire to know" but "all men by nature desire to perceive."

29. The classic demonstration of the implications of absolutizing appearance and so undermining the distinction between knowledge and perception, intellect and senses, is Plato's *Theaetetus*.

30. In fact, precisely *as* appearance it cannot be rendered into concepts. But this fact has mistakenly led some to think that it has therefore no relation at all to the conceptual, which does not follow. A thing can be distinct and yet remain inseparable from another thing.

31. One senses an exasperation over the loss of this perfection in Nietzsche's nostalgia for the ancient Greeks, who had a profound sense of beauty: "O, those Greeks! They knew how to live. What is required for that is to stop courageously at the surface, the fold, the skin, to adore appearance, to believe in forms, tones, words, in the whole *Olympus* of appearance. Those Greeks were superficial—*out of profundity!*" (*The Gay*

In order to avoid having this argument—namely, that we are fulfilled by beauty because we were made to perceive the appearance of things—collapse into a mere tautology, we need to fill out a bit further what is being said. The claim is that beauty represents a perfection in itself, distinct from the perfections of goodness and truth. There is actually a twofold affirmation embedded in this: on the one hand, it means, objectively, that things reach a certain completeness in *showing themselves* in appearance.[32] In beauty, things display their inherent worth and meaning, their glory. To recognize this display as a perfection is to allow their reality to be distinct from their appearance, which means allowing a thing simply to be *in itself*, rather than being significant only relative to us (i.e., to some human need).[33] We will come back to this point. On the other hand, if there is indeed a completeness in beauty, it means, subjectively, that the non-possessive *openness* to things that our contemplative release, our "letting be," implies is not contrary to resolution or closure, but *coincident* with it.[34] We normally tend to set closure and openness more or less in opposition to each other: if I am satisfied and complete, I shut myself up and so off from others and from the world. To keep myself open, I have to "stay hungry," as they say. There is no doubt a kernel of truth here, but certainly not the fully grown fruit. If this were simply true, abiding openness would entail starvation, and we would imply that human perfection is essentially non-relational. To call beauty a perfection, and to interpret it in terms of the paradoxes described by the rich philosophical tradition we have mentioned, is to recognize that my intellect and will, my understanding and appetite, my reason and my senses, my soul and my body, my transcendent spirit and my historically conditioned being, all come to completion at once, coincident with an openness to reality as abidingly other than myself. I feel most myself at the same time

Science, 38).

32. See Adolph Portmann's discussion of animal forms, and his argument that the infinitely inventive displays we find in nature cannot be explained by a "survivalist" etiology: *Animal Forms and Patterns: A Study of the Appearance of Animals*.

33. According to Schiller, man "exercises this human right of sovereignty in the *art of appearance*, and the more strictly he here distinguishes between the *mine* and the *thine*, the more carefully he separates shape from being, and the more self-dependence he is capable of giving to this shape, the more he will not merely extend the realm of Beauty but even secure the boundaries of Truth; for he cannot purify appearance from actuality without at the same time liberating actuality from appearance" (*Aesthetic Education*, 127).

34. C. S. Lewis famously observes, through his character Psyche, that "It was when I was happiest that I longed most" (*Till We Have Faces*, 74).

that I am open to what transcends me, according to the whole spectrum of the meanings of "transcendence" here.[35]

Let us now look a bit more closely at the "objective" side of the event of beauty. Of the countless things one could say about the object, the thing that is beautiful, there is just one that I will highlight in the present context, namely, the role of *nature* in beauty, specifically, the connection between art and nature. This connection is an ancient theme: not only did Aristotle famously affirm that "art imitates nature"[36]—though he meant "art," *technē*, here in the broader sense of skill or contrivance—but already Plato had described the poetic or productive arts as generating imitations of things that exist by nature, first of physical things and through them of eternal forms.[37] It is in the light of such views that the classic "mimetic" theory of art was formulated, which has become an object mostly of derision in postmodern discussions of aesthetics, in part because of an assumption that it implies a reduction of art to the slavish copying of nature. In this case, art is beautiful only if it is crudely "realistic," an implication that we all recognize as inadequate, if not simply false. But to reject the slavish copying of nature does not require us to reject any relation to nature at all. There is a more paradoxical approach, which we find, for example, in Kant's affirmation that nature is beautiful when it looks artificial (i.e., expressive of order or intelligent design), and that art is beautiful when it looks natural—i.e., not simply the contrived product of a foreordained plan, in particular foreordained for some utilitarian purpose.[38] For Schiller, beauty occurs when freedom comes to appearance in and through a natural form;[39] for Heidegger, its essence lies in the tension generated by the human work to transform a thing of nature that simultaneously aids and resists that effort.[40] What we find in all of these

---

35. The most fundamental meaning is religious transcendence, that is, man's relationship to God. For a longer discussion of the role of beauty in religious worship, see my essay, "The Loss of Beauty and the De-Naturing of Faith." Kant attempted to explain the disinterested pleasure caused by beauty by making the human faculties self-directed in this experience. According to him, the faculties that are usually directed to the world simply *play* with each other when we make a judgment of beauty. Our point is not at all to deny this play of the faculties, but rather to insist that it is founded, so to speak, more deeply on the play that is occurring between subject and object, or better: between man and world.

36. Aristotle, *Physics* 2.2.194a22.

37. Plato, *Republic* 597dff.

38. Kant, *Critique of Judgment*, §45 (Pluhar, 173–74).

39. Schiller, "Kallias or Concerning Beauty," 166–70.

40. Heidegger, "The Origin of the Work of Art," 194–95. It is for example the materiality, the natural earthiness, of stone that resists the formation into a wall—not absolutely, but as part of its contribution to that formation—that makes a stone wall

is an interplay between freedom and nature, in which the natural reality provides an anchor and guide for freedom, setting the terms for it, as it were, even as it is being transcended, elevated, enhanced, transformed, creatively interpreted, and so forth.

It seems to me that our earlier reflections offer a way to interpret this delicate interplay. We have dwelt on the fact that beauty is a matter of appearance rather than reality simply in itself, and have emphasized the distinction between appearance and reality. But we have also emphasized that, properly understood, an appearance is not really an appearance unless it is *of* a reality. A crass realism in aesthetics fails to recognize the goodness, as it were, of the distinction between appearance and reality; it seeks to close the difference by making the copy as perfect a representation of the original as possible.[41] "Anti-mimetic" aesthetics, on the other hand—the pure formalism of abstract art, for example, or surrealism in its various expressions—radicalize the difference to the point that it disappears. It is not an accident that such aesthetics tend to reject beauty, which the postmodern "iconoclasts" take to be bourgeois, and aim instead at a radical distortion or even obliteration of natural form—a kind of violence to finite form that Kant associated with the sublime.[42] Appearance ceases in its absolutization to be appearance, since it is thus no longer *of* some reality. These aesthetics—crass realism and abstraction or surrealism—however opposed they may seem on the surface, turn out to be flip sides of the same coin; they both agree in the denigration of appearance. One would thus expect that they would tend to co-exist in a culture, and reinforce each other even in their apparent opposition: the "edgy" side by side with the purely "sentimental." And because they both rest on the denigration of appearance as such, one would also expect that this alliance between the postmodern radical and the bourgeois would coincide with a general cultural despair over the reality of reality.

---

infinitely more beautiful than a concrete wall, in which the resistance of stones has been altogether wiped out by artifice.

41. Hegel humorously criticizes the view that art seeks to be as perfect as possible a reproduction of nature by recalling the famous story of the ancient Greek painter, Zeuxis, who painted grapes in such a lifelike manner that doves descended on them and began to peck: "But when we reflect on these and similar instances, it must at once occur to us that, in place of commending works of art because they have *actually* deceived *even* pigeons and monkeys, we ought simply to censure the people who mean to exalt a work of art by predicating, as its highest and ultimate quality, so poor an effect as this. In general, we may sum up by saying that, as a matter of mere imitation, art cannot maintain a rivalry with nature, and, if it tries, it must look like a worm trying to crawl after an elephant" (*On Art, Religion, and the History of Philosophy*, 72).

42. See Lyotard, *Lessons on the Analytic of the Sublime*.

By contrast with all of this, an affirmation of, consent to, and trust in beauty cultivates an ethos of objectivity, in which the givenness of nature finds respect. In beauty, nature is affirmed in its integrity, even as it is transcended or brought to a level that exceeds so to speak its natural capacities.[43] We have in artistic re-creation a stunning foreshadowing of the transformation of nature by grace, which presupposes the givenness of the nature it elevates. (*Gratia praesupponit naturam.*) A beautiful image, artfully crafted, is one in which human freedom has mediated, as it were, between reality and its appearance. But beautiful freedom does precisely that: it *mediates*; it does not collapse or separate, but creatively brings out something genuine in reality.[44] To recognize the significance of beauty as a distinct perfection, as something valuable in itself, to learn to see beauty and appreciate it, is not just to acquire the capacity to have privileged experiences, here and there, of great works of art. Insofar as beauty tells us something about appearance *tout court*, it follows that learning to love beauty opens up a depth dimension in our experience of reality more generally.

We will elaborate this theme in chapters 5 and 6 below. For now, it suffices to note that, in learning to love beauty, we develop our capacity to receive sense experience as a communication of reality, not just the reporting of information, but the event of a presence. Roger Scruton has spoken of beauty as the display of something like a *face* in things, the revelation of something like a soul in the things of nature.[45] George Steiner, in a similar spirit, has interpreted beauty as a sort of "exchange between freedoms."[46] In beauty, we could say that we experience reality as *revealing its inner being*, as presenting itself to us in a manner that would be analogous to personal self-disclosure.[47] When I disclose myself to another in personal communication, I am making myself known to the other, but the self that I reveal is really distinct from the revelation, so that the other person is not simply imposed on, as the passive recorder of the impression of my meaning, like soft wax

---

43. As Robert Spaemann puts it, "A transcendence of nature occurs only when nature is recalled as it is in its truth" ("Nature," 36). Spaeman's essay "Nature" provides one of the most profound, and also succinct, philosophical accounts available of nature, as the notion developed in history.

44. We might introduce here the analogy of procreation: the child is certainly different from the mother and father, but is nevertheless an expression of them, their nature, their distinctive individuality, however unanticipated.

45. See Scruton, *The Soul of the World*. Schiller similarly spoke of beauty as manifesting "as it were the person of the thing" ("Kallias or Concerning Beauty," 163).

46. Steiner, *Real Presences*, 166.

47. Spaemann offers an extended description and argument on behalf of natural things disclosing themselves as real in a manner analogous to persons in "In Defense of Anthropomorphism."

receiving a stamp. Instead, if the communication is good and proper, I offer my meaning in a form that is full of sense, into which my listener is invited, so that he can come out of himself in freedom to receive the disclosure, and indeed his accepting this invitation is in part what brings my disclosure to a certain perfection. Similarly, in beauty, nature manifests itself, perhaps with the direct help of human freedom, but in any event always analogous to it, and, in order to receive the disclosure properly, we have to arise, to come outside of ourselves to meet it, and in a sense to *indwell* it. Reality is not supplied in abstract packets of information so directly into our brain that we lose the distinction between the world and mental sensation (i.e., we lose a sense of the *reality of reality*). A genuine sense of beauty will coincide with a sense that the things of the world have their own depth, their own significance, to which we are offered access through appearance and perception in the manner of an encounter between real beings of substance. A sense of beauty demands that we extend *courtesy* to things. In such a world, things may indeed serve human purposes, but if they do so it is not in abject slavery; rather, they offer themselves for this use in something analogous to a noble freedom in which their own reality preserves its integrity. Their service takes the form of a gift gratefully received.[48]

It is in this sense that beauty sets the horizon for a genuine human existence: horizon is the proper image, here, because it implies, on the one hand, a kind of limit, a determination or constraint, without which there can be no perfection or coming to completion. On the other hand, this completion is not a termination, which would put an end to all activity. Instead, a horizon opens up a world, it erects a stage on which the drama of encounter can be played out. Our thesis has been that beauty enables a real encounter between man and the world. In the presence of the beautiful, which is a sort of open embrace—both truly an embrace and truly open—a space of existence emerges that is wide enough for the world to be actually present to us and for the full unfolding of our acts of intellect and will, from their origin to their proper term, as we will see in the two following chapters. To switch metaphors, beauty helps to root us in place, to involve us deeply in the reality there where we find ourselves, or in Heidegger's words, to set us in the earth. But it does not do so in a way that would trap us, isolate us, shield us from what is other. Instead, beauty effects a completeness that strengthens our capacity to be open and hospitable.

It is fitting, in this respect, that we tend to think of giving the quality of beauty, more directly than the quality of truth or goodness, to our background surroundings, the encompassing atmosphere inside of which

---

48. See Schiller, *Aesthetic Education*, 111–12 fn. 1.

our existence unfolds. We adorn the spaces in which we live and grow—our houses, our places of education, the public spaces of social intercourse, our churches, our centers of common life—not to "entertain," to provide distractions or occasions for momentary escape, but precisely to enable us to live with each other, with the things of the world, and ultimately with God, more deeply. The presence of beauty is not at all exclusive of truth and goodness or a threat to the seriousness they represent; instead, it is what helps create propitious conditions for their flourishing and proper expression.[49] In a word, our love of beauty is not a symptom of a pathological drive to escape the otherwise flat and stifling world, the lifeless givenness of the things around us; instead, it is a sign of our most natural need for the real.

49. On the evacuation of truth and goodness that arises from the loss of beauty, see Balthasar, *Glory of the Lord*, vol. 1, 18–19.

3

Goodness: Freedom as the Gift of Self

In a commencement address to the graduates of Kenyon College, which was published as an op-ed piece under the title "Liking is for Cowards: Go for What Hurts,"[1] the novelist Jonathan Franzen attempted to summarize a distinctive contemporary cultural phenomenon by illuminating the distinction between liking and loving. Both terms designate a certain positive disposition toward some reality, be it a thing or a person, but that is about as far as their similarity goes. Liking, Franzen explains, is a kind of approbation or affection that does not imply any sort of attachment, or any real commitment of the self. It therefore does not entail a deep involvement with things; in liking, I engage only their surface, and I do so only with my surface. Because of the lack of commitment, I am able to accept only what immediately pleases me, and I can dismiss the rest, ignore it as if it didn't even exist. It is not an accident that the verb "to like" has been able to be so readily appropriated as a technical term by social media, indicating the bestowal of totally inconsequential approval from the safe, anonymous distance of a technological device. In a "world of liking," to use Franzen's expression, things become mere objects of immediate desire, manipulation, and consumer choice. They respond immediately to our impulsive wishes and so never offer any real resistance to our whims. In the "world of liking," things become nothing more than an extension of ourselves, which is to say that such a world provides no escape from, and in fact encourages, reinforces, and so habitualizes, our native tendencies to narcissism.

As a contrast to the false and facile "world of liking," Franzen presents not the *"experience"* but what he tellingly calls the *"problem"* of love." Drawing, whether consciously or not, on Iris Murdoch's understanding—Murdoch famously defined love as the "extremely difficult realization that something

---

1. *New York Times*, 29 May 2011, page WK10. This piece was eventually included, with the new title, "Pain Won't Kill You," in a collection called *Farther Away: Essays*.

other than oneself is real"[2]—Franzen describes love as a genuine drama in which some real, specific thing or person draws us outside of ourselves and makes a claim on us, a reality to which we find ourselves committing ourselves, in some basic way without knowing exactly what it is we are doing. We are thus carried in love far beyond the surfaces and limits of "liking." "[T]o love a specific person," Franzen says, "and to identify with his or her struggles and joys as if they were your own, you have to surrender some of yourself."[3] Note that Franzen characterizes love here as an *identification* with the other and for that very reason a kind of *surrender* of the self: to put it somewhat crudely, the image he evokes with this description is that of a kind of transportation of the self into the other, so that the self now exists, at least in part or in some respect, in a new place, beyond the self's original borders.[4] What "hurts" here is this growth and the expropriation it entails.

In the previous chapter, we reflected on beauty as a kind of open invitation to reality; our focus in the present chapter will be on our relationship to the transcendental with immediate kinship to beauty, namely, goodness. The theme that Franzen's reflections raise turns on two different conceptions of the good, and two different conceptions of the will that correspond to them. In classical metaphysics, beauty opens the world to us, so that, as we will explain below, the desire at the root of our acts of will originates already from *within reality*. Goodness, here, is a property of being. For the modern mind, by contrast, what is good is essentially a *subjective* quality. Rather than drawing the person out of himself and involving him in the world as a matter of course, the good, in the modern sense, is simply an adjective one uses for things that one "likes"; it is reduced to a set of options that parade themselves before the "chooser," and have no intrinsic meaning, that is, no significance, until they happen to be selected.

One of the ways to get at this difference is in reference to the possibility of *identifying oneself* with another, which we just alluded to above. Is the image we used of the transportation of the self a mere metaphor, a kind of poetic exaggeration, or does it express something real and true? Do we, in fact, *actually* join ourselves to another in love? Is there a genuine truth to the frequently-heard notion that, in love, "two become one"? What is ultimately at issue in this question, I wish to suggest, is the structure of the volitional act and what it implies regarding the nature of the good at which that act aims. The argument we will make in this chapter is that what we tend to take

2. Murdoch, "The Sublime and the Good," 215.

3. Franzen, "Pain Won't Kill You," 9.

4. See Aquinas: "love transforms the lover into the beloved as love moves the lover toward the very thing beloved" (*De malo* VI.1ad13).

for granted, mostly unconsciously, as the usual, and indeed *normal*, sense of the will is captured by the phenomenon Franzen characterizes as "liking." The will, we generally believe, may be elicited in some sense by the things we perceive, but its ultimate business is with the self alone. Through our acts of will, we direct ourselves in one way or another, we cause ourselves to engage some action, and so may make contact with things, but the will does not *in reality and of its essence* reach beyond itself. We do not, in other words, think of the will as a place of intimate encounter with a reality that lies beyond ourselves. In a word, we have an essentially "egocentric" model of the will. If this model represents the actual structure of the will, then the notion of "identifying with another" can in fact only ever be a metaphor, a merely subjective experience that may be sincerely meant, but has no objective correlate to give it real substance. But this implies that what Franzen describes here as love is in fact just a higher degree of "liking," a positive disposition that is simply more intensely felt than the usual sort. If this is the case, it means that the "world of liking" is in fact the way the world really is, no matter how much we may want or try to approach it differently. It seems to me that to get beyond the radical human poverty of the superficiality that Franzen describes here (and in his novels) it is not enough just to try to live differently; we need to dig deeper, and address our understanding of the very nature of the will, and of the good that lies at its root. One needs to *think* differently if one wants really to *live* differently.

In order to make a case for this thesis, we will first present in somewhat simplified terms the difference between the modern and the pre-modern conception of the will, and reflect on some of the implications of this difference. We will then show that if freedom is the perfection of the will, these two different conceptions of the will will entail two radically different understandings of freedom: on the one hand, we have freedom interpreted as *a sort of power* (paradigmatically, the power to choose), and on the other hand, we have freedom understood as *the gift of self* (in both the objective and subjective sense of the genitive here: in freedom, we receive ourselves as a gift and we genuinely give ourselves to another). I will conclude by suggesting that we need to recover this latter sense in order to have a fully flourishing human life.

1. Locke and "Will Power"

The modern notion of the will has its classic exposition in the work of John Locke, whom we mentioned in the previous chapter as one of the fathers of the modern school of philosophy known as empiricism, which has been a major influence on the intellectual tradition in Britain and America.[5] In his most theoretical work, *The Essay concerning Human Understanding*, Locke presents the human will as the paradigm of "power": he proposes that the *experience* of the will is the one that most clearly illustrates what power means, because we discover power expressed here in an active form, which is the form most proper to power, namely, the ability to effect a change. This is distinct from the passive form of power, the ability to *be* affected, which we find everywhere else. The longest chapter of Locke's *Essay*, a book that seeks to trace the origin of all of our most basic ideas to their original experiences, attempted to work out precisely what it means to think of the will as "active power." It sought to think through the implications this understanding has for classic problems such as the challenge of harmonizing free will with the determinism that characterizes natural events, the problem of accounting for "weakness of will" (*akrasia*), that is, the strange capacity we have to fail to choose a thing that we really want, and so forth. That Locke's definition of the will was a truly revolutionary one is demonstrated in part by the fact that it took him some time to see clearly the novelty of its implications. In response to questions raised by both friends and critics, he was compelled early on to revise his thinking on the matter and to re-write this already-long chapter repeatedly for a series of new editions, which appeared in fairly quick succession. While he had initially tried to harmonize his understanding of the will with a number of traditional ideas associated with this particular human power, he gradually came to realize that the concept of will he was proposing required a clean sweep of the old notions, and a new interpretation of the whole matter of freedom from the ground up.

People are no doubt more familiar in general with the new ideas concerning the nature of freedom as they are expressed in his political writings, the *Second Treatise on Government* and the *Letter on Toleration*, both of which were published in the same year as the *Essay* (though Locke sent these more obviously revolutionary texts into the world without his name on them). But the deepest roots of all his new ideas lie in the *Essay*.[6] We will focus here on just two of the changes Locke made in his revisions, though they are especially fundamental and bring us directly to the heart of the matter that concerns us in this chapter. The first lies in the answer Locke gives in response to the question, What is it that most basically determines the will in the choices that it makes? In the first edition of the *Essay*, Locke

5. Thomas Jefferson famously included Locke, with Bacon and Newton, on his list of "the three greatest men the world had ever produced" (Jefferson, *The Writings of Thomas Jefferson*, vol. 11, 168).

6. For a more in-depth exposition and analysis of what follows on Locke's account of free will, see the first two chapters of D. C. Schindler, *Freedom from Reality*.

answered this question in what he later admits is the traditional way, affirming what he said was the most common interpretation of the will: what
determines our choices is the greatest good among alternatives, or at least
what we perceive to be the greatest good.[7] This is indeed, with some nuances
and variations, a tradition of interpretation one can trace back to Plato.[8] In
the second and subsequent editions, Locke changed this response to fit better with his new definition of the will as *active* power, as a cause that brings
about some external effect or effects, the *first source* of change, rather than
as the recipient of change or transmitter of causal "energy" received from
elsewhere. To say that the greatest good determines choice, Locke came to
see, makes the will secondary, dependent on something outside itself (the
goodness it perceives in some object), and so appears to compromise its
character as *active* power. Locke therefore amended his response in the new
edition, now saying that it is the *mind* that determines the will, which is to
say that the will is not first responsive to an object outside of the agent, but
is directed by nothing other than the agent himself: "For that which determines the general power of directing, to this or that particular direction, is
nothing but the agent itself exercising the power it has that particular way."[9]
By virtue of the active power it possesses in itself, the agent is principally
and ultimately "*self*-determining."

The second change I wish to highlight here is a subtler one, but is
crucially important for the problem of egocentrism that we alluded to at
the outset. In presenting his second edition, when Locke confesses that his
intellectual integrity and courage compelled him to change his mind about
his precise formulations of the nature of the will, he explains somewhat
cryptically that all of his revisions could be summed up as a "very easy and
scarce observable slip I had made, in putting one seemingly indifferent word
for another": whereas he had originally written that *things* were the objects
of the will, he ought to have said that *actions* were.[10] Scholars have typi-

---

7. Locke, *An Essay concerning Human Understanding*, book II, chapter 21, §29 of
the first edition: "*Good, then, the greater good, is that which determines the will,*" (p.
376), and §33: "the preference of the mind [is] *always* determined by the appearance of
good, greater good" (p. 377).

8. See, for example, *Protagoras* 352aff.; *Symposium* 205a–206a. The classic formulation of this principle can be found in Aquinas: "The will can tend to nothing except
under the aspect of the good" (*ST* 1.82.2 ad 1).

9. Locke, *An Essay concerning Human Understanding*, §29 (p. 330). The matter
becomes quite complex, of course, once Locke begins to elaborate what he means: he
specifies that the will is directed by the *mind*, and the mind in turn by the motive of
avoiding "uneasiness," but this motive is ultimately subordinate to the mind's discretion.

10. Ibid., §73 (p. 366). Locke does not say in the text itself what word this is, but
explained in a letter to his main correspondent regarding the *Essay*, Molyneux, that the

cally observed that Locke was exaggerating or oversimplifying the matter in describing the needed change thus, because it is not at all clear how this single shift of terms suffices to sum up all of the rethinking and rewriting he most evidently did between editions. It seems to me, however, that the appropriateness of Locke's characterization comes to light when we set his view of the will in contrast to the pre-modern conception. Doing so allows us to see how this little word is actually a big deal. In anticipation of the description of the classical notion of the will that we will provide shortly, we may point out here that, by saying the will is directed not at *things* but at *actions*, Locke reveals that he is restructuring the scope and nature of the will in a fundamental way. In a word, rather than acknowledging that the will is directed to—and indeed *into*—a reality in the world, which would imply an extension of the will beyond itself, Locke shrinks the will, so to speak, and limits its reach. It now no longer stretches out beyond the agent, but extends only as far as the boundaries of the self: "the will or power of volition is conversant about nothing but our own *actions*; terminates there; and reaches no further."[11] This limitation of the will's scope corresponds to the definition of will Locke sought to establish. If we think of the will specifically as an active power, which manifests itself by being the "unoriginate" first cause of some external change, it does not make sense to say that I will some *thing*, some object outside of myself. Instead, I have to recognize that the only thing I have direct power over, the only change I can make immediately through the exercise of my will, is in myself, or more specifically: in what I do.

To take a simple example as an illustration: I do not, in Locke's view, set my will on the apple as its object, but rather my will points only at myself. Through my will, I effectively cause an action, namely, eating, which entails in turn the consumption of the apple. To put it simply, I do not will the apple, and thereby eat it, but I will my action of eating, an action that happens to be set, in this case, on the apple.

This may seem like a minor inflection, and thus a point too fine to be all that significant. But we will see in a moment how enormous and weighty are the implications of Locke's revision of the meaning of the will. For now, it suffices simply to point out the way these two changes we described tend to absolutize the self in isolation from everything else in the world. On the one hand, to say that the *self* determines itself—perhaps *to* the greatest good as perceived, but not *by* the greatest good—is to say that the will *originates exclusively in the self*. Its determination comes from within itself; it is not first responsive to reality, but is wholly spontaneous, possessing the capacity

---

mistake was "having put *things* for *actions*": see his letter written 15 July 1693.

11. Locke, *An Essay concerning Human Understanding*, §30 (p. 331).

to set itself in motion without any necessary prompting or causal influence from anything outside its borders. On the other hand, the self not only *begins* its act of will from itself alone, but that movement likewise *ends* exclusively in the self as the will's proper object. I have no control over things in the world outside of me, but have control only over myself. This may seem like a perfectly obvious and true claim. But note: to say that I ought therefore to limit the scope of the will to myself alone is, by implication, to concede that the will is essentially *a matter of control*. The basic image here is the will as a power source that resides inside the private sphere of my self, and causes things incidentally outside in the world as consequences of my internally and spontaneously generated actions. There is, in this image, no *intrinsic* relation to things outside, no genuine connection between the self and the reality of the larger world. It is easy to see, I think, how this image encourages the sense of the "world of liking": the image translates quite effortlessly into that of a self, sitting behind a screen, at a distance from the real world, "arbitrarily" expressing approval and disapproval with very little personal involvement or cost. What we have here is precisely the original "egocentric" model of the will.

2. Anchoring the Will in Reality

For the "pre-modern" alternative to Locke's view of the will, the most obvious thinker to turn to is Thomas Aquinas, who set out a view of the will that synthesized elements from the classical and Christian tradition in a succinct way in the *Summa Theologiae*. His notion of the will reflects a robust and specifically transcendental conception of the good. Rather than spell out his whole philosophy of the will (and how he appropriates from the tradition or traditions he inherits), we will focus simply on his take on the two points we highlighted in Locke. At first glance, one might think that Locke and Aquinas are not very different from each other,[12] insofar as Aquinas clearly states that the will (or more specifically: *liberum arbitrium*) is *causa sui*, cause of itself, which sounds very much at first like Locke's notion of the will as a purely spontaneous, active power.[13] To say that the will is *causa sui* would

12. It is interesting to note that Mortimer Adler, in his massive survey, which attempts to synthesize the main philosophies of freedom in history, ends by presenting Aquinas, Locke, and Montesquieu as the three classical philosophers who offer a comprehensive interpretation of freedom: see *The Idea of Freedom*, 594.

13. Aquinas: "Free-will is the cause of its own movement, because by his free-will man moves himself to act" (*ST* 1.83.1 ad 3). Note that Aquinas distinguishes the power to choose (*liberum arbitrium*), translated here as "free-will," from the will itself (*voluntas*), as a derivative power thereof. As we will explain below, the will itself is not defined

appear to be to make the agent the principal cause, the most original source of determination. But in fact, for Aquinas, the will's self-determination is just one aspect of a more fundamental and comprehensive determination, or configuration of determinations, that occur in every choice we make. In addition to the will's self-causation, there is, on the one hand, the influence of the body and its desires, as well as the mind and its understanding, but there is even more fundamentally an influence of what lies beyond the agent, namely, the *good* itself, and, indeed, most ultimately, God.[14] The act of will, for Aquinas, can be seen as a sort of "joint work," a "co-operation," between the will, the self more holistically, and a determining power that lies beyond the self, indeed, infinitely so. *All* of these factors are involved in every choice made, which is why we need always and from the first to view the agent, not as an isolated, sheer power to choose, but as a subject embedded always in concentric circles of relations, that is, as organically connected to the world from the first.[15] The motion of the will, according to Aquinas, *does not originate in me*, but in fact originates in the actual good in any given situation that attracts me to itself. The will moves itself only in its already being moved by the good that draws it, which means that the will's own active motion is in a certain sense *given* to it. The will does not make its choice in a vacuum, we might say, through a spontaneous burst of "active power," but rather rides a movement that begins, so to speak, deeper than itself. Its choice is therefore more a consent than a directive.

One of the most immediate consequences of this relatively simple point is that it implies already an *internal* connection between the self and the outside world. For Aquinas, the better the good that faces me—which means the more powerfully and comprehensively it attracts me by virtue of its correspondence to who and what I am by nature—the more it enhances my will's own power of self-determination. For Locke, by contrast, because the will is an active power, and so essentially a matter of effective control, it is threatened by any outside influence, and this includes the compelling attraction of a true good. If we think of the will most basically in terms of

---

by free choice but rather by its natural ordination to the universal good.

14. In *ST* 1-2.9, Aquinas explains that the will is moved, in different ways, by: the intellect (art.1), the sensitive appetite (art.2), the will itself (art.3), and an extrinsic principle, namely, the good (art.4), which is identified ultimately with God (art.6).

15. Note that the image of concentric circles needs to be qualified; it seems to imply a kind of extrinsic relation, according to which the various levels make contact at their outer edges, as it were. This would mean that that which is furthest away from the center has *least* influence on it. But in fact, for Aquinas, the movement of the will *begins* from the good/God, which means that God, as infinitely transcendent, and so "furthest" from the center, nevertheless most intimately operates in the will, in all of its acts (*ST* 1-2.9.6).

power, rather than in terms of the attraction of goodness, a kind of dialectical tension becomes inevitable: anything that calls on the will from the outside sets in play a power struggle, a conflict of forces, a competition in a zero-sum game. This is why the first matter of business for the will, according to Locke, is a kind of detachment, a cancellation of any attractive forces, so that the will can be free to make its own choice.[16] We will come back to this point in a moment. Aquinas's definition of the will—in perfect contrast to Locke's "active power"—is "intellectual appetite,"[17] which means it is *essentially* a desire for what is good in truth (as the intellect reveals it). To think of the will as an appetite is to think of it, not primarily as a spontaneous power, but most basically as receptive: the will is our power to be attracted by the good, and to move ourselves *inside* of this attraction. It is a movement whose *principle* lies beyond the soul, and as such is able to initiate a movement that allows the will to reach beyond itself: "appetite" comes from *ad-petere*, to move towards and seek out. From this perspective, it is not the case that I make contact with the world solely as a result of my choices, a view that would place not only me, but in a certain respect also the world, under my control. Instead, the world is always already active in me, shaping me, helping to make me who I properly am, and my will is a means by which I make this movement my own.[18]

We can make sense of this claim—namely, that the world is always already operating within me, which is to say that I am always already involved in reality—best by recalling our discussion of beauty in the previous chapter. As we saw there, and will deepen in chapters 5 and 6, we do not stand before the world first in detachment, as if it were an object toward which we are initially and most fundamentally indifferent. We would be able to overcome this fundamental indifference toward reality only by our deliberate action in its regard: we *make* it meaningful by *choosing* it through the "power" of our

16. Locke comes to say (in the second edition of the *Essay*) that the "source of all liberty" lies in the "power to *suspend* the execution and satisfaction of any of [the mind's] desires": §48 (p. 345).

17. Aquinas, *ST* 1.82.5.

18. One might ask whether the world might in fact be already active in me, not as helping me be who I am, but in hindering me, distorting who I most truly am by disordering my desires and pulling me in an improper direction. There are two things to say in response: first, it is indeed the case that the presence of the world in my self can be destructive because of the effects of sin, both in myself and in those around me. Second, however, one must insist that the attraction to true goodness always remains *the most basic* character of will, which is by definition the "intellectual appetite." Sin corrupts the will, but does not make it a different thing. This does not imply that the effects of sin are superficial. Rather, it implies that the order God created remains absolute, even in the fallen state, which is why man can in fact be transformed by the grace of redemption.

will. If, by contrast, we affirm beauty as a transcendental property of being, we are thereby recognizing that our fundamental relation to the world is not that of detached indifference. Instead, we see that reality has disclosed itself in its appearance to us, so that our every sense experience is already in some sense an acceptance of an invitation to intimacy. It is in light of this "acceptance" that we can make sense of Aquinas's description of the will (*voluntas*) as an appetite, that is, a movement originating in reality to which we join ourselves through free choice (*liberum arbitrium*).

In light of Aquinas's definition of the will, we can see why he is able to offer a description of its proper object that is radically different from Locke's. As we saw above, for Locke, the *end* of the will, the destination in which its act reaches its completion, is the agent's own action. This description, we said, implies that the will never in fact gets beyond itself, never attains an object that transcends its strict self-relation. For Aquinas, by contrast, the act of the will comes to completion in the *real thing itself*, at which it is directed. In technical terms, the *terminus ad quem* of the volitional act is *in re*. To go back to the apple example: for Locke, the decision to eat the apple comes from myself alone, I move myself to eat through an act of will, and, if all goes well, if the external world cooperates, the apple gets consumed in the process. This may seem like I am making intimate contact with the world—I am taking the apple *into* myself after all, and transforming it into a part of my body—but in reality this contact is extrinsic and accidental: the spiritual act of any exercise of will begins in myself and ends in myself, and the apple just happens to be, as it were, in the wrong place at the wrong time. The apple is simply something that provides the occasion for me to relate to myself in an ultimately exclusive way (*ex-cludere:* to close out). In the Thomistic understanding, the act of eating an apple, which may look essentially the same from the outside, yields a profoundly different meaning. For Aquinas, my act of will is first set in motion by the goodness of the apple itself: the apple takes an active role, you might say, calling to me, drawing me toward itself. In this case, my choice takes a principially receptive form, more like the accepting of an invitation than the seizing of a prey.

Because the act of will originates beyond the will it also terminates beyond the will. My choosing to eat the apple is a willing of the apple itself, and my action is not the *end* of the act but the *means by which* the proper end is attained.[19] In this case, there is a profound intimacy in the act of will, by which I come outside of myself and have a genuine encounter with something *real* that is not a mere extension of myself. Though it lies beyond

19. In more technical terms: the will (*voluntas*) is set on the end, and the will's power to cause itself (*liberum arbitrium*) concerns the *means* by which the end is accomplished: Aquinas, *ST* 1.83.4.

our present context to explore this further, for Aquinas, the intimacy in this act is not simply between the soul and the goodness presented by the reality of the apple, but in a certain sense ultimately an encounter with God: in every single act, it is not just goodness that moves me and so allows me to move myself, but *God himself* does so.[20] Every act of will is an intimate encounter with God.[21]

Now, however that may be, the more immediate dimension to draw out in the present context is that to say that the soul exceeds itself in every act of will, which terminates not in the agent but in the reality itself, is in fact to say that the soul *"gives itself away"* in a certain sense in each of these acts. If it is the case, as we argued last chapter, that beauty is an open invitation to intimacy with reality, and, as we will argue next chapter, that truth represents our reception of reality into ourselves, it is also the case that, in the acts of will rooted in goodness, we are actually "giving" ourselves to what is other than us, we are genuinely involving ourselves with an other. In the light of beauty, we have to understand knowing and willing as a kind of intimate exchange between the world and the self. When we think of the matter in these terms, the common philosophical notion of the will as the power of self-determination acquires a new—indeed, a perhaps disturbingly weighty—sense. While in using this phrase we normally mean to underscore our *power*, the *control* we have over ourselves, Aquinas's sense of the will prompts us to reverse the significance in a certain respect: in my choices, I determine myself in the specific sense of committing myself to something, making myself in a certain way something new by binding myself to a reality that lies beyond my merely self-related subjectivity.[22] The reality *to which* I determine myself is thus one that, as other, calls out to me and thereby sets me in motion, carrying me even in my own act of will. Obviously, some acts of will are more decisive in this regard than others:

20. Here we see why we can talk about predestination without implying anything like man as helpless puppet in the hands of an omnipotent God. "Puppet strings" are, however, inevitable insofar as we conceive the will's activity as a matter of power rather than first as a matter of goodness.

21. "Because God is the last end, he is sought in every end, just as, because he is the first efficient cause, he acts in every agent" (Aquinas, *De ver.* 22.2).

22. Behind this lies a profound metaphysical difference: the modern notion of being is decisively *non-analogical*, and so the dynamic it implies tends to take the form of continuation in the same (see e.g., Spinoza's *conatus*). For Aquinas, by contrast, there remains a kind of self-transcendence even in the love of self: the goodness of being, which truly belongs to any given thing as its own, is never simply identical with its essence in any given instance (cf., *ST* 1.6.3 ad 3). Thus, continuation in the same is for Aquinas the lowest kind of natural activity (see *ST* 1.78.1 and 2), but even here it is self-transcending insofar as it implies a kind of new achievement in every moment.

eating an apple is not the same as choosing one's spouse or one's vocation. But in *every one* of our choices, we are nevertheless making a gift of self to one degree or another. Every act of will, in this respect, represents a kind of attachment. This means that in reality there is no such thing as a "world of liking" in the sense of a safe, isolated space from which to dispense uncommitted approval or disapproval. Even remaining "non-committal" is a kind of self-determining commitment.

3. Freedom versus Autonomy

One of the most illuminating ways of showing forth the stakes of this difference in conceptions of the will is to think through, however briefly, their implications for our understanding of freedom. Freedom is, of course, an ideal that is particularly dear to Americans. The model of freedom that we carry with ourselves, mostly unconsciously, has, I wish to suggest, a profound influence not only on what choices we make, but *how* we make those choices, and indeed how we think of ourselves as human beings. And this understanding lies at the basis of how we order civilization. The way that we relate to ourselves, to nature, to other people, and to God all rides on this question: What is the nature of freedom? While it is not possible explore this question fully here of course, our reflections up to this point on the nature of the will allow us at least to try to say something essential.

Whatever else freedom is, it represents the will in its most perfect condition, which is of course why we have made it an ideal that we strive after, that we seek to foster and preserve, even at the cost of great sacrifice. But it seems to me that, if we interpret freedom in line with the modern notion of will that we have described here, this "ideal" becomes quite ominous.[23] If the will is nothing more than the power to choose—power as spontaneous, and so non-receptive, effective causality—then it exists in its most perfect condition when it is completely separated from anything outside itself. The "natural state" of the will, we might say, is detachment. Attachments, in this case, or indeed any sort of commitments understood as genuinely binding, become a threat to the will in its freedom. To be sure, from this perspective,

---

23. Incidentally, both the author we presented at the outset of this chapter, Jonathan Franzen, and the one we will present next chapter, David Foster Wallace (who happen to have been good friends), have made the question of freedom a particularly important theme of their art. Jonathan Franzen, for example, entitled his novel, which depicted the ills of modern suburban life, *Freedom* (2011), and David Foster Wallace discussed the meaning of freedom in what is arguably a central dramatic point of his great novel *Infinite Jest* (2006), 440ff. Both authors, in different ways, have sought to overcome in particular the isolation and egocentrism dominant in modern culture.

one might still talk about freely choosing to commit myself to something or other by virtue of my power to choose, but in this case we are forced to say, to the extent that I do *in fact* bind myself, I am giving up my freedom, so that, if I wish to retain freedom, it will be in the form of the power to rescind my commitment as a result of a new choice.[24] Of course, in this case, it is not really legitimate to speak of a "bond" in any proper sense. The outcome of this view of freedom is *egocentric isolation*: a conception of the self as radically disconnected, essentially detached and free-floating, ultimately caught up in a (usually) secret war with everything in the world outside of the self (the body, the earth, the social and political order, friends, family, spouse, God, and indeed even with itself). Freedom gets identified with independence as non-commitment. To foster this notion of freedom, to make it a culture-forming ideal, is to cultivate and reinforce the habits of isolation and irresponsibility. In this situation, it helps little to multiply connections, to improve communication technologies, to accumulate "friends" in one's account, because, without a deeper understanding of the nature of the will, and so of the human person more generally, none of those "connections" will involve the self deeply. They will be insubstantial, and so inadequate to the real human self that we all inescapably *are*.

From the perspective of classical philosophy, by contrast, freedom is seen as an intrinsic participation in the goodness that belongs to reality in its very being. Freedom in this respect is *always* a kind of involvement in reality. It has its paradigm in total, irrevocable gift of self, by which the self also comes to its proper perfection. The self is a gift we give and at the same time a gift we *receive*. The most complete human instance of this exchange, of course, is in marriage, by which two people make vows—an act of the will—by which they bind themselves together forever, in a way that is fruitful and so never ceases to call on them to renew the gift of self and to find it renewed.[25] The will, here, is called out *by* the other, and comes to comple-

---

24. One might object that there should be no problem with freedom interpreted as the power to choose as long as we subordinate this *instrumental* good to the higher intrinsic goods it ought to be used for, a subordination that might amount in some cases to a sacrifice. This objection might be sustainable in principle, but only if we recognize that freedom, from this perspective, does not belong to the *will* per se, but only to the power to choose (*liberum arbitrium*). Holding this objection, moreover, requires that one not separate means from ends, recognizing that means as such already participate intrinsically in the ends they seek, and also that one deny the various affirmations of freedom as an intrinsic good, as opposed to a mere instrument, which can be found not only in contemporary thought but throughout the tradition.

25. There is also, of course, the religious vow by which one consecrates oneself to God. A full sense of the meaning of freedom as gift of self would require interpreting the two forms of vows—religious and marital—in light of each other.

tion in a complete and irrevocable devotion of the self. In the traditional language that comes from the creation story in Genesis, two people in marriage becomes "one flesh," which is to say that they come together to form a single existence. An ontological transformation occurs here. According to the modern concept of the will, this notion cannot be real: if it is more than a romantic metaphor, it is only because it represents, in addition and more objectively, a legal entity—i.e., a fabrication that has its reality in an institutionalized public recognition. But for the classical view of the will, the legal status is itself simply an acknowledgment of the ontological reality. The classical view is able to recognize marriage as an ontological reality because, for this view, the profound intimacy of the one-flesh union is simply the perfect expression of what occurs analogously in every single choice we make. This gift of self may not be as clear in the trivial choices that occur on a daily basis—to eat an apple, to wear a particular pair of shoes, etc.—but the dramatic engagement of the self that occurs in the great decisions that define our lives reveals the *truth* of the will, even in its normal exercise. In the realization of freedom that is the marriage vow, we exercise a total self-determination; we transcend ourselves definitively and only thus come to discover who we genuinely are.[26]

The will is therefore not a "power to like"; instead, its very *essence* is love. To think of the will as the non-committal power of the modern egocentric self is, in one sense, to make self-protection and the pursuit of self-interest the normal meaning of existence. This pursuit may be interrupted from time to time by some unusual event, but the interruption cannot ever manage to be the expression of reality, of some essential and authentic truth. Sooner or later, the interruption will pass, its effects will fade, and reality will reassert itself, smoothing these castles out once again. The "world of liking" is the world conceived as nothing more than an extension of the self, and in this world I never give myself to anyone or anything.

Or so it seems. At a deeper level, if the pre-modern view of the will that we have been arguing for is the true one, it follows that we *cannot help* but give ourselves away in some sense in everything we do. To live in the "world of liking," then, is not to hold onto ourselves, but rather to give ourselves away cheaply and indiscriminately, to turn ourselves into a trafficked commodity rather than what it is and is meant to be: a gift. To recover a sense of the self *as* a gift, we must reawaken in ourselves the desire for freedom that lies in all of us, and to recognize that this desire will not find its proper fulfillment in the constant battle for detached independence (which is not

---

26. For a more thorough discussion of this point, see my "The Crisis of Marriage as a Crisis of Meaning."

only a battle we will invariably lose, but one that has always already been lost). Instead, freedom, finally, has its truth only in love, in which to lose oneself is in fact to gain everything. And this understanding of freedom is itself the fruit of a recognition that reality *itself* is a gift, that it is good in its very being.

4

Truth: Knowledge as Personal Presence

1. Habits of Isolation

In a recent book entitled *Friendship as Sacred Knowing*, Samuel Kimbriel makes the following observation: "Ours is an age of lonely-mindedness. We are haunted, I suggest, by a certain habit of isolation buried, often imperceptibly, within our practices of understanding and relating to the world. . . . To call the age 'lonely-minded' is to say something more than simply, as many others have done, that it is an age of loneliness, however true that may be."[1] After alluding to the various sociological phenomena people often bring up in this context—the breakdown of families, the fragmentation of communities, the hyper-pluralism that dissolves traditional social bonds, and so forth—the author insists that the problem has a deeper root. Drawing on the work of Charles Taylor,[2] Kimbriel explains that, in contrast to the pre-modern sense of the self as naturally and inextricably embedded within concentric circles of relations, so that we could not isolate the individual conceptually without radically distorting who he is and the reality in which he participates, the modern world tends to take this distortion for granted: we think of the self as an isolated center of consciousness, cut off from the world, from deep relations to other people, and even from ourselves. Ironically, this new sense of the self as isolated subjectivity has in many ways made it easier to "make connections," which is why we have seen in the modern world, and especially now in what is often called the "postmodern" one, such a great expansion of our knowledge of the world, of cultures previously regarded as altogether foreign, and indeed of the intimate lives of other people. But these connections are easy to multiply precisely *because* they

---

1. Kimbriel, *Friendship as Sacred Knowing*, 1.
2. Kimbriel makes reference above all to Charles Taylor's *A Secular Age*.

are superficial; underlying this great web of interconnections there remains a picture of the self that is powerless to reach beyond its own subjectivity.

To respond to this "lonely-mindedness," Kimbriel continues, it is not enough to renew efforts to foster community or increase our knowledge of others. Rather, the deeper root is a *habit of mind*, an interpretation of the nature of the intellect that underlies all of our thinking and doing, and tends to encourage certain patterns of isolation. If this is the case, we cannot *really* address the problem of "lonely-mindedness" without going to the root, re-imagining the nature of reason. What we need, the author says, is a "shift in what counts as 'knowledge' or 'reason.' "For modernity," he continues, "enquiry becomes a remarkably insulated and indeed self-defined affair manifesting a basic tendency towards isolation, or, indeed, loneliness. From our way of knowing, habits of isolation then ripple outward into nearly every corner of modern life."[3] If the *way* of knowing lies at the root of the problem, as Kimbriel suggests, we need not to know more things but to re-think what it means to know at all. Indeed, if our conception of knowledge itself presupposes a certain conception of the nature of truth, we ought to add that a full response requires rethinking the question "What is truth?"

To get a sense of the urgency of this problem, we might consider the tragic case of the extraordinary writer David Foster Wallace, who was a friend of Franzen, whom we mentioned last chapter. A central theme in his work is the importance of genuine human contact, the need to overcome loneliness and encounter the world and other people in their reality. In his own commencement speech, delivered to the graduates of Kenyon College in 2005,[4] Wallace spoke movingly about the tendency to fall into a habit of detachment, to switch into "auto-pilot mode" in our living. At one of the climaxes of the speech, Wallace remarks on our propensity to get stuck inside of ourselves, and says that the "old cliché about . . . the mind being an excellent servant but a terrible master," though it may seem, "like many clichés, so lame and unexciting on the surface, actually expresses a great and terrible truth. It is not the least bit coincidental," he goes on to observe, "that adults who commit suicide with firearms almost always shoot themselves: in the head."[5] As we see here, Wallace presents the mind as a potential enemy, something we need to outwit or evade, if not to eliminate altogether.

If Kimbriel is right, however, what we need to do is not find some way to get *out* of our head and *into* the world, as David Foster Wallace urges, but rather to ask ourselves what sort of assumptions we have about the head

---

3. Kimbriel, *Friendship as Sacred Knowing*, 1–2.
4. The speech was published as *This is Water* (2009).
5. Ibid., 56–58.

that make it something we feel we need to escape, something that takes us away from the reality of things. According to the classical philosophical tradition, the mind is what most properly defines our humanity, but at the same time it is precisely that by which we are most profoundly united with things other than ourselves. The mind is our capacity to participate in the truth that belongs to the very nature of things. If we wish to connect with the greater world, this tradition encouraged us to cultivate the very thing that distinguishes us as human. If, by contrast, we believe that the mind is a kind of isolation cell, an interior place locked up in itself, it implies that the very thing that defines us as human beings is a problem that needs to be overcome. And this is quite a tragic conception of man. We will of course never know what caused Wallace's own suffering, but, given the persistent themes of his fiction—the primary purpose of which, he once said, was to provide "a way out of loneliness"—we might well wonder whether this tragic conception contributed to generating the culture of isolation and thus to the despair that caused Wallace himself finally to take his own life just three years after delivering the commencement speech.

Now, Kimbriel's description of the postmodern condition prompts us directly to ask: What are the assumptions we make about "what counts as 'knowledge' and 'reason'" in our age that create and foster habits of lonely-mindedness? As Esther Lightcap Meek has argued in *Loving to Know*, our "default" conception, the view of knowledge that we cannot help but presuppose in the contemporary setting regardless of whether or not we have ever thought about the matter ourselves, is that knowledge is essentially equivalent to information.[6] We go about the task of knowledge by gathering data and recording facts,[7] and, if we are sufficiently methodical and thorough in our efforts, we believe we can thereby come to know everything that is relevant: it is through this process that we thus achieve knowledge of the event, the thing, the matter at hand.

So, what is wrong with this view? As innocent as this default conception of knowledge may seem, it is not just inadequate in the sense that we need to "fill in" whatever might be missing, further aspects of knowledge that this conception leaves out; instead, as Meek proposes, this conception of knowledge actually undermines our connection to the world in a profound way. The "information-model" of knowledge represents a distortion of things, and at the same time an impoverishment of our relationship to

6. Meek, *Loving to Know*, 5–8.

7. Technical treatments seek to distinguish information from data: see, for example, Floridi, "Is Information Meaningful Data?" But this distinction is not relevant to the argument we are making. Both fall on the side of what we are describing here as "information," in contrast to the classical notion of form, as we will propose.

those things in their actual reality. It isolates us even as it pretends to facilitate interaction.

At the root of this model is a failure to recognize truth as a *transcendental*, which means as a property of being itself, reducing it instead to a quality of knowledge alone, the mere "correctness" of information. If truth is a property of being, our knowing takes the form of a conformity to reality. To know, in this sense, is to make genuine contact with things, to take into ourselves the reality *in* which we have always already been involved in beauty and goodness. It thus entails an aspiration, beyond episodic contact, to a more constant fidelity, a kind of "belonging" to the real or a habitual devotion, involving not just our minds but the whole of our lives. Such a deep conformity is what the classical tradition meant by the term "wisdom," and it is just this that has fallen to the margins in our reconception of truth. As T. S. Eliot famously asked, "Where is the wisdom we have lost in knowledge? Where is the knowledge we have lost in information?"[8]

To try to show why the reduction of knowledge to information is problematic, I will first make some brief observations regarding what information *is*, and then consider some of the implications of taking it as a primary model of knowing. Finally, I will recall an older view of knowledge as a grasp of form,[9] which I will suggest offers a more hopeful alternative. Obviously, a good deal will have to be left out of the argument given the constraints of this book, and I will not try to provide a definitive "proof" for one view or another, but I hope nevertheless to say enough to set into relief the concrete stakes of this question, which may initially seem so abstract and technical.

2. Too Much Information

What, then, is information? I propose that the distinguishing mark of information is its "transferability."[10] Albert Borgmann observes that the decisive characteristic of information is that it "can be produced and distributed."[11] The English word "information" is derived from the Latin, *informare*, which indicates a transmission of intellectual content ("*in-*," in the accusative sense

8. From the opening stanza of T. S. Eliot's choruses from *The Rock*.

9. It is worth noting that "grasp of form" is meant as an *essential* definition of knowledge, but not an *exhaustive* one; a more complete treatment of the theme would require that the essential definition be complemented with several other aspects.

10. See Gleick, *The Information*. Note that Gleick begins his book on information with a discussion of the invention of the *transistor* by Bell Telephone Labs in 1948, and Claude Shannon's coining of the term "bit" to designate the unit of measure for information.

11. See Borgmann, *Holding onto Reality*, 9.

of "motion towards," and *"forma,"* or intelligible object).[12] The intelligible content that constitutes information is defined by, and thus limited to, what can be conveyed across a distance and into other contexts. This tends to imply a breaking down of intelligible contents into moveable bits, that is, into as simplified a form as possible so as to be able to be carried into new arrangements and contents.

Let us reflect on this in a more concrete way. Everything that is intelligible has meaning, but it becomes quickly evident upon reflection that not all meaning is able to be translated without remainder into "information." To see this, we might consider a simple example. If we were to try to call to mind an experience we have had that we would describe as meaningful, many of us would point to a personal encounter, for instance, spending time with family or an old friend. Now, clearly, there is a great deal of information one could report about this encounter: the time and place, the number of minutes or hours it lasted, details about who the person is and why the meeting might be considered significant, statements about the sort of things we thought or felt in response to the meeting, and so forth. There is probably not a single aspect of this event that could not be recorded as information, and yet we recognize immediately that the mass of information is not at all equivalent to the experience we had. It is the experience *itself,* rather than some aspect of it or fact about it, that we designate as meaningful. We all would spontaneously deny that recording all of this information would be just as good as having been there and undergone the experience in person. What is missing is precisely the "actually being there," and this is no small matter.

The information about a thing remains exactly the same, whether one is or was there or not. The reason it remains the same, regardless of context, is that information is, so to speak, essentially detachable; there is a fundamental separation between a reality and the variety of information that can be recorded about it. The preposition is crucial here: *about.* It indicates relation or reference from a distance.[13] Information is knowledge *about* something, as distinct from direct acquaintance.[14] Now, to be sure, it is just

12. The word thus is at least distantly related to "form," which is what defines intelligibility in the classical sense, as we have already mentioned. But the emphasis in "information" lies on the aspect of *transmission,* and so on what can be transmitted. It is revealing that a primary (modern and ancient) Greek word for information is πληροφορία, which has no reference to form (either εἶδος or μορφή). Instead, the word consists wholly in the reference to transmission: φορία, comes from φέρω, which means "to carry" or "to convey," and πλήρες means, "fully."

13. The first chapter of Gleick's book is on the "talking drums" of Africa, used to communicate a message from one village to another.

14. Borgmann points up the difference between "information and presence,"

this separation that makes information so useful: the meaningfulness of a face-to-face encounter is something accessible in the most proper sense only to the two people involved, whereas the information about it can be communicated to anyone at all. Indeed, as data, the information can be recorded and incorporated into statistics for psychological or sociological analysis, and so forth. The possibilities for use are endless, and this is just because so little is contained in each extracted "bit" of information. The meaningful encounter, by contrast, might mean *everything*, but if it does it will be only for a limited circle, perhaps just one person. It is only such an experience that could be said to have great human depth, but it is precisely this that keeps it from being useful for further projects and purposes. The "human depth" is just what does not survive the translation into "information."

An illuminating analogy can be drawn between information and processed food. It is somewhat surprising, at first, to note that food seems to get cheaper the more work is done to it or on its behalf. If we go regularly to the grocery store, we know that the food bill tends to go up the more fresh produce we have on the list. How can it be the case that a frozen dinner, with its sprawling list of ingredients, costs less than what one would pay to buy the real items pictured on the box and make the meal "from scratch"? Why is chopped and frozen broccoli cheaper than its fresh counterpart, and cheaper still than the broccoli grown without pesticides, especially if it is from a local farm?[15] The reason things get cheaper the more they are worked upon is in large part that processing liberates things, so to speak, from the restrictions of their original constitution. The further they are wrested from their *natural* roots, the more they can be manipulated, the more they can be made into a variety of other products, packaged and transported, broken down into their most useful components, made into ingredients of more complex items, taken up and rendered serviceable for purposes nature would have never conceived herself, commodified, and so forth. Michael Pollan, the well-known food writer, brought our attention not too long ago to the shocking array of products made out of America's most plentiful crop

---

which lies at the basis of the "decline of meaning" that coincides with the "rise of information": Borgmann, *Holding onto Reality*, 9–16.

15. Note, incidentally, that it is precisely *chopped* broccoli that is typically frozen and bagged: one does not normally freeze whole crowns of broccoli or of course the whole plant, or the clod of soil in which it grows, even though these are essential to what the broccoli is. To the contrary, it only really makes sense to freeze and package the *bits*: transferability implies reduction. The broccoli, in this example, is not regarded as a plant, a reality in itself, and becomes primarily a food item in this process. To eat broccoli grown in a backyard garden, by contrast, we must first attend to it as an organism, a living being in its own right, and only turn it into food from inside of this prior context.

(which turns out to be *why* it is the crop produced in such great abundance), very few of which in the end bear the least resemblance to corn.[16] And that is the very point we mean to make: the further from the roots, the less of a connection with what a thing really is. This is not an exceptionless principle, of course, but it is a fairly reliable rule of thumb.

Now, the suggestion is that "information" is to intelligibility what frozen dinners are to food. Information, in other words, is what intelligibility looks like when it is, so to speak, processed, packaged, and served up in a manner that attends principally to convenience (rather than, say, nutrition, taste, or traditional cultural custom—or the epistemological analogies to this). It is meaning that has been broken down into the most relevant and useful units, which can be transported and taken up into foreign contexts. The implication is that, given this analogy, to the extent that we make the recording, processing, and storing of information the *model* of what it means to know, our sense of reality suffers, our relationship to the world and to ourselves will be impoverished. Food concerns a very basic part of our lives, but only one such part; knowledge is involved in every single aspect. Arguably, our conception of knowledge as information lies at the root of our treating of food as we do.[17] However this may be, it remains the case that, in a world of mere information, identities become fragile and tenuous. Ironically, in such a world, we simultaneously increase our sense of power over things, since they have been reduced in their significance to essentially manipulable bits of data, and we radically undermine our confidence, our trust in the meaning of the world. The reason for this is the "separation" from reality that information implies.

Let us look at this more precisely. There are two forms of separation that occur in information. On the one hand, as we noted above, there is a distance between a real thing and the data that is extracted from it. Information can never be fully adequate to the reality it is "about" precisely because it is itself only a part, a separable *bit* of the intelligibility that is taken to be relevant according to some external purpose, some standard that lies outside of the reality in question. The reduction to information tends to oversimplify a reality or state of affairs in a way that can be quite misleading. A talented, and very conscientious, student of mine a few years ago entered a prestigious graduate program in psychology and was immediately

16. See Pollan, *The Omnivore's Dilemma*, especially chapter 1, "The Plant: Corn's Conquest," 15–31.

17. See Michael Pollan's argument that unhealthy eating habits in the modern world have grown from a reduction of food to a conglomeration of "nutrients," which is itself an expression of the reductivistic thinking that characterizes modern science: "Unhappy Meals," *New York Times Magazine*, 28 January 2007.

given the task, along with other new students, of gathering data for a major, well-funded study his professors were conducting. Data gathering meant, in this context, meeting with patients, asking a list of questions, making a judgment about the responses, and assigning a numeric value to the responses. This student came to me after a few months of participating in the program because he was undergoing a crisis of conscience. The reason for his crisis was not just the shock that *he*, a first-year grad student without any experience or training, was being asked to make determinations that would lie at the very foundation of the study; what disturbed him even more, he explained, was that most of the cases he was recording represented what one would call "borderline" with respect to virtually every question he asked, so that he could give an argument to justify assigning a whole range of different values in most instances. But once he settled on a value, arbitrarily—or so he felt—determining the case to be a one, a two, a three, and so forth, the information was taken as an absolute fact at the next level, precisely because of the separation between the knowers (the research professors in this case) and the actual realities being studied (the patients and their psychological conditions). This student was abstracting, processing, and packaging the intelligibility into digestible and manipulable bits, and making his delivery. The professors received the packages, without a concrete sense of their origin, and set to work on making some sense of it all. (The stress here is on the *making* of the sense.) In the reduction of intelligibility to information, something necessarily gets "lost in translation." And the greater the separation, the more manipulable meaning gets: we all know how statistics can be made to say virtually anything one wants them to say.

At a subtler level, there is in information a separation between the source of the information and the recipient. We have just seen an obvious example in the psychological study, in which the people who carry out the work of the study are different from the people who originally gather the information. But there is an even more profound separation between source and recipient that we have to consider. If we penetrate to this level, we see that the information-gatherers themselves stand at a distance from the meaningful reality they are attempting to know, precisely to the extent that this knowledge is conceived in the form of information. I suggested at the outset that the distinguishing mark—indeed, the very essence—of information is "transferability." Information is produced or conveyed; it is abstracted and extracted intelligibility that moves from the source to a recipient, who lies outside of that source. According to the model of information, this relationship is understood in the order of efficient causality, in which there is a separation between cause and effect.[18]

To get at the meaning of "separation" in this context, we may return to our discussion from chapter 1. We have all learned to conceive of sense experience as a conveyance of information in the form of a causal event. Thus, we may speak as if leaves were green, but we will all admit if pressed that in reality we know that green is just a subjective sensation produced in our brains by the frequency of the light waves that reflect off of the surfaces. In other words, quantified information is produced by a set of circumstances and transmitted (i.e., sent, *mittere*, across a distance, *trans*) to the appropriate organ that then translates it into terms that are meaningful to the neural system that receives and interprets it. As one school book puts it, light terms are translated into nerve terms. Leaves are not *really* green, we have learned to say; in fact, we have no idea what color they "really" are, and indeed have no possible way of attaining such an idea. Or, more adequately, it makes no sense to say that things in the world have any "color" at all, because color is a name given to an event produced in our brains rather than a quality that inheres in some real thing out there in the world. This event in our brain is separated by an infinite chasm from the thing out there that causes the event—the chasm is literally infinite because there is no determinate connection, no unity that could provide commensurability, no intrinsic relationship between the objective mechanism and the subjective sensation. In a sense, the "loss in translation" that we saw occurring in the psychological experiment is here happening at a micro-level: recordable bits are gathered, packaged, delivered over, and taken as a starting point by the nerves, which they process and translate so that this data can be made meaningful for the brain.

When we attend to the world's *beauty*, to the marvelous spectrum of colors we see in our everyday experience of things, the smells, the textures that enter into our sense perception, we may think that we are touching the world, or the world is touching us. But the information-model of perceptive knowledge implies that this is not so: all of this sense experience, it says, is not a revelation of the world itself, but simply an experience of something going on inside of me, which happens to have been caused by some distant transmitter. Thus conceived, the sense experience does not open us to the world but rather traps us, so to speak, in our heads. It follows that, if all meaning takes the form of information, bits of data gathered from a distance and translated into terms that have no intrinsic relation to the *source* of that

18. Wikipedia states that, "at its most fundamental, information is any propagation of cause and effect within a system."

information (i.e., the reality of the world in which we live) then our thinking and knowing does not bring us any more into contact with things than our sense perception does. This is what the term "lonely mind" is meant to indicate: not just a feeling of loneliness because of a potential lack of affection or personal regard from other people, but a radical isolation from everything, an objective, structural separation from reality that remains in place even in our moments of great subjective experiences of intimacy, as long as we think of truth as facts, and so hold to the model of information as characterizing most fundamentally what it means to know.

In the early modern period, in which the information-model of knowledge was on the rise, the image emerged of human subjectivity as a sort of self-enclosed sphere, into which data from the outside world was transmitted through a variety of causal mechanisms.[19] The result is what Robert Sokolowski has dubbed the "egocentric predicament," and which he has described in terms that are both easily recognizable and, upon reflection, quite disturbing.[20] But it seems to me that the sense of subjectivity has evolved a step further from this modern predicament. If the modern predicament is a trapping of the self inside a bubble of the self's own making, the postmodern predicament is a dissolution of the bubble—and the self along with it. In the contemporary mindset, the predominant image of the mind is not so much a closed sphere as it is a computer—not so much a machine as a kind of function. The mind, for us, has become an information processor, which is a function that can be in principle performed by other machines.[21] We have become obsessed with the possibility of producing Artificial Intelligence because we have made intelligence artificial: if the mind is like a computer, why can't a computer be like a mind?

There is an even more radical disembodiment here, far beyond the problem of the self-enclosed sphere of subjectivity that dominated modern thought. The distinction between image and reality (i.e., that which the image is an image *of*) is being increasingly blurred. We need only think of

19. Marjorie Grene, for example, describes the reduction of sense experience to motion that occurs in Hobbes's materialistic re-reading of human nature: "Hobbes and the Modern Mind."

20. Sokolowski, *An Introduction to Phenomenology*, 9–11.

21. There is no room to explore the issue here, but it is worth noting that there is a new danger that the isolation of the mind will coincide with a total absorption of the person into functions—in a way similar to the "disappearance" of the internet that was recently predicted by the president of Google, Eric Schmidt. It is not that the internet would no longer exist, but it would be totally pervasive and essentially identical to the processes of things going on in the world. With respect to this problem, it is not enough merely to insist on the intentionality of consciousness, to say that the mind is always open to things in the world. What we need is a new metaphysics of the person.

the confusions that are being generated more and more by social media regarding personal identity. Identity theft is becoming, not just an occasional event, but a way of describing the nature of one's participation in social media *tout court*. There is confusion not just with respect to the personal identity of those with whom we interact, but even with respect to our own sense of who we ourselves are. A contemporary philosopher, Luciano Floridi, has argued—with all of the excitement of a scientist who has stumbled on an epoch-making discovery—that we are in fact in the end nothing more than our information.[22] This same philosopher says that in fact the world itself is finally *equivalent* to the information it conveys of itself, which is to say that the meaning of things is just as plastic, just as manipulable and so vulnerable to distortion, as the personal identity created in and by social media. Everything has been detached from its originating roots, from its *nature*, and so things lose any real reference point, which would provide a kind of anchor of identity. This observation holds as much for things in the world as for the persons that interact with them and each other. Unsurprisingly, Floridi celebrates the coming ability, which he believes is just around the corner, to "upload" our personality and save it, so that we can become incarnate in any number of new bodies, and indeed in more than just bodies (which is to deny that we ever *in fact* are "incarnate" in the proper sense). This departure from the givenness of origins brings home the point that we have been seeking to make all along: if we reduce intelligibility to information, we lose the reality of ourselves and the world; we undermine any genuine connection between persons, between us and our own selves. One can readily understand, from this perspective, the almost desperate need to get out of our heads in order to have some genuine communion with what is other than ourselves, which David Foster Wallace described with so much pathos.

22. Floridi, "The Informational Nature of Personal Identity." As Floridi argues here, the world is simply the "totality of informational structures dynamically interacting with each other." Everything in the world, in other words, is nothing but a collection of information. This includes selves. The human self is different from other instances of information simply because it is able to recognize information as such. The article is concerned with deriving a revolutionary new theory of the self (the fourth revolution, he says, after the Copernican, the Darwinian, and the Freudian ones) from the phenomenon of social media, and the other "information and communication technologies," which he dubs "egopoetic technologies." Floridi, an Oxford don, is no doubt the leading exponent of the new field known as the "philosophy of information."

3. The Form of Truth

As an alternative to the modern fragmentation that arises from a view of truth as the correctness of information, we may consider again the classical view of truth as a property of being, and of knowing as a reception of reality that brings one's mind into conformity with it. Aquinas defines truth as the *"adequatio intellectus et rei,"* a proper joining together of the mind and reality.[23] This definition may initially seem to reduce truth to a quality of knowledge, or in any event to reduce truth to an attribute of our minds, since it suggests that truth is not there in things to begin with, but exists only insofar as things are *known* by us. In fact, however, Aquinas explains that there is an ontological truth that precedes our knowing, and indeed makes that knowing possible in the first place: *that* truth is the unity things have, not with our mind, but with God's mind. But God does not know things in an accidental way, as so many "pre-given" objects that he happens to encounter. Instead, his knowing is what makes things be at all. Because it is precisely God's knowing of things that makes them be, intelligibility belongs to the very core of reality. It is in a certain respect identical with being *tout court.*

It is just this theological background that allows us to understand the classical view of knowledge. In contrast to data or information, the principal "vehicle" of intelligibility in classical philosophy is *form.*[24] In a nutshell, form is at the same time an epistemological and an ontological principle. The form of a thing is not only what answers to the question *what* a particular thing is, but it is also what makes the thing *be* that "what," that particular thing. The term "form" is another way of speaking about the intelligibility of things, their translucence or availability to the mind, which is present in them, or indeed *as* them, because of God's creative knowledge.

Let us explain more concretely what it means to connect the intelligibility of a thing and its being in this way. Whenever we identify a thing, we are naming its *form.* Note that this identity, this form, is not just one feature of a thing as distinct from other features, a part that is separable from the rest. Instead, the form is the whole itself, it is the basic meaning that gathers up all of the features and parts and sets them, as it were, in their proper place in relation to each other. The object of our knowledge, for the classical mind, is the form, and this is the integrating reference point for everything else, all the disparate features, qualities, and indeed information and the like. In the first chapter, we spoke of the "what is . . . ?" question, how it

23. Aquinas, *De ver.* 1.1.

24. "Vehicle" is in quotations because, as we will see, it is not the right word, since the classical view does not see knowledge as something primarily *transmitted.*

opens the mind to the heart of things and keeps it from settling on anything incidental. What the "what is . . . ?" question aims at is precisely the *form*.

There is a wholeness to form; it represents, as Plato recognized, a kind of discrete simplicity.[25] As a *simple* whole, the form of a thing is greater than the sum of its parts.[26] In order to get the whole, in other words, it is not enough to collect all of the "bits" of a thing, and then add them together. (To think this way is actually to revert back to the information model.) It is not even enough to talk about the parts *and* their organization, though this point is often missed: because organization is possible only in reference to a unity that transcends the parts. Form is not, in other words, a function of the organization of parts, but rather organization is a function of the form. The form of a thing is absolute in itself in the sense of being irreducible to anything else.[27]

Because form is not reducible to any one of the parts of a thing, or to all of the parts discretely added together; because, that is, the form presents a unity that transcends its material parts, it was dismissed at the very origin of modern thought as a kind of occult property that was unnecessarily mysterious: What does form "add," it was asked, that isn't captured by a thorough enumeration of all the parts?[28] We answer: what is "added" is the *presence* of the *whole as such*, which may not seem to matter if we are interested only in the useful information that can be extracted (i.e., data that can be transferred into separate contexts), but it matters a great deal if we wish to retain an understanding of knowledge as intimate contact with reality. It matters if reality matters. Once form is dismissed, the "what is . . . ?" question begins to lose its ground; it gets supplanted by secondary questions concerning function and causal history.

---

25. See Plato, *Phaedo* 78d.

26. Michael Polanyi describes the grasping of a whole, not as an assembly of discrete, identifiable parts, but as an "indwelling" of the parts in such a way that the whole that transcends their sum becomes evident: see for example, "Faith and Reason."

27. This point is especially evident in organisms, even if biology does not typically recognize it. On this, see Hanby, *No God, No Science?*; cf., Webster and Goodwin, *Form and Transformation*. Organization in the proper sense implies internal relations among parts, which cannot be produced *a posteriori*, but can only be an actuality *presupposed* by the parts even in their contribution to its realization.

28. The decisive break with the classical tradition on this point might be identified with William of Ockham's rejection of the *forma totius*, which would be in any way distinct from simply an enumeration of all of the *forma partis*. On this, see Maurer, *The Philosophy of William of Ockham in the Light of its Principles*, 393. A rejection of Aristotelian form or essence becomes, then, a common early modern trope, as can be seen in the writings, for example, of Francis Bacon and Galileo Galilei.

This notion of the presence of the whole as such leads to the other aspect of the description of form: it is, we said, an *ontological* principle, which means form constitutes the very *being* of things. To grasp the significance of this point requires a radical conversion from the postmodern condition of the "lonely mind": According to classical philosophy, form is not just an object of thought in the sense of being an idea that is in our heads, or a mental concept or category that we apply to one thing or another. Instead, form is an internal principle that belongs to the reality of things, or better: just *is* that reality, in a certain respect. This is what is entailed in the notion of truth as a transcendental. A thing's form is what makes it *be* the thing that it is; it is the internal *essence*, the real being of the thing. According to Aristotle, the form of the living thing is its *soul* (for Aristotle, this is not exclusively a religious term, but a biological one: the living principle of organisms), which means that, what the soul is to a living being, form is to everything that exists. Form, in a word, is the intimate reality of a thing.[29] If we recall what we said a moment ago—namely, that the form is not a separable part or simply the totality of the parts of a thing, but the whole that exceeds their sum, and as such a unity that transcends the diversity of the material components—then coming to know the form requires us to go beyond what is given on the surface, beyond the external and recordable information. If beauty is a reception of the being of a thing in appearance, which is a kind of *invitation* into reality, truth is an *entry* into the reality itself, which coincides with a receiving of the reality into oneself. In this case, to define knowledge as a grasp of the form of things is to conceive of the act of knowing as an intimate encounter with a reality "outside" of ourselves. To know is thus to enter into the inmost being of a thing, and to allow that being to enter into our own inmost reality.[30]

It is not at all an accident, then, that the images of the mind, its cognitive acts, and its knowledge of reality in classical thought so often strike the note of organic intimacy. Aquinas was appealing to the common medieval understanding when he analyzed the etymological roots of the word *"intellectus"*—which refers both to the agent (the intellect or mind) and its proper act (the mind's actual understanding of something)—as "intus" + "legere,"

---

29. This is not to say that it is the *most* intimate reality of a thing: as we will explain in chapter 6, being, and God, is what is most intimate.

30. When Aquinas argues, after Aristotle, that the truth of things lies most properly *in our minds* rather than in things themselves, this is not because he has a "subjectivistic" conception of truth. Instead, the point is that the truth *of things* enters into our soul in our knowledge (see *ST* 1.16.1ad3). For a recent account of the unity of mind and reality in truth, according to Aquinas, see Cory, "Knowing as Being? A Metaphysical Reading of the Identity of Intellect and Intelligible in Aquinas."

which means to read or understand *into* a thing, or, better, *to penetrate into the interior reality of a thing with one's mind*.[31] Aristotle's observation that the human soul is "in a certain sense all things" (πῶς πάντα, which Aquinas eventually translates as *"quodamodo omnia"*[32]) was taken over as obvious by the whole Western tradition. What Aristotle meant by this phrase is that we *become*—in a certain respect, but nevertheless *in truth*—the things that we know. We do not simply record information *about* things that remain forever separate from us, but we genuinely *join* with them in our intellect.[33]

Perhaps most vividly we have Plato's description of knowledge. Though he of course famously emphasizes the transcendence of forms, he nevertheless does not think of them as simply "detachable" from things, like so much data. Instead, he uses the words "presence" and "communion" to describe the relation between physical things and their intelligible forms.[34] This insight into the immanence of forms leads him to present the act of knowledge as a kind of erotic encounter between the mind and reality:

> The nature of the real lover of learning [is] to strive for what *is*; and he does not tarry by each of the many things opined to *be* but goes forward and does not lose the keenness of his passionate love nor cease from it before he grasps the nature of each thing which *is* with the part of the soul fit to grasp a thing of that sort. . . . And once near it and coupled with what really is, having begotten intelligence and truth, he knows and lives truly, is nourished and so ceases from his labor pains, but not before.
>
> (*Republic* 490a-b)

When author of the *Book of Genesis*, conversely, describes sexual union as a form of knowledge—"Adam *knew* Eve his wife, and she conceived" (Gen 4:1)—he is drawing on what we may think of as the general sense of what it means to know in the pre-modern world: knowledge is intimate encounter, it is personal presence.

If we manage to see the act of knowing as concentrating, so to speak, around form rather than around the abstract data of information, our

---

31. Aquinas: "intellective knowledge penetrates into the very essence of a thing, because the object of the intellect is 'what a thing is,' as stated in *De anima* 3.6" (ST 2–2.8.1).

32. Aristotle, *De anima* 3.8.431b21; Aquinas, *SCG* 3.112.5.

33. The word "genuine" and "knowledge" are in fact etymologically connected (along with "generate" and its cognates), all related to the Indo-European root "gn." This connection can be traced through Greek, Latin, and many modern languages. See Shipley, *The Origins of English Words*, 129–33.

34. See Plato, *Phaedo* 100d. The words he uses are παρουσία and κοινωνία.

understanding of human nature undergoes a shift. We no longer think of the mind as an obstacle to our connection with the world and other people, which has to be outwitted, if not simply cancelled through arbitrary acts of will or the emotions that we think of as altogether irrational. Instead, the mind becomes a privileged place of encounter: a window into which the light of the world streams, rather than a separate stage, with the implication that the real reality always remains somehow behind the curtain. In modern thought, we might say, reality does nothing more than put on a show for us (or better: pop up on our screen). In this case, no matter how expansive our knowledge or numerous our apparent "contacts," we can never transcend the limits of our own experience or our concepts, which is to say: we can never get outside of our heads, as David Hume conceded. We may contrast this view with that of Aquinas, for example, who writes that concepts are not *what* we know, but that *by which* we know.[35] A simple shift of case makes all the difference here: what Aquinas means is that, instead of being themselves the principal objects of our knowledge, our concepts mediate the proper objects, which is to say that they open up a connection with real things in the world. Reality itself becomes present—in person, so to speak—in the medium of our concepts, and by extension, our experiences and sensations, not to mention our very language.[36]

To make this more concrete, let us consider the perception of leaves that we discussed earlier. For the classical mind, the sensation of green triggered by my brain is not the *terminus ad quem*, not the endpoint of my sight, but is a mediating aspect of my vision: the internal sensation is that by which we see the green that belongs *to the leaves*. The green is, so to speak, a revelation of what the leaves *are*, even if the leaves require a receptive sense organ to express their color. As Balthasar puts it:

> A tree without its green, its autumnal variety, the pink and white display of its spring blossoms, its fragrance, its hardness and tenacity, its size, its relation to the surrounding landscape, in short, without the thousand qualities that make it what we know it to be, is simply not a tree. It needs the sensorium as a space in which to unfurl itself. It unveils its color within an eye that sees color; it whispers only in an ear that hears sound; it presents its unique flavor only in the mouth of another capable

35. Aquinas, *ST* 1.85.2.

36. See, for example, the text *De natura verbi intellectus*, 1. Though this text seems to have been falsely attributed to Aquinas (and most likely written by Thomas de Sutton), it nevertheless expresses a "thomistic" sense of the word. As for sensations, these are the most obviously related to external things, since the "terminus" of the act of sensation is the *res* rather than the *anima*: see, e.g., Aristotle, *De anima*, 2.5.417b20–27.

of tasting. It makes use of the space furnished for this purpose just as surely as it makes use of the soil and the ambient air in order to develop. Without the subject's sensory space, it would not be what it is; it would be incapable of fulfilling the *raison d'être*, the idea that it is supposed to embody. The object finds its—essential—completion only outside of itself in the world of subjects that allow it its full growth.[37]

If things present real images of themselves to the subject in the beauty accessible in sense experience, it is in truth that they offer their very substance. Things can fully manifest themselves in their being only in an intellect that is naturally ordered to being. For classical philosophy, the mind or the reason that defines my humanity and so makes me most properly who I am is simultaneously the "place" wherein I am most profoundly joined to what is other than myself.

Our proposal is that recovering the classical sense of intimate personal presence as a paradigm of knowledge would contribute in a fundamental way to the renewal of our humanity and our sense of reality in the face of the onslaught of cultural forces that threaten to eclipse it. Recovering this paradigm, it should be noted, does not require the complete elimination of information and the evident benefits it can bring, but only a serious relativizing of its significance. Instead of thinking of information as the paradigm of knowledge, we ought to see it as a relatively adequate substitute for knowledge, which may be necessary or useful in particular circumstances, when knowledge is not possible. But this relativizing, as subtle as it may seem, would entail a profound shift in our understanding of the nature of the human being, and a reordering of our cultural patterns from the ground up: if we thought of knowledge as personal encounter, of the mind and its senses as the place wherein the world comes to present itself, "personally" to introduce itself, to show itself for what it truly is, it would entail a radically different approach to education, a certain liberating distance from technologies, above all those referred to as "information and communication technologies," a different way of organizing space—be it the physical space of architecture and city-planning, or the economic space of market structures and institutions—and indeed a re-interpretation of the private-public distinction in politics, not to mention the subtle and pervasive shift in cultural expressions of human nature.

In short, the question of the nature of truth and our access to it in knowledge is not first and most fundamentally just a question of the degree of certainty we are able to attain—which is what the question became in

37. Balthasar, *Theologic I*, 63.

modern philosophy. Instead, it is a more comprehensive question about the shape of our culture and the quality of man's relationship to reality that it is able to provide and foster. If beauty represents an *invitation* to the real, and goodness our *involvement* in it in freedom, truth is above all our *reception* of reality, on its terms. It is for this reason a living relationship, one with the capacity to transform.

PART II

Love and the Transcendentals

5

Beauty and Love

1. The Reduction of Love

Several decades ago, Josef Pieper remarked on the trivialization that the word "love" has undergone in the modern world.[1] The word has been stretched to cover such an extreme span of meanings—we use it to describe everything from God's sacrificial death to a special preference for strawberries—that it seems void of any determinate significance of its own. After seeing it on the cover of every single magazine in the sitting area at the barber's, he observes, one is tempted to renounce ever using it again oneself. Even if we restrict our consideration of the term to the use we make of it to characterize personal relationships, we tend to find its sense reduced to just a shadow of its classical significance. When we employ the word in a contemporary setting, we generally identify it with an emotion, by which we mean above all a particular psychological state, a subjective experience: Love is something we *feel*.

To be sure, those who interpret love especially as a particular emotion do not necessarily *intend* thereby to trivialize it. While there are certainly some who translate subjective experience into its physiological substrate and subsequently, in effect, "explain love away" by describing its "scientific" causes—its evolutionary benefits, for example—others continue to idealize love precisely *as* a subjective experience. Believing that it is just our feelings that constitute the most *personal* aspect of our existence, some are inclined to think that to call love an emotion is to offer an excellent reason to pursue it, perhaps excessively, even to the point of great personal cost or in defiance of all social conventions. Insofar as it is an emotion, the specifically subjective quality of love—the "lived experience" [*Erlebnis*]—apparently cannot be explained by anything else. Even the scientific account of what causes

1. See the introductory pages on love, in Pieper, *Faith–Hope–Love*, 145ff.

such feelings and what biological purpose they serve has nothing to do with the actual revolution in our interior life, the overwhelming feeling of "being in love," which thus becomes a kind of absolute in itself that does not fit with anything else. It is just this discontinuity with everything else that leads people to cherish it as supreme—even divine.[2]

There are several problems with this conception of love. If love is reduced to nothing beyond a feeling, a purely subjective state, then, in spite of the distinctiveness of the "lived experience," there is ultimately no substantial reason it could not be turned into a physiological "illusion," traceable back to its "scientific" causes, whether these be understood principally as neurological, chemical, biological, evolutionary, or even generally sociological elements or factors. In this case, one would have to admit that a drug, electrical stimulation, or any other generator of virtual reality, would be capable of producing, not just a feeling that imitates the experience of being in love, but in fact love itself. If love is just a feeling, what is the difference between a feeling that is like love, and the reality it is meant to mimic? The fact that we all recognize a difference here, even just enough to make the question intelligible, suggests that love cannot be simply a physiological event.

But even if one were to continue to insist on the *personal, lived-experience* dimension of love as something different from a physiological condition—to say, in other words, that the *feeling* is the point, regardless of how it may have come about scientifically speaking—the situation is no better. Love, as pure subjective experience, remains wholly disconnected from any reality; the more value one gives to love, understood in this way, the more one sequesters oneself from others and from the everyday life of the real world. We will tend to regard love as a departure from reality, a kind of entry into an alternate world. This is the notion of love we find, for example, in many of Terry Gilliam's movies.[3] Along similar lines, in his well-known novel based on his experiences in World War II, *Mother Night*, Kurt Vonnegut presented love as an escape or a radical separation from everything else in the world: a "nation of two."[4] One of the clearest examples of the confusion in our contemporary view of love appears in *The Silver Lining Play Book*. In this popular film, love appears as a strange abstraction of the social from the properly public: while love saves a man from an unhealthy

2. This tendency has existed since the beginning. See Benedict XVI, *Deus Caritas Est*, 4.

3. The clearest example of this is *Brazil*, but the theme turns up in one way or another in most of his other films; it is not a surprise that Gilliam had such an interest in producing a film version of Don Quixote, which is in a sense the classic instance of love as creating a dream world even more real than "reality."

4. Vonnegut, *Mother Night*, 34 et passim.

introversion, it betrays at the same time a deeply anti-social dimension, as if love is all the more real the more discontinuous it is with social conventions, that is, with human culture in its normal manifestation. The point of all of this is simply to highlight the curious paradox, or indeed, the contradiction, in the general status of love: it is revered in some respects to hyperbolic degrees, and at the same time trivialized to the point of having no bearing whatsoever on the reality of existence. And there is no reason it cannot be both at once.

Given such a de-substantializing of love, it is not surprising to discover that, while the theme of love had such a prominent place in classical thought—from one of the very first philosophers whose writings we still possess fragments of,[5] to the epoch-making figures of Plato,[6] Aristotle,[7] and Plotinus,[8] to the great treatises on love by the fathers of the church and the medieval theologians, philosophers, and poets—it rarely appears as a central theme in the philosophy that has shaped the modern world: Montaigne detaches it altogether from the order of reason;[9] Bacon dismisses it as a distraction from the serious pursuits of life, to the extent of claiming that greatness is incompatible with love;[10] Descartes allows it only as a promise of gratification;[11] Rousseau romanticizes it as a beautiful escape

5. See Empedocles, *Diels-Kranz*, B17, which presents love as one of the great cosmic forces that holds together all the physical elements. This idea can be found in some form in the earliest Greek mythology.

6. Plato, *Symposium, Phaedrus, Lysis*. It is interesting to note that, in the *Symposium*, Phaedrus laments the absence of love from the writings of any great Greek poet or philosopher (*Symposium*, 177a-c), which is what occasions the speeches on love that make up the body of the dialogue. In the *Phaedrus*, Plato presents love as one of the great *gifts* from the gods (*Phaedrus*, 244a).

7. Aristotle's *Nichomachean Ethics*, a treatise on human excellence, arguably culminates in a great treatise on friendship (books 8 and 9), before its denouement in the reflections on pleasure and happiness in the concluding book 10.

8. Plotinus, like Empedocles (and Eryximachus in Plato's *Symposium*), presents love as a kind of cosmic power, but for him it is a *metaphysical*, rather than essentially *physical*, reality, and arrives, as it were, "from above" (see "On Love," *Ennead* III.5).

9. Montaigne trivializes any natural or social foundation for friendship in what he takes to be its truest sense, as exemplified in his own relationship with Etienne de la Boétie, and proposes that there is ultimately no intelligible reason for friendship. If he and de la Boétie became friends, it was "because he is he, and because I am I" (see *Essays*, 104–10).

10. Bacon, *The Essays*, 41–43. Bacon also gives a primarily practical (and what would have to be called physiological) justification for friendship in 103–12. He may thus be said to take the exact opposite position of Montaigne.

11. See articles 79, 85, and 90 in Descartes, *Passions of the Soul*, 62–69.

that condemns the real;[12] Kant reduces it to a feeling, namely, the desire for immediate gratification, which he opposes to the more serious human passion of respect;[13] and it scarcely receives mention in the major modern political philosophies of Hobbes and Locke. Whether these modern thinkers make love something worthy or unworthy of pursuit, they all agree on separating it from reality.

How did we get to this point? It would be presumptuous to claim we could identify a single cause of the impoverishment of love, or lay out the history of the development in even the broadest of strokes, especially within the limited scope of the present context. What we intend to do here is the following: in the next chapter we will discuss the relationship between love and being; in the present chapter, we will simply offer a thesis concerning what seems at least to plant a seed for the later impoverishment. Our approach to this theme is somewhat different from that taken in other chapters of this book: rather than contrast the modern view and the "classical" understanding, we will instead indicate what seems to be a departure from classical thought in its more *ancient* form that occurs in the medieval period. To put the thesis in a nutshell: we propose that the impoverishment of love begins—or at least the initial door to such an impoverishment is first opened—in the "relegating" of love to the order of goodness rather than interpreting love principally as related to *beauty*.[14]

At first glance, it is clear that Thomas Aquinas—to take him as a basic reference point—has an extremely rich sense of love, which is profoundly different from the contemporary reduction of love to a feeling or an arbitrary act of will that we just presented. The notion of love in Aquinas is fully

---

12. Rousseau's wildly successful romantic novel, *La Nouvelle Héloïse*, originated in his frustration over the impossibility of finding a woman that corresponded to his fantasies. As he explains in his *Confessions*, 398ff., he thus invented a fictitious world peopled with ideal beings, a world that drove him to ecstasies and enabled him to endure the banality of the real world.

13. Kant, *Metaphysics of Morals*, 161, 198–99.

14. Plotinus offers an excellent statement of what we take to be the classical position, elements of which appear in Aquinas, as we shall see, but under the sign of the *good*. According to Plotinus, "the origin of love [is] the longing for beauty itself which was there before in men's souls, and their recognition of it and kinship with it and unreasoned awareness that it is something of their own" (*Ennead* III.5.1; Loeb edition, 167–69). Note that the desire for beauty is for something that transcends the soul, but is *already present* in it (πρότερον ἐν τας ψυχας), that the desire comes before a proper understanding, that our grasp of it is therefore a kind of re-cognition (ἐπίγνωσις) of what is already acting in the soul; that it generates a *connaturality* (συγγένειαν) with the beautiful thing, which one perceives as belonging most intimately to one (οἰκειότητος) in spite of its transcendence.

analogous: if in its most precise sense it is one of the concupiscible *passions*,[15] Aquinas says that in fact every appetite of the soul can be described as a form of love, since they all designate an ordination of the soul to goodness in *some* respect.[16] In this case, love includes not only the desire for what is good (*amor concupiscentiae*), but also the more "generous" affirmation of the good of another, which we recognize in friendship (*amor benevolentiae* or *amor amicitiae*).[17] Moreover, love, for Aquinas, is not merely a human affair. In a manner that does not fit so readily inside the modern imagination, but makes immediate sense within the classical tradition, Aquinas explains that all things participate to some degree in love:[18] we can speak of any natural inclination of a being—whether it be the impulse of an animal to mate, the imperceptible turning of the flower toward the sun, or perhaps most surprisingly even the rolling of a rock down a hill in accordance with the laws of its nature—as love in its natural mode, insofar as all natures without exception seek the good that is fitting for them. Human love, in this respect, is simply a higher-level appropriation, the living out at the level of intellect and will (*amor rationalis*), of the love that pervades the cosmos, or as Dante so famously put it in *Paradiso* 33, the "love that moves the sun and the other stars." But love, for Aquinas, does not only extend through the whole of the cosmos, it also transcends the cosmos: love—as *caritas*[19]—is a divine reality,[20] which is to say it is most perfect in God, as the very name of the Holy Spirit,[21] but also God's greatest gift to man as the theological virtue of charity, which Aquinas defines, with the tradition, as "friendship with God."[22] This is a special kind of union, which is the supreme aim of all our strivings.[23] As such, love represents the form of all the virtues,[24] which

15. Aquinas, *ST* 1-2.26.2.

16. Aquinas, *ST* 1-2.28.6.

17. Aquinas, *ST* 1-2.26.4.

18. Aquinas, *ST* 1-2.26.1.

19. It should be noted, though, that Aquinas uses the word "caritas" not only to indicate the theological virtue, but also to designate a particularly intense love: "Charity denotes, in addition to love, a certain perfection of love, insofar as that which is loved is held to be of great price, as the word implies" (*"carus"* = "dear" or "precious") (*ST* 1-2.26.3). Without confusion, there is nevertheless no overly simplified distinction between the natural and supernatural.

20. Aquinas, *ST* 2-2.23.2.

21. Aquinas, *ST* 1.37.1.

22. Aquinas, *ST* 2-2.23.1.

23. Aquinas, *ST* 2-2.23.7.

24. Aquinas, *ST* 2-2.23.8.

is to say it is the crowning of all other human excellences, as giving them an inner form and ultimate purpose.

This display of the rich diversity of love is a refreshing contrast to the modern impoverishment we have been discussing. And yet our suggestion is that there is a certain tension in Aquinas's understanding that, if resolved in a one-sided way, opens the door to that eventual impoverishment. To formulate the tension concisely: Aquinas is generally understood to have identified love with the *appetitive* order, that is, with a movement toward, and rest in, the good, which is a final cause. On the other hand, he describes love in terms that often exceed, in subtle but decisive respects, the order of appetite.[25] We will suggest that the more ancient view of love as connected with *beauty*—a quality that has a notoriously controversial status in Aquinas's thought[26]—does more justice to the full diversity of meanings that Aquinas gives to love, whereas a *reduction* of love to the order of the good *rather than* beauty threatens to endanger that diversity, and sets the stage for the modern impoverishment. In order to get a sense of all that is at stake here, it will be helpful to consider for a moment some implications of interpreting love *exclusively* as appetite, before exploring in more detail Aquinas's own more "textured" view.

To state the general danger in a single formulation: reducing love in an exclusive way to the order of the appetite threatens to relativize love entirely

25. In an illuminating book, *By Knowledge and By Love: Charity and Knowledge in the Moral Theology of St. Thomas Aquinas*, Fr. Michael Sherwin, OP, argues that Aquinas's view of love undergoes a development as his thought matures: while there was a tendency to interpret love in terms of form in his early writings, he eventually achieved a much clearer distinction between the intellect and the will, to which love belongs, interpreting the latter, no longer in terms of the formal order (which is more properly the order of the intellect), but now in terms of efficient causality. This clear distinction allows a better sense of the co-operation of intellect and will in moral action. Our proposal, here, is that the early association of love with form is a remnant of the older tradition that connected love with beauty, and so there is a certain impoverishment in the notion of love that coincides with the gain in properly distinguishing the will from the intellect, and subordination of it thereto, an impoverishment that can be avoided if we reject the assumption that love is *simply* a matter of the appetite.

26. Aquinas does not include beauty in the *locus classicus* of his presentation of the transcendentals in *De veritate*, 1.1., but he describes it elsewhere in terms that would seem to warrant its inclusion. The classic text defending beauty's place among the transcendentals is Kovach, *Die Ästhetik des Thomas von Aquin* (1964). The general tendency in the mid- to late-twentieth century was to include beauty on the list, as we see for example in James Anderson's standard textbook: *An Introduction to the Metaphysics of St. Thomas Aquinas*. It seems that the more traditionalist turn of Thomism in the late twentieth and early twenty-first century has been more inclined to remove it from the list: see Aertsen, *Medieval Philosophy and the Transcendentals: The Case of Thomas Aquinas*.

to the subject, so that love *shrinks*, as it were, to fit the subject's measure. This "shrinking" will appear in a variety of forms: on the one hand, love will tend to be interpreted as the pursuit of gratification, the aim to satisfy my desire, my need, which will give love a certain "possessive," if not an outright, "selfish," quality. To some extent in reaction to this reduction, one will also affirm love as the very opposite of selfishness, as a kind of altruism detached from any ulterior motives.[27] But this is just the flip side of its putative opposite, which turns out to be equally a reduction to the subject: such altruism is, in the first place, a purely arbitrary act of will, a movement of the subject toward its end, which is wholly spontaneous since it arises in no way from the attraction of the object. Instead, it is a movement produced altogether by the subject, and so a sheer imposition on the object. This motion of love fits "naturally" with the modern view of the will as "active power," which we described in chapter 3. In the second place, since there is in actuality no such thing as pure spontaneity, since an act of the will, in other words, that is wholly unmotivated would be absolutely unintelligible, the altruistic act will always in fact inevitably have some ulterior motive. But, as we will see in the next chapter, because this motive is ostensibly denied, altruistic love can only cast the shadow of hypocrisy to the extent that the motive comes to light at all, all the more so to the extent that the notion of altruism concedes a selfish form to the pursuit of goodness. Moreover, if we continue to maintain that love is a passion, then the more it is relativized to the subject, the more it will come to be seen as a *feeling*, or *emotion*, in the contemporary conventional sense of the term, that is, as a psychological phenomenon, a wholly internal event, which is not a disclosure of the world in any genuine sense, but principally an expression of subjectivity. So, gathering these various subjectivisms together, we have love as desire for immediate gratification, love as altruism or sheer spontaneous and unmotivated act of the will, and love as mere feeling or emotion. All of these are views of love one commonly encounters today.

2. Under the Sign of Beauty

Having considered the potential problems that arise if we identify love simply with appetite, the power of movement toward an end, I want to suggest that there are a variety of movements, so to speak, in Aquinas's interpretation of love that resist this reduction, and even push away from it, to such an extent that tensions appear. As I mentioned above, it will become apparent

27 The clearest example is Anders Nygren's absolute distinction between *agape* and *eros* in his book *Agape and Eros*.

that the tensions can be relieved if we interpret love principally in terms of beauty rather than principally in terms of goodness. Indeed, it will turn out that founding love in beauty ends up doing more justice to the extraordinarily rich array of qualities and characteristics that Aquinas presents in his discussion of love. After attempting to demonstrate this point, we will finally consider more generally what seem to be the great benefits of recovering the more ancient view of love's connection to beauty, especially in the light of some of the later developments in the interpretation of beauty we discussed in chapter 2.

As we have already indicated, Aquinas defines love principally as a passion, which is a movement of the sensible appetite;[28] the reason he describes the movement of this appetite as a *passion* rather than an *act*—which is the word he will use to describe, for example, the movement of the intellectual appetite, namely, the will—is that it represents the soul's being *affected* by a particular sensible good in a way that causes a change in the matter of the body.[29] In other words, it is a passive being moved rather than an active self-motion. As he explains, "the word 'passion' implies that the patient is drawn to that which belongs to the agent" (*ST* 1–2.22.2). This "being drawn," though it implies a being acted *on*, is nevertheless different from a coercive *push*, as it were, merely from the outside. A properly internal movement—that is, a being moved from without that is not simply imposed externally—is possible only on the basis of some apprehension,[30] which implies a reception into the soul of a certain aspect of a thing, in this case, its sensible species. Because the sensible species is not the thing *itself*, in its reality,[31] it follows that our apprehension awakens a movement toward the thing in its reality, which movement bears the name "appetite." Appetite is an aiming at the thing as a desirable good; it seeks to come to rest in the *reality* of the object as it is in itself. Sensible appetite is directed specifically to sensible union, i.e., a sensible satisfaction (eating, drinking, intercourse). Love, then, is our being moved, our being physically disposed, to regard that union as something good.

Now, though Aquinas defines love as a passion in this sense, he explains at the same time that the word has a broader meaning that extends beyond the range of the sensible appetite. If love were simply a passion, we could not ascribe it to God, who is immaterial and so is not "physically"

---

28. Aquinas, *ST* 1–2.22.3.

29. Aquinas: "Passion is properly to be found where there is corporeal transmutation" (*ST* 1–2.22.3).

30. Aquinas, *ST* 1.80.2ad1.

31. Aquinas, *ST* 1.78.1ad3.

affected by anything; we could not ascribe it to the angels, for the same reason; and indeed, we could not ascribe it in human beings to the *will*, since
the will is part of man's *spiritual* nature, as distinct from his bodily nature.[32]
But of course the activity of the will, for Aquinas, is essentially love, and love
exists in pre-eminent way in God.[33] Thus, Aquinas extends the meaning of
love analogously by associating it most essentially with goodness as such,
not merely in its particular and sensible aspect. In this respect, we can call
any and every occurrence in the universe, at some level, an event of love, or
at least an event due to love of some sort, as Aquinas himself clearly states:
"every agent, whatever it be, does every action from love of some kind."[34]
Love, in this sense, is an ordination to the good, not just as an object of sensible appetite, but also as an object of the intellectual appetite.[35] Nevertheless, it remains a matter of appetite, and so, as we saw in chapter 3, a matter
of being drawn *to* some object: an attraction. In this case, it remains true
that the appetitive motion is initiated by some apprehension.[36] According to
Aquinas, every act of will is preceded by an act of intellect.

Now, as straightforward as all of this seems to be, I want to suggest that
there are some difficulties, recognition of which requires further clarification and work of interpretation. The first and most general difficulty is that
this description of love as a movement of the appetitive power essentially
subordinates love to reason, since there can be no such movement without
a prior apprehension and also because every movement is ordered to rest
as means to the proper end. The ultimate subordination of love to reason
does not fit obviously with the Christian tradition, which certainly does not
separate love from reason as some might think, but nevertheless invariably
crowns love as supreme, above all other things—even knowledge (cf., Eph
3:19). Such a status does not seem to be warranted for a *passion*, which resides indeed in a lower part of the soul.[37] It is interesting to note that, when

32. Aquinas defines "spirit," in contrast to the "soul" qua form of the body, as the
soul precisely in its transcendence of the body (*ST* 1.97.3). Because the agent of the
operations of intellect and will is the soul considered in its distinction from the body
rather than in its unity with the body (which is the agent of the operation of the sensible
appetite, for example), these operations are therefore *spiritual* activities (*ST* 1.75.2).

33. Aquinas, *ST* 1.20.1.

34. Aquinas, *ST* 1–2.28.6.

35. Aquinas: "includes intellectual, rational, animal, and natural love" (*ST*
1–2.28.6ad1).

36. Even the movement of non-rational and non-sensitive beings is still due to
reason—in this case, the divine intellect (*ST* 1–2.27.2ad3).

37. One might point out that Aquinas does indeed make charity the *form* of all
the other virtues, set as it is on the highest end—namely, "adherence to God"—which
contains and so integrates the ends of all the other virtues. But this affirmation by itself

Aquinas defines love as a passion in *ST* 1-2.26.2, he cites "the Philosopher" (Aristotle) as his authority, over against the three objections he raises, all of which are drawn from Church Fathers: Dionysius, Augustine, and Damascene.[38] It would seem that he is privileging a pre-Christian understanding of man, specifically in relation to the meaning of love, at least in its human dimension.[39]

Moreover, the description of love as a simple passion, or a movement of the sensible appetite, does not upon reflection seem to do sufficient justice to our experience, or even accord smoothly with other affirmations that Aquinas himself makes about love, even if we acknowledge an analogous extension of the term. Let us consider an example.[40] Aquinas apparently tries to honor the status of love by making love not just one passion among others but the *first* of the passions,[41] and indeed, as we have cited above, in a broader sense the proper cause of all of the other affections. (Incidentally, he cites Augustine in this case as an authority.[42]) But in his explication of the claim that love is the first of the passions, he clarifies that it is first only

---

is insufficient for two reasons: First, there would need to be a natural analogue to the supremacy of the theological virtue of charity, or else the elevation in grace would not represent a fulfillment of nature, but only a reversal of it. Secondly, the logic of nature would nevertheless tend to reappear even in the ultimate state, so that the same difficulty would recur: without a deepening of the "natural" meaning of love, even adherence to God would tend to take on the *primary* sense of the satisfaction of an appetite—love of God as a means to the enjoyment of God, an act of intellect that represents the *essence* of eschatological union. We will return to this point at the end. It is worth noting that the famous "pure love" controversy in early modern French thought turned on the ambiguity of just this issue in Aquinas. See Robert Spaemann's discussion of this in *Philosophical Essays on Nature, God, and the Human Person*, 45–59. Whereas Spaemann attributes the controversy to a splitting apart in the eighteenth century (ultimately because of an impoverishment in the general conception of nature) of what Aquinas had held together, we are suggesting that there is an ambiguity already in Aquinas.

38. It should be noted that Dionysius and Augustine are the most frequently quoted in Aquinas's discussion of love; they seem to be the primary representatives of the Catholic tradition on this theme.

39. Max Scheler famously raises this charge, perhaps most succinctly in his essay "Love and Knowledge," (cf., also, *Ressentiment*, chapters 2 and 3). Scheler's position is *decidedly* different from the one we are going to present, as we will explain below.

40. Another example of a tension, which we will not develop here, is the fact that Aquinas *defines* love as a passion, while at the same time offering friendship as representing the absolute sense of love (*ST* 1-2.26.4), even though friendship is itself *not* a passion. Moreover, the highest instance of love—the love of God, and indeed the proper name of the Holy Spirit—is also not a passion. It is not clear what basis there is for the analogy. If we define love, instead, simply as movement toward the good, then it simply coincides with appetite, and loses its distinctness.

41. Aquinas, *ST* 1-2.25.2.

42. Aquinas, *ST* 1-2.27-4 *sed contra*.

in a certain respect; it turns out to be last in what is arguably a more decisive one: love, he explains, is a certain aptitude for the good, a positive
disposition toward it, or in the technical scholastic term: a *complacency* in
the good.[43] This positive disposition comes first *in the order of execution.*
In this order, it is followed by the movement of desire, and comes to an
end in enjoyment, the actual satisfaction of the appetite. But in *the order of
intention,* by contrast, love comes last, as entailed by the end that is principally sought, namely, pleasure, the direct enjoyment of the good: "But in the
order of intention, it is the reverse: because the pleasure intended causes
desire and love."[44] What love finally *aims* at, and so what determines the
scope of love, is the satisfaction of appetite. As a rule, the order of intention
carries more ontological weight for Aquinas than the order of execution.
Aquinas is saying, here, that we first apprehend intellectually the pleasure
we wish to enjoy, which will require the movement of desire in the appetite,
and this movement in turn cannot occur itself without a positive disposition
toward the object desired. The *reason* for love is derived entirely from the
enjoyment it makes possible.

The question we need to consider here is: Is this true? Is love a function
of pleasure, a mere means to the end of enjoyment, as this description, at
least crudely interpreted, implies? No one who has any experience of love
would think so, and, as we will see in a moment, Aquinas himself does not
believe it. But I submit that it is an affirmation that will tend to impose itself
to the extent that we define love in an exclusive way as an appetite for the
good. In this case, because appetite denotes movement, and because, for
the classical tradition generally, movement is always subordinate to rest as
means to end, love will inevitably tend to shrink into an instrumental good,
which, again, does not appear to do justice to what we know love to be.
In the light of this problem, it is instructive to see that Aquinas seems to
reverse his position only a few pages after the affirmation just noted. When
Aquinas specifically addresses the question concerning whether some other
passion of the soul can be a cause of love, he intends to answer *no,* because

---

43. "Complacency," in the scholastic usage, means a "being pleased with" (as distinct from the modern connotation of smug self-satisfaction). The "com" (i.e., "con")
is an intensifier of the root *placere,* to please; but it also indicates an abiding difference
between subject and object. While the direct enjoyment of pleasure, in other words,
occurs only in *actual* (i.e., "real") contact, complacency denotes a state of being *with
respect to* an object. The modern sense of "complacency" naturally arises within the
conceptual horizon of positivism, which can conceive of no other possible union apart
from that of direct, physical contact. In this case, the absence of such contact could only
mean *isolation:* hence, static self-satisfaction.

44. Aquinas, *ST* 1–2.25.2.

he wishes to insist on the primacy of love over all other passions.[45] In order to clarify his understanding, he raises as an objection the very point that he himself had declared a few pages before: if we love for the sake of enjoyment or pleasure, this would make pleasure a cause of love (*causa finalis*), which would imply that pleasure takes a certain precedence over love, or, in other words, that love is a means to the end of pleasure. In his reply, Aquinas concedes that pleasure can be a cause of love—because we intend rest in some good it entails a positive disposition toward that good, or in other words, it brings about love—but then he makes this astonishing statement: the very pleasure that causes love in a particular instance "is caused, in its turn, by another preceding love; for none takes pleasure save in that which is loved in some way." Rather than interpreting this response as leading us into an infinite regress, where we would have to acknowledge an intention of pleasure as preceding *that* prior disposition of love, an intention that arises in turn by yet an earlier disposition of love, and on and on, it seems more sensible to see this claim as reorienting our conception of the relation between intention and execution described above: it becomes clear here that if pleasure comes generally first in the order of intention, love represents an order that *precedes* that of intentionality itself; it sets the fundamental context *within which* one would come to seek any particular good.

We will return to elaborate what this means in just a moment, but before we do it is good to see that there is a general "drift" in Aquinas's formulations that move away from the notion of love as simply an appetite for the good.[46] I will eventually suggest that this drift makes more sense if we conceive of love *most basically* in terms of beauty, though of course, as the tradition has generally recognized, there is a very close relationship between the two.[47] The point, in other words, will be not so much to deny the relation of love to the good as to set that relation into the more fundamental context of beauty. After making this suggestion, I will conclude by proposing what seem to me to be the significant benefits of reconceiving love in this way.

45. Aquinas, *ST* 1–2.27.4.

46. We speak of a "drift" in order to make clear the modality of our argument: we do not intend to offer a necessary demonstration of the position we are presenting, which in any event is not usually possible for fundamental hermeneutical claims, but rather an argument of "fittingness," which we offer, for reasons that will become clear, as an alternative to the traditional interpretation, without denying that there are solid textual grounds for the traditional interpretation. In other words, we concede that the traditional view is a possible interpretation, with strong textual support, but wish to propose that it is not the best interpretation.

47. Plato famously substitutes "good" for "beautiful" in the course of an argument, without apology, in the *Symposium* (204e). In the *Divine Names*, Dionysius speaks of the two, as it were, in a single breath: "the-good-and-the-beautiful."

As for the "drift": it is remarkable how, in subtle but significant ways, Aquinas will resist a simple identification of love with the appetite ordered to the good in some of his formulations. Rather than affirming that love simply *is* appetite, for example, he will say on occasion, more cautiously, that love *pertains to* (*pertinet ad*) appetite, which is to say that it has a certain relation to appetite, or it is connected with appetite in some way, without necessarily being identified with it or having its proper place simply *inside* of appetite.[48] In other words, to say love "pertains to" appetite is not exactly to say that it *is* appetite *simpliciter*, though it would seem that this latter formulation would necessarily follow if we defined love *just as* relation to the good, since goodness is finality, that toward which all things strive.[49] It may perhaps seem that we are "picking nits" by insisting on distinguishing clearly between "pertains to" and "is," but the importance of this distinction will emerge more clearly as we proceed.

Our insistence on this distinction already gains support when we note that Aquinas also avoids calling love a *movement* toward the good, which is just what defines appetite (*ad-petere*, a *pursuit*, which is a movement toward).[50] Instead of calling love a motion, he calls it more precisely, and quite significantly, a *principle of motion* (*principium motus*).[51] But, of course, the principle of any motion transcends that motion as its cause; the origin of motion does not itself move (unless it be as an effect of some other cause).[52] If appetite is itself a "movement toward" (*motus*), then love, as the principle of motion, would be a *principle* of appetite, and so to that extent would *transcend* appetite. As Aquinas puts it, the appetible object "gives the appetite, first, a certain adaptation to itself, which consists in complacency in that object, and *from this follows movement* [*ex qua sequitur motus*] towards the appetible object."[53] Love is the moment of adaptation, not the movement itself.

What is it, in general, that functions as the principle of appetite, of motion toward the good? As we saw at the very beginning of our discussion of Aquinas, every act of the appetitive power is preceded by an act of

48. Aquinas, *ST* 1–2.26.1.

49. Aquinas, *ST* 1.5.4.

50. The appetite moves toward (and into) the appetible object: *"tendit in"*; *"motus in appetibile"* (1–2.26.2).

51. Aquinas, *ST* 1–2.26.2ad1.

52. Aquinas, *ST* 1–2.26.2ad1; 1–2.36.2: "The first principle of appetitive motion is love." There is a difference between "*principium*" as the initial moment of movement, i.e., the "start" of motion, and "*principium*" as the principle, or cause, of movement. Love is this latter.

53. Aquinas, *ST* 1–2.26.2, emphasis added.

apprehension.[54] Let us note that the order in which the acts of apprehension fall, for Aquinas, is the order of the intellect, the order of the true, which is logically opposed to the order of the good.[55] Designating love as a principle of motion, rather than being itself a motion *simply*, would seem to connect it in some way with the apprehensive power. So we may ask: Does love pertain not only to the appetitive order but *also* in some way to the order of apprehension? Does Aquinas characterize love in a way that would warrant such an interpretation? Indeed, he does—overwhelmingly, in fact. After having initially defined love as a passion, Aquinas affirms in the very next article that "We find four words referring in a way to the same thing: viz., love, dilection, charity, and friendship." Each of these bears a relation to reason, and indeed one that is not an accident, but turns out at least arguably to belong to the very essence of love. We have already discussed love, *amor*, which is a passion in a unique sense. As a *principle* of the passions it would seem to share the position of the act of apprehension, which is itself the principle of every movement of the sensitive appetite. Second, dilection, Aquinas says, is love with reference to choice (*electionem*), and therefore makes obvious reference to the power of reason. Third, friendship, according to Aquinas, includes—as defining of its very essence—the *apprehension* of our unity with another person to whom we will some good. In this case, it is not sufficient to characterize love simply as the will of some good, and therefore as an act wholly circumscribed, as it were, within the appetitive power; instead, love would seem to designate a prior context *within which* the appetitive acts unfold, a context that we act within only because we have *apprehended* it as belonging to us. Charity, finally, is defined specifically as "friendship with God," and so shares in an analogous way the form of friendship we just described: it includes, as part of its very essence, an apprehension of unity with God.[56]

It is also worth noting that an essential reference to the apprehensive power is included directly in the first three "effects" of love that Aquinas discusses in question 28 of the *prima secunda*, which we may call the principal effects.[57] In his explanation of the effect of union, Aquinas writes: "Now

54. See Aquinas, *ST* 1.82.4ad3; 1.80.1ad3; 1.80.2.

55. "Logically opposed," here, does not of course imply any sort of incompatibility, but is meant only to indicate the different "directions" of the operations.

56. In the specific article, he defines charity "non-theologically," as the perfection of *amor*, but this does not make a difference with respect to the point we are making.

57. We call these "principal effects" not only because they are the first three mentioned, but because, in contrast to the two other effects Aquinas mentions, these seem to reveal something about the nature of love. The fourth effect, "zeal," concerns only the intensity of love; and the fifth, the "wound" of love, speaks of psychological effects.

love being twofold, viz., love of concupiscence and love of friendship; each of these arises from a kind of apprehension of the oneness of the thing loved with the lover. For when we love a thing, by desiring it, *we apprehend it as belonging to our well-being*."[58] Note, he is not just saying here that, prior to the act of love that is an appetitive movement toward the good, there is first an act of apprehension, as the first part of this passage may suggest.[59] This interpretation would make love simply an appetite, which is always thus preceded by an act of intellect. Instead, Aquinas points here to the simultaneity of the two orders of appetite and apprehension: *when [cum] we love*, we are both desiring a thing *and* apprehending that we are in a sort of union with it, in the sense that the act of love includes in itself the acts of both of the other powers. The sense of simultaneity is reinforced when we consider the next two effects of love. Regarding the second effect, "mutual indwelling," Aquinas begins his response thus: "This effect of mutual indwelling may be understood as referring both to the apprehensive and to the appetitive power." Notice: it is *both*; there is an emphasis once again on the simultaneity. As for the third, "ecstasy," Aquinas begins his response thus: "To suffer ecstasy means to be placed outside oneself. This happens as to the apprehensive power and as to the appetitive power."

It is worth pointing out something subtle, perhaps, but profoundly significant, as we will attempt to elaborate below. Early in our reflections, we noted that one of the dangers of conceiving love solely in terms of the appetitive power is that it would entail a tendency to reduce love to a one-sided form, making it a function of the subject, giving the object significance only in its relation to the subject. It is interesting to note that these three primary effects of love—namely, unity, mutual indwelling, and ecstasy—are all "supra-subjective"; they all involve a movement of the subject beyond himself or a *reciprocal*, rather than unilateral, relationship, and they all contain reference to *both* the appetitive and the apprehensive powers, both the order of the good and the order of the true.

---

58. Aquinas, *ST* 1–2.28.1, italics added. Cf., "the proper nature of love is seen to consist in this, that the affection of the one tends to the other as to someone who is somehow one with him" (*SCG* 1.91.4).

59. To be sure, he does seem to say exactly this in *ST* 1–2.28.2ad2: "The apprehension of the reason precedes the movement of love." Our claim is that there is an ambiguity in Aquinas, a drift toward the reduction of love to the order of the good, and another drift that resists this. We are suggesting that the text just quoted, for example, is inadequate taken in isolation, and are attempting to qualify it by highlighting texts that point in the other direction. We want to say that there is a kind of apprehension of reason that is *part* of love, of its essence, and that *this* apprehension precedes, not love strictly speaking, but appetite.

Here we approach a decisive moment in our argument. We are suggesting that love pertains not merely to the appetitive power alone, but somehow *both* to the appetitive *and* to the apprehensive power; it is a matter simultaneously of cognition and desire. As it turns out, this "double reference" *is precisely how Aquinas characterizes our relation to beauty:* "The beautiful is the same as the good, and they differ in aspect only; . . . beauty adds to goodness a relation to the cognitive faculty: so that *good* means that which simply pleases the appetite; while the *beautiful* is something pleasant to apprehend."[60] As we saw in chapter 2, beauty involves both the intellect and the will, but not in their "consummate" mode of knowledge and enjoyment. Instead, they are involved in relation to appearance, not to reality first of all—*im*-mediately—in itself, but to reality specifically through the mediation of appearance. In other words, as we elaborated in chapter 2, in beauty, the intellect and will are involved in the mode of receiving reality as it "freely" offers itself to us. If it is true that love includes a reference to both orders, intellect and will, it would seem most fitting to say that properly speaking love signifies our relationship, not first to goodness, or for that matter to truth, but implicitly to both at once, which is to say that *love is a relation most specifically to beauty; beauty is the proper cause of love.*

At this point I would like to suggest how this interpretation seems *in fact* to accord better with Aquinas's own interpretation of love, and then I will suggest in a more general way, beyond our reading of Thomas, a number of reasons why it would be good, especially in the contemporary situation, to recover the more ancient tradition that roots love in beauty. As we have seen, Aquinas presents love as a positive disposition toward a good (*complacentia, connaturalitas*), which precedes both movement toward it and rest in it. He uses the word "aptitude" or "proportion of the appetite" to describe this disposition, which means that, in love, the soul is "tuned," as it were, or "adapted" (*co-aptatio*) to the particular good it encounters as something suitable to it and for it. Why should such a moment be necessary? It would seem that, if the good is a true good, then it already corresponds to the soul's nature; there is already a "proportion" of the appetite to it. On the other hand, if there is by contrast no such proportion presupposed, then there would seem to be no possibility of "instilling" it. The good either corresponds to a given nature, or it does not, in which case it cannot be said in fact to be a good for that nature. What Aquinas defines as love would seem therefore to be altogether superfluous, either preempted by a "built-in" natural inclination and so unnecessary, or simply unnatural and so without purpose. But this dilemma arises only if we conceive of the

60. Aquinas, *ST* 1–2.27.1.

soul's relationship to goodness in a wholly one-sided way, as the good's being good by "fitting" into a "pre-given" need on the part of the soul. This is
just the sort of reduction to subjectivity that we spoke of at the outset, which
we said will tend to impose itself to the extent that we conceive of love as
belonging *wholly* to the order of the good, and so simply as an appetite. Everything changes, however, if we recognize love as *preceding* in some sense
the appetitive order of the good (*principium motus appetitus*), which is to
say as corresponding most basically to beauty.

How does this work? When Aquinas denied, as we saw above, that love
was itself a movement of the appetite in the sense of being a pursuit of its
object, which pursuit is more properly designated by "desire" (*ST* 1–2.26.2),
he nevertheless conceded that love *does* in fact represent a *kind* of movement of the appetite: "Although love does not denote the movement of the
appetite in tending towards the appetible object, yet it denotes that movement whereby the appetite is changed by the appetible object, so as to have
complacency therein" (ad 3). This is a movement of *a radically different sort*
from the movement that generally characterizes relation to the good: we
might say it represents a movement "of a different order." Rather than being
a change *of* the appetite—a "horizontal" change, designating a difference in
"place" so to speak along the line that crosses the distance between subject
and object—it is instead what we might call a "vertical" change, a change *in*
the nature of the appetite itself. Aquinas describes this change as a certain
formation of the appetite (*formatio quaedam appetitus*), a specification of
the appetite in the formal order.[61] We could say it effects a connection between the appetitive order (final causality) and the cognitive order (formal
causality). This specification is brought about by the action of the object
on the subject of appetite, though of course it is the object specifically as
appetible and so as related to the subject's appetite, rather than being some
wholly foreign entity. There is thus a kind of "reciprocity" between the subject and the object, which overcomes in principle the reductive unilaterality
we have been criticizing. Aquinas describes this as "a certain union of the
lover and beloved."[62] Note that this union involves the importing of a real,
internal change (*immutatio*); it entails a difference between the "before" and
the "after"—Aquinas describes the object's action on the subject as *resulting*
in complacency (*ut . . . complaceat*), which means that the complacency is
not presupposed as a prior condition for the union—though this "event" is

---

61. Aquinas, *De ver.* 26.4. We recall that, as Fr. Sherwin has observed, Aquinas had
laid greater emphasis on this aspect in his earlier work, most evidently in the *Com-
mentary on the Sentences*.

62. Aquinas, *De ver.* 26.4.

something other than the simple movement from potency to act that we find in the movement of desire or other sorts of change.[63]

It seems to me that this moment would tend to get marginalized to the extent that we remained within the two orders, truth and goodness, since the moment does not clearly fit either. But it stands out as a distinct moment in itself when we recognize beauty as a fundamental "property" of being, one of the basic transcendentals. In this case, the "moment" of love ceases to be a mere "preparatory" moment inside of the sensible appetite, which precedes its more obvious movement, and thus a mere means to some other end; instead, it becomes a *perfect* condition *already* in itself, which does not need to justify itself, so to speak, by the "real" consummation of the appetite. If beauty is a transcendental property to which love corresponds, then love becomes a revelation of being: to unfold this theme will be our task in the chapter that follows.

In our second chapter, we interpreted beauty as an "encounter between two freedoms," a kind of union between two distinct and integral realities, man and the world. This interpretation of beauty "fits" with a basic drift in Aquinas's description of love. As we previously mentioned, Aquinas describes love in terms of: (a) *union*, a relation between two in which they become one without losing their distinctiveness from each other; (b) *mutual indwelling*, in which subject and object are not only present *to* one another, but indeed present *in* one another; and (c) *ecstasy*, a movement beyond the self. With regard to this latter, Aquinas describes it specifically in relation to the subject, man as lover, but we may point out how "beautifully" this corresponds to what we described in chapter 2: beauty does not lie in the reality simply in itself, but the reality in its *appearance*, which we may now describe in terms of the *ecstasis* of love: in the appearance, the object comes as it were *outside* of itself, and joins with the *ecstasis* of the perceiver of beauty. In this way, *ecstasis*, like the first two effects of love, namely, union and mutual indwelling, would represent a reciprocal exchange between subject and object. In a sense, we might say that each of these three signifies the very same thing, but from a different perspective, and the very same thing they signify is: love.

---

63. Aquinas describes concupiscible love precisely as entailing the movement from potency to act (*ST* 1–2.27.3). Of course, every change presupposes potency, but the change of love being discussed here is quite unique with respect to the typical order of events: it presupposes not a potency that is "already" ordered to actuality, which is the usual shape, as it were, but rather a potency that is capable of receiving a potency for a particular actuality. In other words, there seems to be an extraordinary analogy here in the natural order to what later scholastics call the "obediential potency" in nature for grace. We will return to this point at the end.

Now, one might object at this point that Aquinas presents these not, as we have just insinuated, as descriptions of love but specifically as "effects" of love, which are brought about by a passion in the subject's soul.[64] In this case, we would say that love most basically is a movement of the sensible appetite, but the various forms of reciprocity we just discussed occur specifically as a *result* of this passion, which presumably takes place in each of the subjects involved individually. There are two responses to make to this objection. First of all, though Aquinas does indeed present union as an effect of love in question 28, in his explanation he observes that "union has a threefold relation to love": in one respect, it is a *cause* of love, and in another respect, it is an effect of love, but in a third respect, "*There is also a union which is essentially love itself.*"[65] Love can be conceived essentially as a unity between a lover and a beloved.[66] In an earlier question, he had used a formulation to describe love that corresponds perfectly to the argument we are making. In contrast to the "real" union of subject and object, which bears the name "joy" or "pleasure" and represents, as we saw in chapter 4, the terminus of the appetite for the good, Aquinas observes that "there is also an affective union, consisting in an aptitude or proportion, insofar as one thing, from the very fact of its having an aptitude for and an inclination to another, partakes of it: and love betokens such a union. This union precedes the movement of desire" (i.e., precedes the order of the good!).[67] Note

64. Another significant objection might be raised on just this point. According to this objection, one could observe that the brunt of our argument has turned on the inclusion of the cognitive order inside of the essence of love, rather than the reducing of love to a part simply of the appetitive order. But, for Aquinas, the appetitive order *always* follows the cognitive, and so always presupposes it in its own operation. (This objection has as its correlate the rejection of beauty as a transcendental property, since in fact there is nothing in beauty that is genuinely distinct from goodness: the connection to the cognitive order that Aquinas indicates is what distinguishes beauty in fact concretely already belongs to goodness insofar as the good always follows the true: see Aertsen's argument on this score in *Medieval Philosophy and the Transcendentals*.) Love as the first of the passions stands, so to speak, right at the moment of *transition* between the two orders (though specifically *on the side of* the appetitive), and so it is natural that the reference to apprehension would stand out especially clearly here, even though the reference to the cognitive would be presupposed in the whole movement of the appetite. Thus, there is no need to make the moment of love transcend the appetitive order; we need only emphasize the close connection between intellect and will/appetite in Aquinas. There are two things to say in response to this objection: first, it makes love *superfluous* in exactly the way we have just described; and, second, one might say it is precisely the prioritizing of love, to which the integration of intellect and will is *essential*, that preserves the intrinsic connection between the two orders.

65. Aquinas, *ST* 1–2.28.1ad2. Italics added.

66. Cf., Aquinas, *De ver.* 26.4.

67. Aquinas, *ST* 1–2.25.2ad2.

that this union can also be described as a mutual indwelling by virtue of the participation it involves, and can be described, in addition, as an *ecstasis* insofar as the aptitude or proportion is effected in the subject, which implies a movement of the subject beyond its prior state. It seems to me that one could describe each of the three primary "effects" of love as representing, *in fact*, a cause of, an effect of, and the *very essence of* love itself. However that may be, the principal point is that, as a union, love has its proper place, so to speak, *between* lover and beloved, rather than residing merely in the sensible appetite of the one *and also* in the appetite of the other—i.e., as indicating simply the coincidence of two individual appetites.

The second response is to admit that Aquinas does in fact contradict himself in a fairly straightforward way: while he affirms, as we have just seen, that love is, at least in one respect, essentially union itself, he also elsewhere explicitly denies this: "love is not the very relation of union, but that union is a result of love."[68] It is interesting to note that Aquinas makes this denial in the course of the article in which he is attempting to define love specifically as a passion (and so as a movement essentially located in the lower part of the soul of the subject). This suggests that the difficulty arises precisely when Aquinas *reduces* the meaning of love in just the way we have been criticizing. Union becomes *merely, exclusively*, a result only if we insist on narrowing it in its proper sense to its subjective aspect, making it principally a movement that occurs inside the subject's soul. We are proposing that Aquinas contradicts himself here, not because of any confusion or sloppy thinking—we are speaking of Aquinas after all!—but because he is the inheritor of a broad and deep tradition of reflection on the rich meaning of love, which he is attempting to articulate in terms of what we have been arguing tends to a one-sided conception, namely, love as belonging simply to the order of the good, but which his characteristic depth of insight and intellectual honesty prevents him from over-simplifying.[69]

68. Aquinas, *ST* 1–2.26.2ad2. Note, it would have been possible to say that unity is the result of love in a certain respect, without denying that it is also in another respect itself the union. It is only to the extent that Aquinas excludes this latter aspect in principle that a contradiction arises.

69. A basic question arises, which we cannot address here, both because of reasons of space and also because we are not sufficiently competent in the intellectual history of medieval thought to make a final judgment on the matter. The question is: Why is Aquinas committed to the association of love with goodness rather than with beauty? Without claiming to resolve this exceedingly difficult question, we might speculatively propose three possibilities: 1) beauty is not as central to Aristotle's metaphysics as it is to the conception of being in the Neoplatonic tradition, and Aquinas was part of the new thirteenth-century tendency to read Aristotle *apart* from that tradition, rather than as a natural part of it; 2) along these lines, a "participation metaphysics" begins to cede place to a "substance metaphysics" (which is not at all incompatible in principle

Let us at this point sum up the role we are giving to beauty in love, and what it implies for man's relation to the world. We have suggested, in chapter 2, that man's very first encounter with reality occurs under the sign of beauty. The order of beauty precedes not only the order of goodness *but also the order of truth*. This would seem to be an anti-Thomistic claim, but I want to suggest it is actually in the spirit of Thomas's thought and preserves the significance of some of the foundational affirmations we associate with him. It is fitting to begin with beauty, first of all, precisely because beauty is in a basic respect a matter of appearance. We do not begin with reality *in se* but rather *quoad nos*; we do not first encounter the inner essence of things *as* essence, but, instead, as Aquinas insists, our first encounter occurs through the senses. As it turns out, Aquinas also says that the first thing to fall into the conception of the intellect is being.[70] So we can ask, do we encounter, in the mind's first awakening to reality, first *appearance* or *being*? We may evidently respond "Both!" if we start with beauty, which can be understood as a transcendental property only if the *appearance* in which beauty resides is an appearance *of being*.[71] In this case, appearances—*pace* Locke and Hume—are not "mere" accidents, a veil that would have to be penetrated or shoved aside in order to find the substance hidden underneath, the substance which is precisely *not* manifest. Instead, as we discussed in chapter 2, to acknowledge the primacy of beauty is to recognize that we *first* experience appearance as the manifestation *of* reality, its disclosure *to* us.

Now, if we go on to associate beauty with love, in the manner we have been suggesting in this chapter, we recognize that this reception of reality's self-disclosure is a kind of "attuning," a "proportioning" of the soul to the real. Reality, by giving itself in the splendor of appearance, in-forms the appetite as the pre-condition for the relations that are enacted through the

with a "participation metaphysics"). The interpretation of love in terms of beauty tends to emphasize the reality of love "in itself," whereas in a non-participatory substance metaphysics, a thing can be real only as either a substance in itself (which love is not), or as an accident inhering in a substance (as love, then, must be): thus, love becomes principally a passion of the soul or an act of the will. (On this score, we might compare Plotinus, who begins his treatise on love asking whether it is a passion [*pathos*] of the soul or a spirit in itself [*daimon*], and decides it is both, but principally a spirit; 3) there was a tendency in the high Middle Ages to connect the transcendental properties with the Persons of the Trinity, and, in this model, there is no obvious place for beauty. Instead, we have unity (Father), truth (Son), and goodness (Holy Spirit).

70. Aquinas, *ST* 1.5.2.

71. According to Balthasar, the first principles of knowledge and being are "supraconceptual": "these first principles cannot be abstract propositions because it is precisely not on the basis of abstraction that we arrive at them: they must necessarily be concrete, immediate encounters, not only with the laws of Being, but with Being itself" ("On the Tasks of Catholic Philosophy in Our Time," 180).

intellect and will.[72] The soul is "readied" by beauty for an encounter with reality in itself, through the effecting of a positive disposition (*coaptatio*,[73] *complacentia*). This attuning occurs because the reality offers precisely *itself* in the appearance, so that the soul can be said to be in some sense given a *participation* in that reality through the mediation of its manifestation.[74] In other words, this attunement is a particular kind of *union* between subject and object, a reciprocal *ecstasis* that can be described as a mutual indwelling of sorts. The union is a perfection in itself, but also simultaneously involves in an incipient way the cognitive and appetitive orders. We might say that it "pre-contains" these orders, not in the sense of being a merely provisional place-holder, but as presenting, "unbidden," everything necessary, in a certain respect, in a manner that allows the genuine difference of the other respects, namely, truth and goodness in their specificity.

Love is thus the most original and foundational relation between the soul and reality, and it is inside this profound openness, which precedes every deliberate, self-conscious act, but provides precisely the proper condition for it, that the soul can exercise its distinctive operations. In the movement of desire that has, so to speak, already begun, it can pursue the reality itself as an object of appetite, or, in relation to the radiant appearance that is, as it were, full of the essence of the real, it can reason through a proper distinction between the two and come to a real grasp of a thing as it is in itself. Beauty opens up the orders of both goodness and truth as unfolding this promise, and ensures that both goodness and truth will be understood, not as unilateral relations, but as instances of a true reciprocity between subject and object at every point in just the way we have been proposing in this book. In this sense, because beauty "pre-contains" the other orders, the acts of reason and desire reveal themselves to be a deepening of the love they presuppose. This is why we can indeed say that love *is* a union, is caused by union, and results in union.[75]

---

72. Note, this in-formation, as mediated in appearance, is distinct from the reception of form by the intellect, and it is not simply in the will *rather than* in the intellect, which is why this interpretation does not fall into the confusion insightfully identified by Fr. Sherwin, *By Knowledge and By Love*, 67–69.

73. *Coaptatio*: the adaption of two things to each other.

74. See Aquinas, *ST* 1–2.25.2ad2.

75. See Aquinas, *ST* 1–2.28.1ad2.

3. Restoring Love

In addition to the resistance to any subjectivism and the advantages just intimated, it seems to me that there are several more that are worth listing here in the final part of our reflection. First of all, if we recall our discussion of beauty in chapter 2, we see that associating love with beauty infuses love, as it were, with the comprehensiveness, the constant unifying of extreme differences, that the tradition has recognized as belonging to beauty. (Note, incidentally, the natural fit with beauty in this regard, too, if we conceive of love as a bond, a unity between two that face each other as other: a *coincidentia oppositorum*.) It would be a fruitful exercise to think through love in terms of all of the phenomena of the unity-in-opposition we saw in beauty, but we will content ourselves here with a basic observation: as linked to beauty, love can be understood as involving the whole person, in all of the constitutive tensions that belong to human nature, rather than having its proper place in a mere part of the soul—i.e., the sensitive appetite, or perhaps the will. Thus, love includes body and soul, intellect and will, movement and rest, eternity and time, the infinite and the finite, the divine and human, and so on, while preserving every essential difference. At the same time, this association does not simply eliminate the Aristotelian/Thomistic characterization of love as a passion of the soul, as if this position were simply false. As we saw in our earlier discussion, because beauty is essentially a matter of appearance, the sensible aspect is privileged in a certain respect as paradigmatic, without however being absolutized insofar as appearance is not exclusively sensible, but appears so to speak analogously in all modes of manifestation or self-disclosure. Along these lines, we may say that love has a correspondingly privileged place as a passion, a being physically moved,[76] while at the same time recognizing that its significance always also transcends this physical dimension. Indeed, if love represents the subject's being acted on by the object so as to be disposed properly to respond,[77] the bodily, "passional" dimension would naturally stand in the

---

76. In justifying Dionysius's privileging of *amor* (*eros*) over dilection (*agape*), Aquinas explains that "it is possible for man to tend to God by love, being as it were passively drawn by Him, more than he can possibly be drawn thereto by his reason, which pertains to the nature of dilection" (*ST* 1–2.26.3ad4). In other words, our love of God in a certain respect exceeds our reason. In *ST* 1–2.27.2ad3, Aquinas explains that we can love something perfectly even if we do not know it perfectly, which suggests that love in some respect exceeds knowledge. Such an affirmation makes most sense, in fact, if we characterize the apprehension to which our appetite is subordinated as aesthetic rather than strictly intellectual.

77. We recall that love is a change in the appetite brought about by the acting of the object *on* it (Aquinas, *ST* 1–2.26.2ad3).

foreground. If it is beauty that so moves us, however, our body is stirred not by a mere sensible good, but a spiritual one. As we just observed, because beauty is a transcendental, we ought to say that, in love, it is precisely the being of things in appearance that moves the subject in his body. Love thus involves the whole person in response, from the foundation of our nature to the highest point of spirit. Love—as a union with reality—transcends us, but only as including the whole of us.

Implied in this is a further advantage, namely, the central place of reason in love. We have been criticizing the perspective that would limit love to the appetitive order—i.e., make it a matter of goodness exclusively. Linking love with beauty affirms the essential role, as it were, of the appetitive order, but does not allow this role to be exclusive. Instead, it "adds" to the appetitive an ordination to the cognitive power as part of love's very definition.[78] In this respect, the intellect and its relation to truth becomes essential to love, rather than being at best only a necessary presupposition of the order of love, which remains, even in its necessity, merely accidental. The act of the intellect may be accidental to the act of will—though we will suggest in a moment that the primacy of beauty highlights the intrinsic relation between them—but it is not accidental to love. Beauty involves a delight simultaneous with an apprehension; love thus is a *cognitive* grasp that coincides with a *positive disposition towards*. The implications of this point are endless, but we will just mention briefly three here. First, while we tend to think of sin, and therefore redemption, as a matter exclusively of the moral order, if we understand sin ultimately to be a failure of love, we will be inclined to recognize more directly that the intellect itself is not innocent, so to speak; or, to put the point more precisely, that sinfulness is a failure in both the intellectual and volitional orders at once. For this reason, redemption from sin requires not just a healing of the will, but involves a new understanding—a putting on the *mind* of Christ. Second, because beauty is essentially a matter of *order*,[79] as the classical tradition has always recognized, it follows that love likewise indicates a kind of order—and not just the intention of goodness. In this respect, we can judge the quality of love, and not just its "quantity," i.e., its intensity and perhaps its sincerity, the degree of commitment, and so forth. The quality will turn not just on such things but also on the basic question of the order, nature, structure, or form—in short, the *logos*—of relationship.[80] Love in this case is not first the discrete acts of good will, but

78. Cf., Aquinas, *ST* 1–2.27.1ad3.

79. Aquinas: "beauty includes three conditions, 'integrity' or 'perfection,' . . . due 'proportion' or 'harmony,' and lastly 'brightness' or 'clarity'" (*ST* 1.39.8).

80. On the relationship between love and order, see David L. Schindler, *Ordering Love: Liberal Societies and the Memory of God*, especially the introductory chapter. Cf.,

designates the union within which such acts occur, a union that provides a certain order, logic, or ethos to the desire and the movement of appetite that occur inside the horizon it establishes. Third, along these same lines, once we recognize that beauty, and so love, is a matter of order, it follows that the meaning of love extends into the objective sphere: the sphere of the nature of the body, of relationships in their organization, of institutions, of political and economic systems, and of culture more generally. Clearly, this point in itself opens up into an infinity of other themes and questions, but we wish to point out here only that, when we conceive of love in terms of beauty, and *therefore* in terms of order, the theme of "structures of sin," which became so prevalent in the twentieth-century Catholic Magisterium, becomes natural, and indeed quite obvious.

In an aphorism, Hans Us von Balthasar poses the interesting question, "Which of the two has loved more deeply: Hegel, the great matchmaker, who personified the impatience for marrying off and uniting; or Kierkegaard, who embodied the zealous patience for keeping the parties apart to the end, only to make us fall to our knees more definitively?"[81] Connecting love with beauty allows us to say what Balthasar clearly means to imply by leaving this question unanswered: both set into relief something essential in love. It would be hard to accord a genuinely positive value to the element of *distance* in love, a kind of generous respect that stands back from the beloved rather than simply pressing onward to him or her (or it), if love were simply a matter of the appetitive order. As we have observed repeatedly, appetite means just that, a "movement towards"—as opposed to a "standing back." But beauty implies both a desire and a reserve, which the aesthetic tradition has given the name "disinterestedness." Aquinas, intriguingly, distinguishes love as having regard for goodness specifically in its universal sense (we might say: in its truth), "whether possessed or not" (*ST* 1.20.1). When Plato describes the soul's passionate pursuit of beauty in the famous image of the charioteer driving the pair of horses, he sets into relief a kind of twofoldness to the relation: beauty not only stirs the soul on to possession, but *at the very same time* causes the soul to pull back from its pursuit in a state of awe and reverence;[82] beauty inspires to "let be, in gratitude."

D. C. Schindler, "Beauty and the Holiness of Mind."

81. Balthasar, *The Grain of Wheat*, 11–12.

82. The soul, seeing beauty in the beloved, is driven first by a scarcely containable desire to possess him. But "when the charioteer [of the soul] sees that face, his memory is carried back to the real nature of Beauty, and he sees it again where it stands on the sacred pedestal next to Self-Control. At the sight he is frightened, [and] falls backwards awestruck . . . ." (*Phaedrus*, 254b-c).

Josef Pieper captured this sense in his formulation of the essence of love as consisting in the affirmative judgment—which as affirmation belongs to the appetitive order and as judgment to the cognitive—that "It is good that you exist!"[83] We might describe this affirmation as explicating the content of the utterance "You are beautiful!" Beauty, after all, is not something simply different from the good, but is the good specifically *as* true, in the sense both of manifestation and absoluteness. It is just this that allows the soul to affirm the beloved as prior, in a certain respect, to one's desires, and so without immediate reference to the self, or more specifically to the fulfillment of the appetite of the self—though, of course, it is crucial to add that this does not at all imply the exclusion of such fulfillment as its fruit. It is precisely the "ordination to the cognitive power" in an essential way that causes this "disinterestedness": love is a positive disposition toward the beloved that coincides with an *apprehension* of union, and it is this coincidence that gives love *two* objects, while desire (appetite) itself has simply *one*. In love, we not only will something good, as we do in desire, but we will it *for* an other.[84] In love, desire arises within the more basic context of an affirmation of the other and therefore always inside of an ethos of gratitude.

A further advantage of associating love with beauty—interpreted *metaphysically*, specifically as a *transcendental* property—is that it opens up a potentially fruitful encounter between Aquinas and certain currents in modern thought. Heidegger, for example, described the "attunement" (*Stimmung*) to Being as what allows beings to show themselves in their truth (*a-lētheia*).[85] This insight is not altogether different from Aquinas's description of love as entailing a disposing of the subject by the object. We saw that this disposing of the subject is a kind of elevation of the subject (a "vertical" change in the appetite) that occurs in the perception of beauty. The subject is brought thereby to relate to the object in a new way. Recognizing a certain affinity between the *coaptatio* ("the adaption of two things to each other") and *die Stimmung* ("attunement") opens up ontological depths that are not always evident in scholastic discussions of beauty; it allows us to see that the love pro-voked, called forth, by beauty ought to be understood not just as occasioning a pleasant experience, a delight, but as revealing a thing *in its being*, and thereby opening up being itself in its radical difference from beings.

83. Pieper, *Faith-Hope-Love*, 207 et passim.

84. Aquinas: "although the other operations of the soul deal with only one object, love alone seems to be directed to two objects" (*SCG* 1.91.10). Cf., *ST* 1-2, 26.4. Our interpretation gives a reason why it is unique: love is *not* the act of a single power, but in fact involves *both* intellect and will at once.

85. See Heidegger's lecture, "What is That-Philosophy?" especially 29-31, with relevant notes.

Beauty, after all, is a transcendental! As associated with beauty, love pertains not just to appetibility, but also to intelligibility; in other words, love has an essentially *revelatory*, and not merely moral dimension. It thus concerns the meaning of things in their most profound depths. All of this would find interesting points of dialogue with Heidegger's philosophy. But while Heidegger, as I have argued elsewhere,[86] tends to describe this attunement in predominantly negative, and even violent terms, as *angst* and eventually as *horror*, and arguably swallows up the distinctively personal in the nothingness he identifies with being, Aquinas's notion of love—interpreted in relation to beauty—offers all of the depth of ontological attunement, but opens this depth inside of a genuine *reciprocity*, one that is eminently personal.[87]

Moreover, the view of love presented here resonates with the view beautifully expounded by Max Scheler, who affirmed love as the distinctively Christian contribution to philosophical anthropology. According to Scheler, love is a radical disposition that precedes every act of intellect and will as phenomenologically opening the horizon within which those acts intend their proper objects.[88] In a manner similar to what we have been suggesting here, Scheler argues that love has tended in the tradition to lose the place that belongs to it by rights and has instead been folded into the order of the will and appetite. One of the dimensions that Scheler's view would contribute to the Thomistic understanding of love is both this sense of love as setting the horizon for our intellect and will, and, moreover, the recognition that, in so doing, love is not just a union but for that very reason a kind of *openness*, an unveiling of meaning and an eliciting of desire. But there is a decisive difference between Scheler's view and the one we have been describing here: while Scheler makes love a matter of feeling, and thus radically separates it from the good and the true, and indeed from being itself, in a manner that makes it altogether indifferent to these, we have been arguing for its inseparability from the orders of goodness and truth, and for a specifically metaphysical interpretation of beauty that goes far beyond (though without excluding) the psychological realm. Moreover, while Scheler thus offers his philosophy of love as an alternative to the Thomistic tradition, and thus with only superficial points of contact, our interpretation has arisen precisely from *within* a reading of Aquinas. As a

86. See my "Giving Cause to Wonder," in *Catholicity of Reason*, esp. 197–200.

87. Heidegger is complicated of course, and this is a summary judgment that would require further discussion in another context.

88. In phenomenology, to say that the mind "intends" its objects means that it trains its focus on them, highlighting them against a backdrop. That backdrop, which provides the setting for the mind's relation to its objects, is referred to with the technical term "horizon."

response to the transcendental property of beauty, love is not principally a *feeling*, even if it includes in a particular way a "passional" dimension, as we explained earlier; instead, it is a matter of both intellect and will/appetite simultaneously, and so differs from goodness and truth only as in a certain sense "pre-containing" them. The soul's powers are set in motion in love, but it is a motion distinct from the motion proper to each in its distinctness, a movement directed to a terminus in which it comes to completion.[89] The motion of love is a different sort of motion: it is the opening up of the world.

Finally, we might point out that this interpretation of love connects in a direct way with the one of the main currents of modern personalism, which interprets love, not first as a passion of the soul, but rather as a "union of persons."[90] Karol Wojtyła (Pope John Paul II), for example, presents the first element of love as *amor complacentiae*—the Latin he gives as equivalent to the Polish word "*upodobanie*," which is translated in *Love and Responsibility* as "fondness" and in a later "Meditation on Givenness" as "predilection." This *amor complacentiae* precedes desire and gives it its proper place.[91] Moreover, he identifies it as an act of both intellect and will, though he links it most basically to the intellect, and indeed connects it specifically with beauty.[92] In a later reflection, he explains that this beauty is a revelation of the givenness of creation, and reveals that things thus belong together (i.e., subsist already in love), which is precisely what allows the profound gift of self that is our destiny:

> The yearning of the human heart after this primordial beauty with which the Creator has endowed man is also a desire for the communion in which the sincere gift of self is manifested. This beauty and this communion are not goods that have been lost irretrievably—they are goods to be redeemed, retrieved; and in

---

89. In a manner similar to Scheler, and the argument being made here, Hans Urs von Balthasar in an early work claims that the openness of love precedes, and provides the condition for, truth; but he presents this as a volitional act (though one that he clearly distinguishes from the act of deliberate choice): see *Theologic I*, 109–12. It would seem that the irrationalism, which Balthasar wants unequivocally to avoid (111), could be more decisively excluded if we recognized love as simultaneously an act of *intellect and will at once* (and indeed of the whole embodied person), rather than locating it simply in the will.

90. John Paul II, *Love and Responsibility*, 23.

91. John Paul II, "A Meditation on Givenness," esp. 875–77.

92. See John Paul II: "fondness [i.e., complacency] is most deeply linked to cognition" (*Love and Responsibility*, 58); "It is difficult to explain fondness without granting a reciprocal penetration of reason and will" (ibid., 59); "The object of fondness, which stands as a good in the field of vision of the subject, presents itself to him at the same time as the beautiful. . . . The beautiful finds its place precisely in fondness" (ibid., 63).

this sense every human person is given to every other—every woman is given to every man, and every man is given to every woman.[93]

There would be the possibility here, once again, of a fruitful encounter between this current of thought and the more directly metaphysically-grounded tradition of Thomism.[94]

It is also worth noting that love, rooted in beauty, conceived as "pre-containing" the orders of truth and goodness in a non-extrinsicist manner, enriches each of these orders in turn insofar as it represents a unity that mediates the intellect and will to each other even in their distinctiveness. We might say that it "adds" the movement toward finality (appetite) to the intellect's proper relation to form and it "adds" the predominance of form (apprehension) to the appetite for the good that constitutes will.[95] We cannot unfold, here, in an even remotely adequate way the implications of this point for our understanding of epistemology and ethics, but we may content ourselves nonetheless with a general observation in each case. First, within the horizon opened up by love, we come to appreciate more fully the *contemplative* dimension of the intellect, which we might say is an approach to truth seen from the perspective of beauty: an act of *loving reason*. Contemplation is not a matter (only) of the immediate possession implied by knowledge—which can thus reduce to a storing of information that is "done with" a thing once it is known—but remains in the expectant openness of wonder, an affective longing for the truth known.[96] Contemplation is a knowing that resembles the *beholding* of beauty; it is the shape of reason in, and indeed in some sense *as*, love. On the other hand, the formal dimensions of the relation to the good in appetite come more sharply into focus. We have here

93. John Paul II, "A Meditation on Givenness," 877.

94. For an example of such a fruitful encounter, see David L. Schindler, "Being, Gift, Self-Gift: Reply to Waldstein on Relationality and John Paul II's Theology of the Body."

95. Note: we place "adds" deliberately in quotes. It is improper to conceive of each power first separately and then consider what beauty adds, over and above their natural operation, which would make the relation too extrinsic; rather, the dimensions we are indicating always-already belong to each because they always subsist so to speak in relation to each other as correlates of the transcendentals, which are themselves convertible. The argument is that recognizing the primacy of beauty and love sets these aspects into greater relief, and moves them to the center. There is no tension, in other words, between these aspects being added by beauty and their belonging to each by nature. I am grateful to Fr. Anselm Ramelow for raising a question about this matter, which allowed for clarification.

96. For a more detailed argument on this point, see my "Giving Cause to Wonder," in *Catholicity of Reason*, 163–228.

an approach to the good from the perspective of beauty: *loving desire*. This approach reveals that the appetite for the good does not seek merely the discrete and episodic attainment of satisfaction in one act after another, but wants instead to abide in relation. In this respect, we acknowledge more decisively, for example, the (relative) permanence of affective union, the bond of friendship, and the covenant of marriage. Moreover, at the same time, recognizing the relation to form elevates the natural activities of appetite into the meaningful form of culture, custom, ritual, and the like. Separated from the love rooted in beauty—which, as we recall, concerns reality not in itself but in its appearance—truth and goodness will increasingly become aspirations to immediate union with reality, impatient with regard to any mediations, or what are called "trappings." Inside of love, by contrast, they can celebrate mediation as something positive, and not as an obstacle to immediate intimacy. Cultural form thus takes on a more substantial weight, and so too does the role of the body, and sense experience, in our thinking and knowing. Most basically, because love is union, conceiving reason and will as acts unfolding from within the relation of love highlights the fact that each is a kind of co-act between subject and object—there is generous reciprocity from beginning to end, as we have attempted to show in earlier chapters.

With respect to the Christian mystery of grace and redemption, and the endlessly controverted question of its relation to nature,[97] the notion of love as rooted in beauty rather than being altogether circumscribed within the order of goodness introduces a fruitful starting point. One of the difficult problems in formulating the relationship between nature and grace is understanding how grace can *elevate* nature, which is to say, how grace can fulfill nature without *simply* corresponding "already" to the end that is built into nature, so to speak, or to put it in yet other terms, how grace can give nature a *radically new* end—life in Christ as adopted sons and daughters of the Father, and ultimately participation in God's inner Trinitarian life—without changing nature in a violent manner. The interpretation of love, as rooted in beauty, and so as a distinct perfection that precedes in a certain sense the perfections of truth and goodness, reveals that there is in love a *natural analogy* to the transformation of nature by grace. This analogy

97. The question of the relationship between man's created nature and the grace offered to him in Jesus Christ, for his redemption and as an invitation into God's own life, has been a matter of discussion and debate from the beginning of the Church's theological appropriation of revelation. In the modern, "post-Christian" world, Catholic theologians took up this debate—now typically referred to as the "nature-grace problem"—with a new vigor, especially after the provocative theses of Henri de Lubac (1896–1991).

implies that the novelty introduced by grace, for all its radical difference from nature, is not simply discontinuous with it. The nature-grace problem would be essentially insoluble, I submit, if we had *only* the orders of truth and goodness to work with, as it were. In this case, the end of nature would necessarily be proportionate to the appetite of nature as already given, i.e., as "built into" nature as such. Given such a conception, the only "movement" of the appetite would be toward, or indeed away from, its (due) completion. But we saw that Aquinas describes love as a "movement" of appetite, not "horizontally," so to speak, along the line of its fulfillment, but rather "vertically": it is a change in the appetite as a disposing of it, a *rendering* of it apt, a *proportioning of it* to the object (and indeed *by* the object, which means not as a function of the prior condition of the subject, as would be the case for example in Transcendental Thomism).[98] The fact that Aquinas calls this a *change* (*immutatio*) means that its aptitude is in some respect different after the moment of love from what it was before. We could say that, in love, the object presents itself as the end of the subject's appetite only by, at the very same time, in-spiring, giving form to (*formatio*), the subject's appetite. The object can thus be said, in beauty, to transform that appetite, rendering it one specifically attuned, as it were, to the object, an appetite meant specifically for *this particular beloved*. In this sense, love is not a mere unilateral relation (appetite to end), but involves a union, a mutual indwelling or reciprocity, and an *ecstasis*. It is a *com-placentia* in the specific sense of "being pleased *together*."

To put the point more concretely, the love occasioned by beauty is an elevation of the subject, beyond his previous condition, that opens him up to desire (i.e., will) the beloved object properly—and arguably also to understand the object properly, though we will leave that theme for another time. If this is the foundation of man's encounter with the world, or perhaps more adequately put, if his engagement with the world begins and ends in love, and thus under the sign of beauty, then the notion that grace elevates nature by in some respect giving it a new end, that it satisfies only a desire that it has already transformed, does not represent in any sense a dialectical violence with respect to natural existence in its normal unfolding. The complete *surprise* of grace resonates, as it were, with what nature is already used to as a matter of course. We note here that, perhaps contrary to the more dialectical interpretations that either separate nature and grace or

98. "Transcendental Thomism" attempts in general to solve the problem of nature's capacity for grace by drawing on Kant's notion of the *a priori*, which provides the conditions for the possibility of experience. For an excellent critique along these lines of Rahner's notion of the "supernatural existential," see Ouellet, "Paradox and/or Supernatural Existential."

collapse them into one, this approach reveals the human experience of love as a privileged place of the encounter with God's grace.[99] Fittingly, the openness to grace does not require as a matter of essential principle a breaking of nature, but occurs when nature is, so to speak, at its best: nature discovers a longing for grace precisely when nature is most perfect, most complete in itself.[100] In the fallen conditions of history, of course, it is often the case that nature discovers its need when it is most desperate, that "grace comes somehow violent,"[101] but it is in just such conditions that the experience of human love, too, arrives, if and when it does, as a sort of healing violence.

Finally, by connecting love with beauty, we are able to affirm the sovereign status of love that the Christian tradition has always acknowledged. Such a status would not seem warranted for a mere movement of the sensitive appetite, the lowest "part" of the soul. Even if we extend the meaning of love beyond its strict sense as a passion to indicate any ordination to the good, and in this way to include the act of will, we still identify love with only one of the basic movements of the soul, in contrast to the intellective movement, which Aquinas, along with the whole classical tradition, esteems as the noblest part of man. He thus, somewhat infamously, makes man's highest act, the eschatological vision, to consist essentially of an act of intellect, rather than an act of will[102]—i.e., in the conventional categories, an act of love. The Fransciscan response, which, in an attempt to do more justice to the Christian tradition, makes the eschatological act consist most essentially of an act of the will rather than an act of intellect, appears simply to fall off of the other side of the horse.[103] But if we connect love with beauty, rather than (merely) with the appetitive order of the good, it becomes possible to affirm love as the perfection of all perfections, the highest and most abiding, without the danger of arbitrary voluntarism. Love is then a unity that provides the context for the acts of intellect and will in their proper order, a unity that entails grateful acknowledgment of God's truth and goodness—It is *supremely* good that You exist!—and an elevation of man

99. We might consider, here, John Paul II's reflections on marriage as a "primordial sacrament," almost "naturally supernatural": see, e.g., his *Address to the Roman Rota*, 2001, and of course his catechesis on human love: *Man and Woman He Created Them*. According to Trent, the union of Adam and Eve occurred already through the inspiration of the Holy Spirit (DS 1797); for this reason, Leo XIII claimed, citing previous popes, that *all* marriages, whether of believers or unbelievers, can be considered, in a sense, sacramental (*Arcanum*, 19).

100. We recall the passage from C. S. Lewis cited in chapter 2: "It was when I was happiest that I longed most" (*Till We Have Faces*, 74).

101. Aeschylus, *Agamemnon*, line 183, in Lattimore's translation.

102. Aquinas, *ST* 1–2.3.4.

103. Scheler makes a similar observation: "Love and Knowledge," 160–61.

that allows both a contemplative gaze in wonder (*admiratio*) and the most unshakeable fidelity of a covenantal bond (*adhaerare deo*).[104] Note that the traditional name for ultimate happiness is not "beatific understanding," but "beatific *vision*," which refers implicitly to beauty, *quod visum placet*. This vision is not merely immediate union with the divine essence, but intimacy and distance at once.

Not least, eschatological love as response to beauty sets into relief the vision of the Father precisely in his appearance in the Son,[105] indeed, the *incarnate Son*, in the Spirit who is "One Person in Two Persons"[106]—rather than an impatient rushing past all appearance for the solely satisfying immediate grasp of the divine essence. Love, as the heart of heaven, includes the whole of man, the body and soul with all its powers, in union with the "whole" of God—Body, Blood, Soul, and Divinity—in the Triune life of God, the infinitely fruitful union of the Father and the Son in the Spirit, who is Love-in-Person.[107]

104. See *SCG* 3.62.9, in which Aquinas says that wonder is everlasting in the eschaton, and *De caritate*, 23.7, in which Aquinas, citing Psalm 72, says that man's ultimate end is "to adhere to God."

105. "He who has seen me has seen the Father" (John 14:9); cf., John 12:45.

106. Heribert Mühler, cited in Hans Urs von Balthasar, *Theologic III*, 308.

107. Aquinas, *ST* 1.37.1.

6

Love and Being

1. Expanding Unity

At a decisive moment in his *Confessions*, Augustine famously exclaims, addressing God, "Late have I loved Thee, O Beauty, ever ancient, ever new!"[1] In a spirit of some regret, though suffused with joy—or perhaps more accurately, a kind of looking back on regret from the perspective of joy—Augustine laments that, in relation to Beauty, his love arrives late. It is "late," on the one hand, because it is a response to what has always preceded him: this Beauty has never *not* been present to him ("ever ancient"), even though in its always having been there it has also only ever just begun to disclose itself, with the promise of infinitely more to come, as it were ("ever new"). On the other hand, it is late also because the conscious and deliberate *act* of love is simply the intellectually joining in, so to speak, to a love that has always already been underway, since it is the response to an always antecedent presence.

The point of the present chapter is to flesh out, to a certain extent, what this means and why it is important to recognize. Following up on the argument of the previous chapter, which sought to show that the principal cause of love is not goodness but beauty, we will suggest it is precisely the connection with beauty that reveals love to be a matter of being (rather than first doing, making, feeling, acting), insofar as the perception of beauty involves a disposing of the whole person prior to the deliberate exercise of any of the soul's distinct powers. In order to show this, we will first reflect on the experience of unity that characterizes love, then on the nature of love, and finally on the metaphysics behind all of this, to show the close affinity of love and the act of being in the light of creation.

---

1. Augustine, *Confessions* X.27.38, tr. Sheed, p. 210.

It may at first seem that to connect love with beauty is precisely to identify love strictly with a deliberate and conscious activity. Haven't we in fact emphasized the essential involvement of the soul's highest powers, the intellect and will, in beauty? Indeed, if it is possible to desire goodness without conscious awareness, as we pointed out in chapter 2, it is not possible to experience beauty in this way. The experience of beauty is always a conscious experience. Nevertheless, we have also indicated that, just as beauty transcends goodness and truth, even as it integrates them, so too does love transcend the intellect and will in their distinctive operation. While it is essential—*pace* Scheler—that the intellect and will be included in love, or else love would not involve the whole person (i.e., it would not engage man in his most human aspect), it is also the case, as we have discussed, that love involves man also precisely *in his flesh*, as it were. It engages the intellect and will together, *through* the senses, and so, indeed, through the body. There is something quite profound in Aquinas's definition of love as a passion, a movement of the sensitive appetite, even if this is inadequate specifically as a definition of love: as we mentioned in the previous chapter, without much elaboration, the "passional" aspect of love—which corresponds to the specifically *aesthetic* aspect of beauty, i.e., its being principally a matter of sensible appearance—sets into relief its "passive," or "receptive" character. What we mean by this is that love not only breaks in from above, so to speak, in our experience, but at the very same time (and, as we will suggest, for the very same reason) it "wells up" from below, entering into consciousness from inside of our nature, our very physical being.

Our consciousness of beauty is a coming to awareness of a movement already underway. We *first* experience beauty already as a "recollection," a kind of memory of what we have always already loved ("Late have I loved Thee . . ."). It is unsurprising that the experience of beauty has so often been associated with a kind of nostalgia, not just a longing, but a *wistful* longing, which so evidently, but so inexplicably, seems to exceed the boundaries of the particular thing that has struck us as beautiful. The experience opens us up to "something greater"—we know not what, exactly—because the beautiful thing, precisely *in* its being beautiful, points somehow beyond itself. Augustine presents the beauty of things as their response to the question that the soul's search for God poses in the very attention it gives them, a response that tells the soul, "I am not He."[2] In a similar way, Paul Claudel famously described feminine beauty as a "promise that cannot be kept."[3] What he seems to mean is that beauty dilates the heart, as it were, beyond

---

2. Augustine, *Confessions* 10.6.9.

3. From his play, *La Ville* (1893), end of act 3.

the limits of the particular experiences *of* which are conscious, and so sets the heart on something greater than what lies on the immediate surface of the experience. We cited Plotinus's excellent formulation of the cause of love in the previous chapter: it is a beauty that we long for with an "unreasoned awareness," a kind of knowing (ἐπίγνωσιν) that is not yet rational (ἄλογον), because it is discovered as already present "before" (πρότερον) in the soul. This discovery means that we do not begin the longing for beauty at a discrete moment, in the way in which we might begin an act of intellect or will, but instead we find ourselves already having been moved, and our conscious love is a recuperation, a coming (late) to share in, the movement that precedes us. We experience beauty as an encounter with something *above* us, but it is at the same time something *within* us,[4] and thus it occasions not just a movement (forward) but a "turning around" (ἐπιστροφή: *conversio*) that allows us to move properly in the first place.[5] This quite complex event is why beauty occasions simultaneously a *shock* that disturbs and provokes, and a profoundly satisfying *fulfillment*.[6]

This description admittedly has a sort of "mystical" ring to it, which one might concede is appropriate, at best, for the "lightning bolt" of falling in love that most people experience at some point in their lives, but is hardly a fitting description of the more quiet and ordinary (but certainly no less profound) experiences of love in family and friends, for example. Even in the case of *eros*, one might insist that the language is an apt metaphor, but a metaphor indeed. We wish to suggest, however, that the overwhelming experience of *eros* is simply the intensification of what characterizes love in general,[7] and that the description is not merely metaphorical but expresses the truth about the nature of beauty and the nature of love.

As we argued in the last chapter, love is a union that involves reciprocal indwelling and *ecstasis*. In other words, it is a special kind of union, which is distinct, for example, from the union of parts in the whole of a substance. In distinction from substantial unity, which gathers parts together into a single whole being, love is a unity that *transcends* substance, so as to bring multiple beings together without violating the unity that belongs to each substance in itself. In this respect, it is not *less* of a unity than substantial unity, as one might think by saying it is a mere "moral" unity or "unity of affections," as

---

4. Plotinus, *Ennead* V.8.10.

5. Plotinus, *Ennead* I.6.1; cf., also V.8.11. We argued in the previous chapter that this "turning around" is the *coaptatio* that effects *complacentia*: a tuning of the soul, in its very ground, to the good for which it is meant.

6. Plotinus, *Ennead* I.6.4.

7. This is not at all to deny a difference in *types* between sexual love, familial love, friendship, and so forth. Nevertheless, these represent differences within a basic unity.

opposed to the "real" unity of a particular being;[8] instead, it is simply a higher order unity, one that is more *comprehensive*. It is not a unity that lies at the same level as substances so as to be in competition with them, but in fact has its place *above* substances so as to be able to preserve each in its unity with itself and distinction from the other. In a manner we will present in more detail below, we recognize that *eros* culminates in marriage, which is a permanent unity of two persons in "a single new existence."[9] But in fact, as we will argue at the end, even the most trivial instance of affection is a kind of unity, a joining in a "single existence," between two otherwise independent substances. To say that I have an affection for something—to take a relatively insignificant example: a particular reading chair—is to say more than that it is the object of a particular, discrete act of will, a "liking," or even a host of such acts. It is not even enough to say that the affection I have developed for this chair is a habit—i.e., the condition of the appetitive power that has acquired a certain basic actuality in the form of an inclination or readiness as a result of repeated operation—if we understand "habit" simply as a psychological condition, and nothing more.[10] (While friendliness might be a virtue, a "habitus," friendship itself is more than just this.[11]) Rather, affection is a kind of "extension" of one's being (*ecstasis*), an existing in union with a particular thing, or person, which we interpreted in the last chapter as the essence of *complacentia*. According to Aquinas, as we discussed in the previous chapter, complacency is "a certain union between lover and beloved."[12] This union, in which I partake of a particular object, or in which I "identify" with it so that it correspondingly "affects" me, implies a kind of reciprocal presence or "indwelling": I am present to it in an immediate and unreflective way, and it is similarly present in me—"in my affections," as we say. This reciprocal indwelling, *ecstasis*, and union is why I spontaneously experience a certain pain if my chair gets damaged, and I feel a loss if it gets ruined or otherwise taken away. It is interesting to

8. Aquinas in fact says that the union of love is analogous to "substantial union" (*ST* 1–2.22.1ad2).

9. Commenting on the "one-flesh" union described in *Genesis*, Ratzinger explains that man and woman join to form a "single new existence" (*Called to Communion*, 38).

10. This is the potential problem of concerning friendship as nothing more than a habit: we might say that it represents the interpretation of friendship *on the basis of* love as passion, rather than the reverse.

11. See Aristotle, *NE* 8.5.1158b29–30. Aristotle says that friendly feeling is like a passion, but that friendship itself is like a "habitus," i.e., a fixed disposition (φιλία [ἔοικε] ἕξει), but the comparison rests on its *stability*. He is not saying that friendship is merely a habitus. Aquinas cites this comparison (*ST* 1–2.26.3), but oversimplifies it in some formulations (see, e.g., *ST* 1–2.26.4, first objection).

12. Aquinas, *De ver.* 26.4.

note the particularity involved here: it is *this* chair to which I am attached, and I would not exactly be satisfied with a functional equivalent—though, of course, over time I could develop an equal affection for the new chair. A chair, after all, is not as significant as, say, a pet or, most obviously, a person.

Affection, then, is something that develops *over time*. This note of time is crucial, and sets into relief another dimension of love. Love does not exist as the episodic relation established in the discrete operations of the powers of the soul, whether these be the active operations of the intellect and will or even the passive operations of the sensitive appetite. It cannot so exist precisely insofar as it is a unity. As the philosophical tradition has recognized, unity can never simply be *produced*; one can achieve only an "accidental" unity by assembling parts together, but not the essential unity of form, the sort of unity that characterizes, for example, a living being.[13] Similarly, a genuine unity between living beings can never simply be the result of a particular action, or even inter-action between two agents. Instead, unity can come about, so to speak, only by being pre-supposed as "already" given.[14] Clearly, there is a paradox here, and we will look at the metaphysics behind it in just a moment. For now, we note simply that the "non-constructability" of unity is due to its nature. Unity has an essentially transcendent character, which means that it is not circumscribable simply within the finite limits of physical space and time. To be "one" means to be "undivided"; a thing that is genuinely one—a *per se unum*, to use the technical phrase—lacks the kind of separateness that characterizes matter in its spatial extension: *partes extra partes*.[15] To affirm this transcendence is not to deny that unity exists in space and time, to say that it floats—impossibly—somewhere outside the world. Instead, unity reveals itself in space and time in a very distinctive way: it is not identical with a single moment and with a single point in space, or even with many such moments and points, but instead "enters" into time simultaneously "from above" and "from below." In this sense, unity possesses of its very essence both a "gift" character and an "organic" character, both dimensions of which might be captured by the simple

13. Aristotle famously distinguishes the unity or wholeness that belongs to a proper substance from the conglomeration of parts that forms a mere "heap" (*Metaphysics* 8.6.1045a8–10). Plato affirms that the unity of essence is "non-composite," so that it cannot either come to be or pass away (*Phaedo* 78b-e).

14. A similar insight emerges from Scripture: man and woman are capable of one-flesh union only because they in fact originated in one flesh (Gen 2:21–24). According to Aquinas, man is able to love woman in a profound unity precisely because she was created from him—i.e., it is possible to *forge* a deep union because the unity is *already there* (ST 1.91.2).

15. The phrase was used in the seventeenth and eighteenth century to characterize the *extension* of matter, but it has precedents in the tradition.

adjective "given."[16] It is thus *in* time, but not strictly bounded by it. Instead, unity itself comprehends time in its successive character. We might describe this by saying that unity always has a kind of history, or better, a "tradition" (though this is an aspect we are not able to develop in the present context).

This description, again, may sound "mystical," but if it does it is only because we have grown so accustomed to a materialistic metaphysics, that is, to the bourgeois metaphysics we discussed in chapter 1. In fact, the time-transcending character of unity is a perfectly ordinary part of everyday experience (at the crudest level, we see it reflected in what psychologists call "object permanence"—a recognition of identity, and so unity, that abides through the succession of passing moments—which is taken to be one of the most basic elements of human experience). One of the ways this aspect of love appears is in the fact that unity grows over time, or "spreads out" over a span; we do not decide to attach ourselves to a particular thing or person, or if we do, that decision takes the form of a commitment to spending time with it or with him. The attachment (i.e., the unity) does not occur in an identifiable moment, which can be strictly isolated from the previous moment, in which there was *no* attachment. Instead, we discover in a particular moment that we "already" *are* attached; we come to explicit awareness of a union that, by its very nature, precedes that awareness. Though I can say that this unity did not exist in the past, I cannot say exactly when it began, because its beginning entails a kind of transformation of the antecedent moments, which now become, as it were, parts of *its* story. When it "begins," it does so not as having been produced by the prior set of "pre-unity" conditions at time T_1, but as breaking in or "dawning," and so as an event that is in a certain respect unanticipated. Unity does not have a discrete time; it has a narrative *history*, a qualitative account that gathers together a sequence of moments into an ordered whole (a *unity*). This is why love "takes time," like an organism that has to take root and unfold, since it possesses a unity that is given, not made, a unity that contains more than any one moment or sequence of moments can express.

Given the relationship between unity and time, there is quite a profound insight in the way Aristotle distinguishes friendship from simple benevolence, an insight that prevents us from interpreting "complacency" in too superficial a sense. Friendship is more than willing the good of another or simply being positively disposed in general toward him, for we can quite obviously, and easily, will the good of someone we have never met or have virtually no "connection" with. In addition to good will, friendship implies

16. On all of this, see Lopez, *Gift and the Unity of Being*, 42–50. On the essential givenness of unity, and specifically of love, see David L. Schindler, "America's Technological Ontology and the Gift of the Given."

unity, a union of affection, which can come about only by spending time together, i.e., existing together in a common place over a stretch of time.[17] As we saw last chapter, willing the good of another is an act of love only if it is accomplished along with an apprehension of *belonging* to the other, a recognition of the other as existing in unity with me. And, as we have seen, such a unity for the most part takes a certain amount of time to establish itself.

The significance of time for unity helps us to see that there is more to love, in fact, than the simple "event" of complacency, in which a subject and object adapt themselves to each other (*co-aptatio*). This event is an indispensable first moment, since it plants love, so to speak, in our nature, at a level more profound than the acts of the powers of the soul, especially those of the intellect and will. Nevertheless, if it remains at this level, it can only be a seed of love, but not as it were the mature flower. Love can involve the whole human being only if it *includes* the intellect and will. Thus, the seed can be cultivated, or it can be smothered, according to the discrete, deliberate actions that either promote or inhibit unity. It ought to be seen, however, that the actions that reinforce the initial moment, and so deepen the love, are recapitulations of the *given* unity, which amplify what is already there rather than produce it from nothing. The acts are, in this case, acts *of love*, which is to say that they arise from this ground beneath things, so to speak.

We are beginning to see, here, why love is not just a particular subjective experience; nor is it a mere decision of the will, a commitment one decides to make, though of course this can be an essential element in love's coming to maturity. Instead, love concerns *being itself*.[18] Because of this connection—which we will explain and elaborate in just a moment—love gives *depth* to existence. It opens up a more fundamental dimension of our

---

17. Aristotle: "Friendship is a partnership, and as a man is to himself so is he to his friend; now in his own case the consciousness of his being is desirable, and so therefore is his friend's being, and the activity of this consciousness is produced when they live together, so that it is natural that they aim at this" (*NE* 9.5; cf., 9.12). Note the connection between love (friendship) and being—indeed, being as existing together, or sharing existence. Aquinas: "love differs from benevolence. For love implies a unity of affection between the lover and the beloved. One who loves looks upon the loved one as in a manner one with himself, or as belonging to himself, and is thus united with him. Benevolence, on the other hand, is a simple act of the will whereby one wills good for someone, without the presupposition of any such union of affection" (*ST* 2–2.27).

18. As David L. Schindler has argued, relationality is not something that occurs merely in the operations of a substance (i.e., in "second act"), but is already present in the first act, in the *being* rather than merely in the *doing*, of a substance. For the most recent articulation of this argument, see "Being, Gift, Self-Gift." The argument we are developing here may be read as complementary, making the same fundamental point from a different angle.

knowing, willing, and in short, our living. Love represents, as we argued last chapter, a context that precedes and so opens the horizon for the particular acts of intellect and will. Our awareness is the awareness of a connection that is "always already" there. It is within such a context that knowledge and freedom take the form of genuine communion in the ways we described in chapters 3 and 4. Significant philosophers of the twentieth century have pointed out the necessity of a sort of communion in order to come to proper knowledge of a thing. According to Michael Polanyi, discrete acts of knowing take place within what he happens to call an "indwelling" of the object, which we see now we can give an ontological and not merely epistemological sense.[19] Hans Georg Gadamer described the event of "*Verstehen*," "Understanding," as a process that begins with a pre-given involvement, and deepens through the "give" and "take" of the "hermeneutical circle," into a unity (the "fusion of horizons") that allow a proper disclosure of truth—all of which invites interpretation as love.[20] Perhaps most profoundly, Ferdinand Ulrich has interpreted knowledge as a kind of vicarious representation, a real exchange of place, a brief glimpse of which we attempted to present in chapter 3.[21] Acts of will, similarly, can be understood as a kind of exchange of being, rather than a simple discharge of energy or imposition of arbitrary intentions, if we recognize that they arise inside of a reciprocal relationship that precedes them. Given the prior unity, we can recognize that there is a "built in" affirmation of the *reality* of the other, so to speak, at the very root of the will's own activity. In this sense, too, the will, at its heart, is an expression of love, which, in Iris Murdoch's words cited earlier, is the recognition that something other than oneself is real.

If love is the unity that opens up the proper context for our knowing and willing, and if beauty, as we argued last chapter, is the proper cause of love, then we have to see, in sum, the indispensable role of beauty in genuine human existence. Beauty thus reveals itself to be crucial in pedagogy, which is the formation of the human being.[22] To be surrounded by beauty, in the

19. We do not at all mean to imply that Polanyi rejects an ontological interpretation, but his primary interest was epistemological: see the *Tacit Dimension*. Thus, Polanyi speaks of one's committed involvement as indispensable to knowing, in contrast to the pseudo-detachment of objectivity: *Personal Knowledge*. Esther Lightcap Meek has creatively extended some of Polanyi's ideas on this score, highlighting the bond that we form with things that is a precondition for the genuine disclosure of truth: see *Loving to Know*; cf., *Contact with Reality: Michael Polanyi's Realism and Why It Matters*.

20. Gadamer, *Truth and Method*, esp. part II, 265–379.

21. See, for example, the first section of *Der Tod in Erkenntnis und Liebe (Ein Fragment)*, 147–99.

22. Maria Montessori understood this well: "The place best adapted to the life of man is an artistic environment . . .; if we want the school to become a laboratory

profound rather than in the bourgeois sense of the "aesthetic" (the "pretty" and the "pleasant"), helps deepen one's affection for the things of the world, so that one can live truly. Being surrounded by "profound" beauty means living in a place that is not altogether sealed off by human artifice from the beauty of nature, for which there is ultimately no real substitute; it means having one's home in an *organized* town or city, which has arisen organically in history and is ordered around buildings and spaces that are significant— i.e., truly *signify*; it means living an existence unified by genuine culture, celebrating liturgical feasts in tune with the changing seasons of the year; it means giving beautiful form to the various activities that constitute daily life; it means, as Schiller once observed, according even ordinary, useful objects, a certain dignity and intrinsic value. Obviously, this is an idyllic picture, rarely achieved by anyone in a complete way, but it is clearly a way of living that human beings desire, and naturally seek to realize to the extent that they are able. Beauty establishes the natural love and affection that provides a horizon for genuine knowing and willing, for the intimacy of truth and the true involvement of ourselves that is free action. It "expands" one's being, and roots it more deeply *into* reality, which opens us up to more genuine possibility and richer experience. This has been one of the primary points of this book. Beauty, by calling forth love, brings out the being of things, and so sets the stage for a true encounter between man and the world, man and man, man and God.

2. Creation as Fait Accompli: The "Already-ness" of Love

Now, at this point we take a further step in our argument. We have just suggested that, precisely *because* it is a special kind of unity, love enters into our experience as "always already having been there," so to speak. What we would like to suggest now is that this "already having been there" is not simply one of the many characteristics of love, but in fact expresses something essential about its very nature. We will attempt to explain this, first, by appealing to experience and to decisive witnesses, and then turning to look more directly at the metaphysics, the structure of being that gives rise to the experience.

---

for the observation of human life, we must gather together within it things of beauty" (*Spontaneous Activity in Education*, 114); "It is almost possible to say that there is a mathematical relationship between the beauty of his surroundings and the activity of the child; he will make discoveries rather more voluntarily in a gracious setting than in an ugly one" (*The Child in the Family*, 43). This is of course a theme pursued in depth by Friedrich Schiller, in his *Letters on the Aesthetic Education of Man*.

The experience of love is summed up beautifully in St. John's declaration: "In this is love: not that we loved God, but that he loved us" (1 John 4:10). There is something curious about this well-known formulation. In order to explicate what love *is* (i.e., to state its essence) St. John describes how love "arrives": *love precedes*. The *prius* of love (i.e., its "firstness") thus appears as a basic part of love's nature. As curious as this formulation may be, upon reflection we see that it turns out to reveal something familiar in our experiences of love that great thinkers have consistently remarked on. Let us consider a variety of examples, somewhat at random, of the "firstness," or perhaps "already-ness," of love. A person does not have to explain in detail, justify, and negotiate the terms of a request that he makes to an old friend, because he knows he can count on the friendship: the friend interrupts and says, "Before you go on, first let me say, yes, I'll do it, whatever you need from me." Love's response to the question "Would you do me a favor?" is "Consider it done." What love gives is, so to speak, "taken for granted," not in the sense of ignorant presumption, but in the sense of being given and received as *already there*, as a kind of *fait accompli*. In his interpretation of the annunciation, Hans Urs von Balthasar explains that the depth of Mary's loving yes to the Father reveals itself in the fact that her questions concern the implications of the consent that is already presumed to *have been* given.[23] Charles Péguy relates the nightly ritual of a father's kissing his children before they go off to bed, a ritual that has become so fully expected, it is performed unthinkingly, almost automatically—as an unspeakably profound gesture of love precisely because it is a revelation of its unquestionable "givenness."[24] According to Josef Pieper, "To confirm and affirm something already accomplished—that is precisely what is meant by 'to love.'"[25] As Aristotle saw, but Montaigne denied, it is precisely *because* the relations that constitute the family are "pre-given" that we take them to represent love in a particularly profound way.[26] A child *is* (already) in

23. "Mary's agreement is silently presupposed from the very outset as something completely taken for granted, something that is available to be disposed of without further ado" ("The Mass, A Sacrifice of the Church?" 227).

24. Péguy, *The Portal of the Mystery of Hope*, 32–33.

25. Pieper, *Faith–Hope–Love*, 165.

26. Aristotle, *NE* 8.1.1155a16–21; 8.12.1161b17–1162a4. Compare Montaigne, who cites thinkers in the Stoic tradition to communicate his idea about the difference between friendship (love) and relationships given by nature: "There have been great philosophers who have made nothing of this tie of nature; as Aristippus, for one, who, being pressed home about the affection he owed his children, as being come from him, presently fell to spit, saying that also came from him, and that we did also breed worms and lice; and that other, that Plutarch endeavored to reconcile to his brother, 'I make never the more account of him,' said he, 'for coming out of the same hole'" ("Of

some real sense one's flesh and blood, and this real unity makes the relationship something altogether incomparable. From a different angle, there is Kierkegaard's beautiful statement, which the philosopher Ferdinand Ulrich has meditated on in such depth: "Love builds up by presupposing that love is present," which is to say that love *presupposes* precisely what it *gives*.[27] The recognition of love as already there in the other is an act of generosity, but this generosity is just what love *is*. As Stefan Oster has explained, the truth of this statement is evident to anyone who has raised or educated children; we allow them to grow by showing to them what they already are; we *give them* a capacity by acknowledging it as present.[28] Love does not im-pose, but generates, by *pre-sup*-posing, creatively acknowledging and giving attention to what is already there.

Genuine love is said to be "unconditional"; this means that it does not insert itself, as it were, into pre-established conditions so as to take its measure from them. Instead, love comes, as it were, *before* the conditions; it "pre-empts" them. In this respect, it itself presents the reality to which the conditions must conform. This absolute priority, this "already-ness," is why we associate love with gratuity, a generosity that is not measured by pre-given conditions, but "super-abounds" them. For the same reason, we associate love with *mercy*, a generosity that transcends the "pre-established" limits of justice.[29] At the same time, however, it is crucial to see that this does not imply a disregard for, or dismissal of, limitations. Love is not violence.[30] To think that love's unconditional character means it simply overrides all conditions willy-nilly is to miss the paradox from the other side, so to speak. This view would turn love, once again, into an *im*-position rather than a reality that arrives as already *pre-sup-posed*—taken as the antecedent ground—and so eliminate its generosity. Love is essentially *responsive* to the

---

Friendship," 79).

27. Kierkegaard, *Works of Love*, 207. On p. 206, he summarizes the point thus: "*the lover presupposes that love is in the other person's heart, and by this very presupposition he builds up love in him—from the ground up, insofar as in love he presupposes it present as the ground*" (italics in the original).

28. Oster, "Thinking Love at the Heart of Things."

29 See Aquinas, *ST* 1.21.4. Note the analogy between creation and merciful love: the *ratio misericordiae* comes to expression in the act of creation "*inquantum res de non esse in esse mutatur*" (1.21.4ad4), which we are drawing out here.

30. See Aquinas, *ST* 1–2.28.5. Though love "wounds" in a certain respect, and so shares a certain similarity to violence, insofar as it is a disposing to what is good, it perfects and benefits. Jean-Luc Marion distorts the "unconditional" character of love, making it dispense with all prior conditions, to the point that it becomes arguably irrational and violent: see *The Erotic Phenomenon*. This position is connected with his concern to separate *radically* love from being: *God Without Being*.

other, even if what it responds to in the other is not simply there before it. Love responds to what it elicits. We might say that, in this sense, love *does* indeed insert itself into conditions that are there before it, but without being *measured* by them, so that the very conditions become transformed into an expression of love, rather than its limitation. Part of love's gift is its open reception of the conditions of the other. We can thus say of love what the famous *"Grabschrift"* of Ignatius says of the divine: it cannot be circumscribed by what is greatest, and yet can be contained in what is smallest.[31] In this respect, we can see what is missing, for example, in Anders Nygren's notion of *agape*, which is absolutely unmotivated, and so becomes, as many critics have pointed out, wholly indifferent to the other it is meant to serve. Love, we have to say, *is* motivated, but ultimately by beauty, which as we have seen is the perception of an essentially "pre-given" unity—the unity that is love. In other words, love is wholly motivated . . . by love itself.

In short, love is not a discrete gift, but as Aquinas says, it is the *first* (*prius*) gift, because it is the affirmation of unity with the other *within which* every subsequent gift is made.[32] To make any particular gift at all to another is to presuppose a more basic gift that has "already" been given, namely, the love from which the particular gift springs. And this most fundamental gift is given, as we just suggested, precisely by being at the same time received: the unity with the other is a *co-aptatio*, a being-disposed *to* and *by* the other.

Let us enter into this last point more deeply, turning now more directly to the metaphysical dimension. We saw that, for Aquinas, love is the *first* of the passions,[33] which means it does not itself presuppose any other passion, but is rather itself presupposed by every other passion; moreover, we proposed expanding this priority to include not only (even if paradigmatically) passion as the movement of the sensitive appetite but indeed all relations whatsoever. Every relation that is effected through the actualization of a potency of the soul, whether that actualization comes principally from an agent outside the soul or from the soul itself, presupposes love as the relation most basically *given* in both senses of the word: it is generously bestowed and it is already there ("taken for granted"). Now, to say that "love is first" means that the *co-aptatio* it involves is not preceded by a more basic inclination, or indeed even an intellectual intention of satisfaction, as Aquinas says.[34] Instead, love arrives, so to speak, in some respect before the

31. "Non coerceri maximo, contineri tame a minimo, divinum est." Though this is commonly known as St. Ignatius's "Grabschrift," it does not appear on his tomb.

32. Aquinas, *ST* 1.38.2.

33. Aquinas, *ST* 1–2.25.2.

34. We recall the tension we discussed in the last chapter: Aquinas makes love the *last* in the order of intention (*ST* 1–2.25.2), but then says that no other passion precedes

soul is ready for it.[35] However paradoxical this may appear, it follows strictly from Aquinas's own interpretation.

The question that now arises is: How is such a thing possible? It would seem to contradict what by many accounts is the very heart of Aquinas's metaphysics, namely, the relationship between potency and act, according to which there is an inseparable, through asymmetrical, connection: there can be no potency except in relation to a particular actuality, and actuality is always the realization of a potency. If love represents some actuality, it would seem that this is possible only if it be preceded by the proper potency. In this respect, love would have to be the realization of a capacity already there. How is it possible for love to precede the soul's powers? In attempting to respond to this question, we move to the next stage of our argument. The relationship between act and potency is an insight that has its origin, of course, in Aristotle,[36] and Aquinas adopted it from him as he did many of his most basic philosophical concepts. But there is an aspect of Aquinas's thought that already clearly exceeds at least the most straightforward interpretation of the relation between act and potency, and it is not a marginal one: it is his metaphysics of creation, which is generally recognized as one of his great contributions to philosophy.[37]

As Aquinas observes, there can be no potency in the creature, no "capacity to be created," prior to the actual act of creation because creation is precisely the beginning of all things *ex nihilo*. There is strictly *nothing* that precedes creation; the potency for creation lies simply in God, and not in any creature.[38] This of course does not mean that creation is an act *imposed*—"arbitrarily"—on the world, because in fact to speak of an imposition is to posit, prior to creation, a world that is thus somehow "forced" to be.[39] It is equally false to say that the world has no capacity to exist as to say that it has such a capacity; whether we affirm or deny the capacity, we are

---

love (*ST* 1–2.27.4), and that *everything* anyone does is done out of love, which seems to make love absolutely first (*ST* 1–2.28.6). Note that the absolute priority of love, which we are advocating here, does *not* call into question Aquinas's affirmation that every act of appetite is preceded by an act of apprehension. This objection presupposes that love is simply of the order of the appetite. If, instead, love is a kind of apprehension, affirming its absoluteness *implies* that the appetite is always "responsive" to apprehension.

35. Again, this does not mean there is no potency for love, but, as we explained last chapter, this can *only* be the potency to receive a new potency, or else there is in fact no place for love at all.

36. The *locus classicus* is Aristotle, *Metaphysics* IX.

37. There is some question of the extent to which anticipations of Aquinas's notion of *esse* can be found already in Aristotle, but this does not concern us here.

38. See Aquinas, *De pot.* 3.1ad2.

39. See Schmitz, *The Gift: Creation*, 63–97.

affirming or denying it *of* a world that we suppose to have some sort of existence prior to creation. This is a simple point, but it is crucial to formulate it properly, because there is a great deal at stake here. Insofar as there is a world at all, it (already) has a capacity to exist, but at the same time that capacity is given, just as the world is, in the act of creation.[40] We cannot think of God's act of creation as being due to creatures, but nor can we think of it as contrary to them, as occurring "in spite of them." Ferdinand Ulrich, with an extraordinary profundity on this point, presents creation as a *gift*, along the lines of love, as we just described it: love presupposes what it gives.[41] God thus *gives* being, but does so as something that arises *from* the creature itself: this *esse* is the first *effect* of God's creative act,[42] and at the same time a thing's *esse* "is the act of being resulting from the principles of a thing."[43] In other words, God gives not only being, but at the same time(!), he gives the capacity to receive being, so that the creature may be said to participate in an "active" and intrinsic way in its own existence. In other words, God does not cause being merely "from above" or from the outside, but only simultaneously "from above" and "from below." Here we have the profound root of Aquinas's teaching on "secondary causality," which is such a distinctive part of his metaphysics.[44] *Esse*, "to be" or "to exist," is not a marginal thing in Aquinas's thought; it is the perfection of all perfections and the actuality of all acts.[45] And yet it also does not "fit" the "normal" relation between act and potency. We will come back to this point, but it is interesting to note how this makes *esse* both something extraordinary (i.e., an essentially "unprethinkable" event,[46] as it were) and yet at the same time more perfectly usual, more common and "taken for granted," than anything else.[47]

40. Aquinas: "hence it is necessary that even what is potential in [creatures] should be created" (*ST* 1.44.2ad3).

41. Ulrich's late magnum opus, *Gabe und Vergebung: Ein Beitrag zur biblischen Ontologie*, a massive metaphysical interpretation of the Parable of the Prodigal Son, might be seen as an in-depth meditation on just this notion. See especially 206.

42. Aquinas, *ST* 1.45.1ad1.

43. Aquinas, *III Sent.* 6.2.2.

44. Aquinas, *De pot.* 3.7. At the heart of this position is a recognition of the *generosity* of goodness.

45. Aquinas, *De pot.* 7.2ad9.

46. This expression comes from Schelling's late philosophy; he uses it to characterize *being* as the absolutely positive, which always remains prior to and ungraspable by thought. We ought to note the connection between the tendency toward irrationalism in this conception and the failure to interpret being *as love*. For Schelling, love is not *presupposed*, as absolutely first, but is rather *achieved* as the overcoming of evil. See his *Philosophical Inquiries into the Nature of Human Freedom*, 78–86.

47. Heidegger makes a similar observation: "what is ontically nearest and familiar

Here we arrive at the next step of the argument. We have just described creation as an act of love, which "presupposes what it gives." This is indeed the most radically generous way to give: there is no "wavering" in God's creative act, or hesitation in potency (God may or may not give), but instead the gift is made as *radically* actual, as already having been made, as "taken for (already) granted."[48] It is for this reason that the Christian doctrine of creation, contrary to its nominalist interpretation,[49] is not simply opposed to the classical philosophical vision of the world in terms of necessary essences, as Aquinas takes great pains to show.[50] The human soul, for instance, is *created* by God, and yet what God creates in this case exists by (its God-given) nature; as Aquinas puts it, the soul exists *per se*, by virtue of itself or with its own inner necessity.[51] Something analogous can be said about any essence precisely to the extent that it is an essence. The radical contingency of the world is not opposed to its inner necessity.

Let us explore this point further. That creation is an act of love is of course a teaching more or less as old, at least, as the Judeo-Christian tradition. But we wish to propose that we interpret this ancient doctrine specifically along the lines of the meaning of love that emerged in the previous chapter, as rooted most fundamentally in beauty rather than first in goodness. According to the *Septuagint* translation, when God created the world, he saw that it was *beautiful* (καλόν).[52] While we typically think of creation principally as an act of *will* (and of course it *is* also an act of will), a different sense of things arises if we think of creation in terms of *love*. The difference stands out most starkly, in fact, if we understand will as separate from love-as-union and so in the "episodic" and unilateral sense that we have criticized, namely, as a discrete act that arises wholly from the subject and

---

is ontologically the farthest" (*Being and Time*, 43).

48. More precisely: there is no potency in the world, from the perspective of the world, that is higher than, and able thereby to measure, the world's actuality. God's potency is perfectly coincident with his perfect actuality, and so has no hint of "indecisiveness" or reluctance, as it were.

49. For a recent articulation of the Christian doctrine of creation that moves in this nominalist direction, see Wirzba, *From Nature to Creation*, esp. chapter 4, "Perceiving Creation." The contingency taken to be implied by the divine will lies at the center of Leo Strauss's interpretation of intellectual history, and represents the ultimate cause of the divide between the ancients and the moderns: see his "Reason and Revelation."

50. See his treatise "On the Eternity of the World." Cf., Aquinas: "How absolute necessity can exist in created things" (*SCG* 2.30).

51. Aquinas, *ST* 1.75.6; cf., 1.75.2.

52. Again, it bears emphasizing that highlighting the significance of beauty does not at all imply any exclusion of goodness; "*kalon*" is goodness in its absolute sense (i.e., in its truth).

terminates in an object. From this perspective, there would be a strong tendency toward nominalism, an emphasis on the contingency of the world as, so to speak, hanging precariously on the end of God's will. The permanence of God's will would in this case be imagined as a discrete act that is constantly repeated. What is referred to as *creatio continua*, namely, the denial that the act of creation is a historical event, as it were, which began and ended at a particular, isolated moment of history, means that there is no moment in which the world does not actually depend on God; but it does not mean, as is often thought, that God has constantly to recreate the world in order to keep it from going out of existence. This would imply, by contrast, a kind of impotence in God's creative action, which never really manages to come to fruition. As Aquinas puts it, it is true to say at the same time that the world *is being created* by God and that it already *has been created*: "*simul creatur et creatum est.*"[53] We may interpret this statement as saying that the being of the world is not "up for grabs" at every moment, in the sense that the *power* of God's will—God may or may not sustain the existence of the world—takes precedence over its *de facto* exercise. To think thus would be to elevate the "potency" of God over his actuality, to fear that, regardless of what may be the case at this moment, God may or not sustain the existence of the world the next moment, so that our assumption of future existence becomes a relatively blind act of faith: let us hope he gives again and again what he has given before, which in truth means he never really *gives* it.[54] Instead, the world is a gift that has *always already* been given; it is a *fait accompli*, or indeed *the fait accompli par excellence*. Love means "already-ness."

Let us unfold this point. What we saw in the previous chapter is that love is not in the first place an act of will, traced out inside of the order of the appetite, but instead represents the *always-prior* context within which any particular act of will—or, for that matter, intellect—takes place. In this respect, love is primarily a kind of union. To speak of creation in terms of love, from this perspective, is to think of it not simply as the result of a particular act of will but as a union with God. As it turns out, Aquinas uses precisely this language to describe creation: "But God moves all things to union, for insofar as He gives things being and other perfections, He joins them to Himself in the manner in which this is possible."[55] It is interesting to note that, in this sentence, we see a simultaneously two-fold movement,

53. Aquinas, *ST* 1.45.2ad3.

54. Aquinas: "a gift is properly an unreturnable giving, as Aristotle says (*Topics*, IV.4)—i.e., a thing which is not given with the intention of a return—and thus contains the idea of a gratuitous donation. Now, the reason of donation being gratuitous is love" (*ST* 1.38.2).

55. Aquinas, *SCG* 1.91.6.

which reflects what we have seen in love generally: God *goes out to* things ("by giving things being") and *brings things to himself* ("He joins them to himself"). Thinking creation as love means, as we will elaborate in our final chapter, that God gives in some sense *himself* in giving being,[56] but more directly in relation to our present concern, it means that *to exist at all is to be in union with God*; to "be" is to "be in union." Being *is* love.

Now, we saw above that love represents a special *kind* of unity: not the unity of a substance, of *a* (single) being, but a higher sort of unity that brings into one two beings that remains distinct from each other.[57] Creation is not a mere extension of God's being, so that the world is nothing more than God himself, but is really and truly *other* than God—even though this does not at all mean that God and the world stand over against each other as separate "beings" of the same order.[58] Nevertheless, the independent reality, the *self-being* of each thing that exists, arises from within the unity with God, the love, that is *esse* itself. It is just, we might say, the absolute permanence of this bond of love—which is distinct from the infinite repetition of distinct acts of will—that allows the perfect independence, of creatures; the bond does not depend on the "good behavior," as it were, of creatures, and indeed cannot even be revoked by God himself.[59] There is nothing more *unconditional* than creation itself. In this respect, we can speak of creation as an "act" only in an analogous sense: it is not a discrete event inside of a pre-given horizon—a particular event in history, so to speak—indicating a change from potency to act in something that already exists. Instead, as Aquinas puts it, creation is a *relation*, which characterizes created beings as

56. This is why it is wrong simply to *oppose* "free creation" to Neoplatonic emanation, which, if unqualified, leads an impoverishment of freedom. Aquinas after all uses the word "emanation" to describe creation (see Aquinas, *ST* 1.45, which "concerns the mode of emanation of things from the First Principle, and this is called creation"). As love, creation includes the dimension of natural, spontaneous self-outpouring. Dionysius highlights this aspect of creation ("For as our sun, *through no choice or deliberation*, but by the very fact of its existence, gives light to all those things which have any inherent power of showing its illumination, even so the Good . . . sends forth upon all things according to their receptive powers, the rays of its undivided Goodness," *Divine Names* IV.1) and does not mean in the least thereby to compromise freedom, but only to express God's perfectly noble generosity.

57. There can be an analogous extension to include the unity of a substance: see Dionysius, *Divine Names*, IV.10, in which Dionysius describes the unity of a substance as a thing's *eros* for itself, which is analogous to the love that joins beings that are distinct.

58. In other words, it remains true at the same time that in another respect the world does not "add" anything to God. Robert Sokolowski refers to this paradox as the "Christian Distinction"; see his *God of Faith and Reason*.

59. This is not because God is bound by a higher law, but precisely because of the absoluteness of God.

a whole.[60] Creation, as love, *is* the horizon. We said last chapter that love "opens up a world," by establishing a context within which things become accessible to each other. Creation is thus love in the most perfect sense; it is the absolute opening up of the world.[61]

The significance of creation as love emerges even more clearly when we consider the other fundamental characteristics that we discussed last chapter: love is not only union, it is also reciprocal indwelling and *ecstasis*. As for the reciprocal indwelling, it is of course a classical axiom that God is immanent within his creation. According to Aquinas, God is in things and indeed "most intimately" (*intime*);[62] Augustine famously said that "God is more intimate to me than I am to myself."[63] Augustine's formulation is an even more profound paradox than is often remarked: it does not mean simply that there is a space, a "hole" in my being, where I am not, and which is thus open to be filled by God, for this would make God still *external* to me. There is, rather, a deep metaphysical intimacy implied in Augustine's statement; God's presence is not a displacement of the self. Instead, where I am most fundamentally myself, there in my inmost "heart of hearts," God is present; God and I *coincide* in this most interior "place," but God is present as *already* there before me. It is precisely because God indwells me (and indeed all things whatsoever), in the *order of creation* (as union of love), that we can say, as Aquinas does, that all things love God *more* than themselves, and do so *naturally*.[64] In rational creatures, this love of God that naturally exceeds self-love is spontaneous, and precedes any deliberate choice, as the context within which they make any deliberate choices.[65] It is not merely the case, in other words, that one *ought* to love God more than oneself, as if love of God were simply a moral law, an obligation imposed from the outside on my otherwise self-directed activity. Instead, the love of God is, as it were, an already given reality; it is the union with God that *is* creation. Thus, God does not only indwell creatures, but in fact all creatures always already "indwell" God: to exist is to participate in the being that God *is*, to have a (created) share in God's own *esse* that he has given away.[66] We are

60. On this, see Hanby, *No God, No Science?* 320–24.

61. Pieper also, but in a slightly different sense, characterizes creation as the "comparative of love," i.e., the metaphysical paradigm of what love is in general (*Faith–Hope–Love*, 170–72).

62. Aquinas, *ST* 1.8.1.

63. Augustine, *Confessions* III.6.11.

64. Aquinas, *ST* 2–2.26.3.

65. Note that this natural will is weakened by sin, so that the spontaneity is lost, but the inclination nevertheless remains (Aquinas, *ST* 1.85.2ad1).

66. According to Hans Urs von Balthasar, created *esse* "is the streaming plenitude

right to emphasize the reciprocity here, to see, namely, that this is not a unilateral imposition of being, even if creation does indeed *absolutely* precede the creature, because, as we saw above, creatures exercise their own act of existence; the being in which they share is also—as we will elaborate in a moment—something they actively *do*.[67] The absoluteness of creation does not exclude, but rather (generously) includes, the relative priority of the creature, as always-already given.

As for *ecstasis*, we need only read Dionysius's *Divine Names*, book IV, to see the appropriateness of the word to describe creation, which Dionysius does here specifically in terms of the "beautiful-and-the-good."[68] As he puts it, God *comes out of himself* in the act of creation (though of course without any loss or the least diminishment), in a manner analogous to a lover's exuberance in the presence of the beloved.[69] It is truly an *ecstasis*, because in fact, in some respect, the world represents an excess, something "more" than simply God in himself, which is just to say, in the end, that in creating God gives rise to a world that is other, that is not simply God himself (without ceasing to be in some respect God himself, precisely as given truly away to what is other than himself).

Now, it is crucial to see that Dionysius describes this *ecstasis*, paradoxically, as being elicited by the beauty of the world. To be sure, the world's beauty is not something simply *other* than God's beauty. Just as God knows every particular thing in both its universal necessity and its absolute uniqueness in the one act by which he knows himself,[70] so too is his love of himself coincident with his love of the world. In this respect, Dionysius's description of creation is simply an exposition of the traditional notion that God creates for the sake of nothing but himself, which is to say, simply out of love of (his own) beauty. But Dionysius brings out an astonishing dimension of this notion:

> And we must dare to affirm (for 'tis the truth) that the Creator
> of the Universe Himself, in His Beautiful and Good Yearning

---

of God's being in the state of having been given away to finite receivers" (*Herrlichkeit*, III/1, 961).

67. Aquinas explains that, while in one respect the act of creation has a priority over the creature, in another respect the creature comes before creation as the subject of existence, which makes creation an accident (*ST* 1.45.3ad3). There is clearly a paradox here.

68. Dionysius introduces this phrase at *Divine Names*, IV.7 (pp. 96–97 in the Rolt translation), and uses it regularly for the rest of the book.

69. Aquinas agrees: a lover is "translated outside of himself and into the beloved" in love (*ST* 1.20.2ad1).

70. Aquinas, *ST* 1.14.11.

[*eros*] towards the Universe, is through the excessive yearning of
His Goodness, transported outside of Himself in His providential activities towards all things that have being, and is touched
by the sweet spell of Goodness, Love, and Yearning, and so is
drawn from His transcendent throne above all things, to dwell
within the heart of all things, through a super-essential and ec-
static power whereby He yet stays within Himself.[71]

In other words, God creates by pre-supposing what he gives. His creation
of the world, to say it again, is not a sheer imposition, as nominalism would
have it, but takes the form of an ec-static "response" to the beauty of the
world; it takes, that is, the form of love. God gives so perfectly and absolutely, we could say, that he discovers that his gift of being has already been
given. To exist, as creatures, is therefore to rise up, so to speak, to meet this
love: to ek-sist. As a participation in the being that God has (always-already)
given, creaturely being reflects the "*ecstasis*" that God *is* (already in himself):

And hence all things must desire and yearn for and must love
the Beautiful and the Good. Yea, and because of It and for Its
sake the inferior things yearn for the superior under the mode
of attraction, and those of the same rank have a yearning toward
their peers under the mode of mutual communion; and the superior have a yearning towards their inferiors under the mode
of providential kindness; and each hath a yearning towards itself
under the mode of cohesion, and all things are moved by a longing for the Beautiful and Good, to accomplish every outward
work and form every act of will.[72]

To be is to be *in* oneself only as simultaneously coming *out* of oneself
in both receiving and giving. The union that creation is is a reciprocal—
though radically asymmetrical—*ecstasis*, and indeed there can be no union
of love that is not also in some respect both of these at once.

3. "To Be" in Fruitful Communion

This last comment brings us to a final theme. One of the reasons a person
would have to reduce love to the status of a passion of the soul turns on the
primacy of *substance* in one's metaphysics. We might now explain this reduction by saying that, insofar as the sensitive appetite operates, so to speak,
"below" the faculties of the intellect and will, defining love as a passion

71. Dionysius, *Divine Names*, IV.13 (page 106).
72. Ibid., IV.10 (page 101).

represents an attempt to capture what we have called the "already-ness" of love within the constraints of such a metaphysics. But the metaphysics of creation opens up a more basic way of interpreting this "already-ness": *esse*, the *actus essendi* ("the act of being"), according to Aquinas, has a certain primacy over substance, even if it is a paradoxical one insofar as it represents God's generosity (*esse est similitudo divinae bonitatis*;[73] "being is the likeness of God's goodness"), which presupposes what it gives. The absolute priority of *esse* thus does not exclude the relative priority of substance. In any event, *esse*, as Aquinas interprets it, represents a radically "new" sort of actuality, beyond the essential actuality in which Aristotle's philosophy culminates. In Ferdinand Ulrich's words, *esse* is "super-essential" being, and its superessential quality is precisely what gives rise to the paradoxes we have been discussing. It is a *super*-actuality because it does not lie circumscribed within the order of potency and act, which defines the analogical notion of being founded ultimately on substance.[74] As we have seen, *to be*, as God's *first* created effect (*prius*), is *not* the actuality of some prior potency, but instead is itself the source, in a certain respect,[75] of the very potency that it actualizes: every *essence*, which receives *esse*—i.e., participates in it and gives it determination within the essential order—emerges also *from esse*, since outside of being there is strictly *nothing*.[76] Nothing at all exists that is not in some way made actual by *esse*, or better, given the actuality that *esse* "is."

Now, one will have noticed that this brief reflection on *esse*, the act of "to-be," as "super-essential," that is, as lying beyond the essential sort of actuality, "resonates" in a basic way with a phenomenon we investigated in the previous chapter, namely, the *co-aptatio* of love. In a word, we wish to propose that this "event," which Aquinas presents as the "movement" that love essentially is, is an image of the fundamental love that is *esse* itself. *Co-aptatio*, in the deep sense we have given the notion, is first of all possible only because of *esse*, as we will explain in a moment. Second, as we observed in the last chapter, the *co-aptatio* of love does not fit into the normal potency-act relation, because it is the *formatio* of the potency, *precisely so that* the potency may be ordered to the actuality of its object. In other words, in the "event" of love, the beloved object *gives itself* to the lover precisely by giving the lover the potency to pursue the beloved, which is another way of saying

73. Aquinas, *De ver.* 22.2ad2. We are following Ferdinand Ulrich's interpretation of this notion: see his *Homo Abyssus*.

74. Aristotle, *Metaphysics* 7.1.

75. Created *esse* is not the source of things as first cause, but rather as, so to speak, the creative medium out of which God (First Cause) draws all things.

76. Aquinas, *De pot.* 7.2ad9.

it "pre-supposes what it gives," or gives *itself*, but only *as a result* of the lover's own (preceding) act. This *formatio* is a generous mode of formation, which does not *actually* determine the appetite in the sense of imposing on it a finished form, so to speak, that would bring it to satiety. Instead, it determines the appetite as enabling it, so that it can receive the corresponding actuality as its own act, as belonging properly to itself. On the other hand, this *formatio* is not the realization of an already established potency, with a fixed determination, so to speak, but a re-making of the potency. This interpretation allows us to see once again the deep significance of beauty, which is the communication of form in a distinctive way. It is not essential form in and as itself, which is what is communicated in truth and goodness, but is form precisely *in appearance*, which means as (generously) given away to the other. Third, this *formatio* is not a transitive act, so to speak, that passes in a "linear" way from a subject to an object (as do, in a basic sense, the discrete acts of the powers of the soul), but is precisely a *union* between subject and object, which *allows* them to "act on" each other, now in a far more intimate way. We recall that the word Aquinas uses is co-*aptatio*, a kind of adaptation *of each to the other*, so that they "fit" together in the "fittingness" that describes beauty. As we have seen, it is a union that is at the same time a reciprocal indwelling and an *ecstasis*. Just as *to be* is to be in union with God, so too is every instance of love a union, which reflects that most basic one—creation itself—as its privileged image.

The *com-placentia* of love is a unity that is not simply constructed by any particular act of subjects on objects, or the simple result of a certain set of such acts; nor is it the mere coincidence of each acting on the other in a particular way. Instead, it is a unity *in* which they find themselves, as something, so to speak, "already there." This was the experience of love we discussed above, but we now see more clearly the metaphysical foundations of the experience. We all have some acquaintance with this "already-ness" of love in some respect, not only in the obvious surprise of discovering one has "fallen" in love (the verb is significant here, since it highlights the fact that the act is not a fully deliberate one), but also in the ordinary sense we described above of becoming conscious of an affection for some thing or person that has developed without our being aware of it, and perhaps even without our wanting it. Our tendency is to give this experience a "merely" psychological interpretation. But our reflections up to this point suggest that the experience is the manifestation of a deeper truth, of the nature of existence itself. We observed in the previous chapter that the co-*aptatio* that constitutes love cannot be considered a change in the usual sense, since change, strictly speaking, is always a transition from potency to act. This particular "movement" is, we said, a "vertical" one, rather than a "horizontal" one, insofar as it does not presuppose a corresponding potency (it *is* the very "correspond-ing" itself!). But this means that *love is a "movement" that does not take place in time*, if we understand time to be a succession of moments. Accord-ing to Aristotle, time is "the number of change in respect of the before and after,"[77] which means there can be no time where there is no motion,[78] and the "movement" of love is precisely *not* a motion, as is for example the acts of the appetitive power. In this, love again demonstrates its likeness to *esse*, for, according to Aquinas, "*Esse* does not express the kind of act which is an operation passing over into something external to be produced in time, but rather the act that is so to speak primary" (*prius*).[79] Like *esse*, love is thus, in the strictest sense, a "timeless"—or at least a "supra-temporal"—event, as we indicated in our earlier discussion of the experience of real unity. This supra-temporality does not mean that love is not experienced *in time*, for indeed all of our experiences are in some respect temporal experiences, but it does mean that the temporal unfolding of the experience, as a sequence of discrete moments, does not express the whole of the reality. Love transcends time, even as it unfolds historically.

Wendell Berry expressed this aspect of love quite beautifully:

> Hate . . . always finds its justifications and fulfills itself perfectly in time by destruction of the things of time. . . . Hell itself . . . is the creature of time, unending time, unrelieved by any light or hope. But love, sooner or later, forces us out of time. It does not accept that limit. Of all that we feel and do, all the virtues and all the sins, love alone crowds us at last over the edge of the world. For love is always more than a little strange here. It is not explainable or even justifiable. It is itself the justifier. We do not make it. If it did not happen to us, we could not imagine it. It includes the world and time as a pregnant woman includes her child whose wrongs she will suffer and forgive. It is in the world but is not altogether of it. It is of eternity. It takes us there when it most holds us here.[80]

Such a thing, I submit, would not be possible if we had only indi-vidual substances inter-acting with each other inside of the horizon, so to speak, that is established by their substantiality. *Esse*, interpreted as love, by contrast, opens up a much greater horizon. Within this horizon, we could say that the encounter of love, though it certainly occurs in history, always

77. Aristotle, *Physics* IV.11.219b1.

78. Aristotle, *Physics* IV.11.218b21.

79. Aquinas, *De ver.* 23.4ad7.

80. Berry, *Jayber Crow*, 249.

enters into our being, so to speak, simultaneously *from above* it and *from below* it, which is why we can say both that love "comes upon us" and that it "wells up from within"; love is "most intimate" (εἰκειότητος)[81] even though it is an encounter with what remains abidingly other. *Whenever* love "happens," it *precedes us*, because to precede is its essential nature. It is in this respect a particular recapitulation of the very love, of the unity with God, of the *esse* that makes us *be* in the first place.

Everything that any agent does, Aquinas says, is done out of love of some kind (*ex aliquo amore*).[82] This phrase is normally interpreted as affirming that all actions, of any sort, are aimed at the good in one respect or another. We recall, however, that love is not a movement toward the good, but rather a *complacency*, a *state* of being disposed, a connaturality, which precedes any such movement and makes it possible. We have interpreted this connaturality as a *unity* that opens up the context, sets the proper horizon, for any interaction. If we say that every action, of whatever sort and by whatever agent, is done out of love, we may read this "out of" not only in the sense of "for the sake of" but also, and first, as indicating the presupposed unity from which proper action springs. In this respect, thus, the action will take the form of a *recapitulation* of that unity, a "re-installment," as it were, that serves to deepen the love that is already given. The action undertaken "out of love" will therefore always be, at some level, an inter-action, a genuine involvement of each in the being of the other, as described in chapter 3, no matter how unilateral the action may seem on the surface. And, finally, if love and being coincide, this interaction is a deepening of existence itself—more, it is creative, a bringing into being of something new.

This last point reveals its truth most clearly if we recall that, according to Aquinas, God does not create substances that *then*, in a second moment, act—so to speak—on their own, taking their created existence as a given fact, already complete in itself, simply prior to or outside any activity.[83] In other words, it is not as if God's creative act extends *only* to the *essential being* of things, and not *also to their doing*. Instead, God creates beings-in-action; the terminus of God's creative act is the *subsisting being as a whole* (*totum ens subsistens*).[84] God does not only create beings; he is also the prin-

---

81. Plotinus, *Ennead* III.5.1. Plotinus uses this adjective specifically for the beauty that generates love.

82. Aquinas, *ST* 1–2.28.6.

83. Note the formulation: this is not meant at all to deny that the *substance* that subsists is in a fundamental respect complete in itself as substance, but only that this completeness has its place somehow outside of its relating to what is other than itself in its actual existing.

84. Aquinas, *SCG* 3.1.

cipal cause of every single action originating from every being, and indeed he causes it from within the very same act by which he creates their being.[85] What this implies is that, in being given being, things are at the same time and by the same token given a creative participation in God's single act of creation.[86] While this may seem to stretch the imagination, perhaps beyond the limits of credibility, it is helpful to consider that the denial of this point leads ultimately to non-sense, strictly speaking. A world of self-enclosed monads, merely colliding with each other in a purely extrinsic way, however much such a world may be presupposed, for example, in classical physics, is simply unintelligible.[87] Already to speak of a *world* of such *sui generis* oddities is to posit them as existing together in a greater whole (and indeed even to call them "oddities" is implicitly to compare them to each other, which presupposes some commonality[88]). If such action were simply (i.e., absolutely) extrinsic, in the sense that no change were effected *in* the beings in question, there would be no difference between inter-action and its absence, between action and non-action.[89] The very foundations of thought and speech would give way. To say, by contrast, that things participate in God's creative action in their own operations is to say that their inter-actions affect and indeed (in a certain respect) *ef*-fect each other. Our inter-action is an acting *in*, and not merely *on*, the other, and in our actions we ourselves are made "anew." It is just this sense of existing *as* ourselves precisely *in* our giving and receiving that Dionysius described as the symphony, the ultimate *beauty*, of creation.[90] As we saw above, love "enters" into things simultaneously from above and from below; and so too does every action done "out of love" (*ex amore*), which is every action *tout court*. This is why we develop

85. Of course, he does not create sin; just as evil is a *privatio boni*, not a positive thing in itself but a deprivation, a perversion, or a corruption, of some really existing thing, so too is it the case that sin is best understood not as a particular kind of action but as a *failed* action, a kind of "non-action."

86. For a profound reflection on this point, see Walker, "Personal Singularity and the Communio Personarum."

87. Though it is unintelligible, it thereby becomes supremely "calculable," which gives the deceptive appearance of intelligibility.

88. For a thorough discussion of what is metaphysically entailed in the very thought of a "uni-verse," see Hanby, *No God, No Science?* chapter 2: "A Brief History of the Cosmos," 49–104.

89. See Clarke, "Forward," to *An Introduction to the Metaphysics of St. Thomas Aquinas*, xvii.

90. Dionysius: "From this Beautiful [i.e., God considered specifically under the aspect of beauty] all things possess their existence, each kind being beautiful in its own manner, and the Beautiful causes the harmonies and sympathies and communities of all things" (*Divine Names* IV.7, page 96).

affection for the things we interact with regularly, for the people we spend time with, for the place in which we live; through this interaction, we quite truly *grow* together—we become con-crete (*con-crescere*, "to grow with")—which means that our very being gets, as it were, rooted in the other, just as the other gets rooted in us, and for that very reason, assuming the proper conditions, we come to flourish. In love, things offer themselves to us, and we offer ourselves to them—or better, we are offered to each other by God: creation is a gift *also* in this sense.[91] This is what it means to say that being is love; to be is to exist in love. Love opens up the world.

This line of reflection opens up a new way to think about Aquinas's notion of *esse commune*, common being. Aquinas affirms that *esse* is most intimate in us (*interior omnibus aliis effectus*),[92] and at the same time most common (*comunissimum*),[93] because there is nothing that exists that does not . . . *exist*. Rather than interpreting this claim "nominalistically" as positing a mere coincidence of various discrete exercises of the act of being, we ought to understand the phrase *"esse commune"* as indicating a participation, a sharing in the one act of being, though of course a participation that is *diversely* exercised. On the other hand, however, what is meant here is not a strictly Platonic model of participation, which would imply according the status of a being to *esse* itself. As Aquinas explains, *esse* does not *subsist*, but beings do.[94] There is no *esse* apart from the many things that exist. Nevertheless, *esse* remains, even as non-subsistent, *"simplex et completum"*; it remains "one," and indeed complete or perfect in itself. The only way we can *both* affirm that *esse* does not subsist in itself *and also* avoid reducing *esse* to a mere coincidence of discrete acts is to say that *things exist together whenever they exist*, and that their "togetherness" is always in some respect a unity that is more than the mere sum of its "parts." This unity always in some respect *precedes* each thing in its distinctness, though this does not exclude the complementary assertion that it *always also* arises from things

91. In *Genesis*, we see that the world is made for man, but also that man is meant to tend the garden, i.e., cultivate the things of the world—not first for utilitarian purposes (there is no indication in the text that man is raising his own food before the fall), but first for their *beauty* (the first thing said of the trees is that they are "pleasant to look at"). Moreover, it is quite clear that man and woman are made *for* each other, and the sign of this is their (pre-given!) unity: flesh of my flesh, and bone of my bone! We may say something analogous about the world (though the intimacy here is clearly of a lower degree), for man was formed from the same clay as the things of the world. For a profound reflection on creation as gift, see John Paul II, "A Meditation on Givenness."

92. We recall that Plotinus had characterized precisely *beauty* as most intimate to us: *Ennead* III.5.1.

93. Aquinas, *De pot.* 3.7.

94. Aquinas, *In Boeth. de Hebdom.*, 2.

in their distinctness.[95] Things interact with each other, as we just argued, in a creative way, i.e., as bringing about in history a genuine novelty, something that never existed before,[96] but this action is always a participation in God's creative act—the giving of *esse*—which always also precedes things. In this action, things give rise to something greater than themselves alone, namely, a *unity* in which things come to be, to show themselves, and fruitfully to give themselves, as they really are. Aquinas says that "*vivere* [living] is the *esse* [being] of living things";[97] but the acts by which things live always involve a profound intimacy with things beyond the organism (consider breathing, or eating, not to mention reproduction, and so forth). Our *esse*, our *actus essendi*, is an act we exercise ourselves, as resulting from the principles of our own being, but it is also the case that our very own *esse* is an act we jointly exercise with others; it arises also as a fruit of our acting in them and their acting in us, and the whole of this is God's gift of being, the supreme act of love. We might say that "*amare* and *amari* is the *esse* of all creatures," and we can say this because God, the source of created being, is in himself love.

There are, of course, different degrees of existing, and different degrees of love, which means different degrees of unity with all things, and indeed with God in all things. Let us sum them up in conclusion. There is, first, simple existence, just "being there" in the world. This is a union with God, and a sharing in the *esse* that belongs to all things that exist, but this sharing is at first "rudimentary." This basic unity is why we experience the world as beautiful, if we "open our eyes to it," as it were, and why the beauty of the world strikes us in our very being.[98] When we do *in fact* open our eyes, when we experience particular things as beautiful, the original unity is recapitulated and deepened, our intimacy with things grows. Our affection develops, and we come to *inhabit* the world "for real." In love, we are called out of ourselves, to give ourselves in cultivating the world through action, and we take the world more fully into ourselves in knowledge. All of this is a unity of existence, the profound sharing of *esse commune*. The most

95. On all of this, see David L. Schindler, "Being, Gift, Self-Gift," 241–49.

96. Hannah Arendt famously characterizes human action as an introduction into the world of something totally new, which cannot be taken back (but only forgiven) (*The Human Condition*, 176–78).

97. Aquinas, *In I Sent*, 33.1.1.ad1m.

98. Immanuel Kant saw that there is no feeling more profound than that caused by the contemplation of the starry sky above—and a consideration of the moral law within. For him, this is because of the sublime infinity of freedom. We are suggesting that Kant is recognizing here, in the vision of the stars, an experience that touches on the heart of existence, but this heart is not most basically the infinity of freedom but rather the beauty of love, of our unity with all things, which itself opens up to the *glory of God*.

complete form of this love is the one-flesh union of marriage, which we may now understand to be more than mere metaphor: it is the creating of a new reality, a single existence made up of two distinct persons, and fruitful of more; a new reality that links whole families, and has a natural inclination, through the creation of a home, to become rooted, as it were, in the earth. As unique as the marriage bond is, it is not absolutely different from our relation to all other things; marriage is instead a paradigm that casts light on our existence in the world more generally. Greater than marriage in the natural sense is what Paul calls the "mega-mystery," the unity of Christ and the Church, in which the baptized participate, and which they affirm, realize, and deepen with every reception of the Eucharist. At the foundation of this unity is of course the perfect hypostatic union, between the human and divine natures in Christ, and finally the fecund Unity at the source of all unity, the absolute oneness of the Trinitarian Persons.

Augustine exclaimed, "Late have I loved thee, O Beauty." We may see that, what he said of God, can be said of all things analogously, as all things give expression in a certain respect to beauty. We love all things "late" because our own love precedes us, because we "are" before we "act," and because *being is love*.

PART III

God and the Transcendentals

7

Being and God

1. Guardians of Metaphysics

Does one need to be a philosopher in order to be a good Christian? The answer to this question would seem to be obvious. Scripture presents human wisdom not only as not necessary, but in fact as foolishness, which can puff one up and so present even an obstacle to our faith in God (1 Cor 3:19; 8:1). Moreover, it is said that God has revealed himself to the simple, to babes, rather than to the wise.[1] If the kings from the East, traditionally held to be wise men, eventually arrived in Bethlehem to offer homage to the child Jesus, they were nonetheless preceded by the simple shepherds who came in from the fields. What distinguishes Christianity from the Greek philosophical tradition is that the relationship to God is not a reward reserved to the studious, but a possibility open to everyone. Jesus does not demand that we become learned, but that we become simple: Unless you become like a child you cannot enter the kingdom of heaven (cf., Matt 18:3).

But before we exile the philosophers from the New Jerusalem, as Plato apparently exiled the poets from his ideal city, we need to ask: What, after all, *is* a philosopher, exactly? As the name suggests, and as the greatest philosophers have always held or in any event exemplified, the philosopher is not a self-satisfied possessor of knowledge, but a *seeker* of it. If the philosopher has a wisdom of his own, then, according to Socrates, it is of a very special sort: the wisdom to remain always open to better understanding, the knowledge that one's knowledge is never so definitive and comprehensive that there would no longer be a need for fundamental inquiry. In this respect at least, the philosopher in fact resembles a child, who is especially characterized by a kind of innocence with respect to knowledge, a spontaneous

1. Matt 11:25; cf., "The LORD knows that the thoughts of the wise are futile" (Ps 94:11).

149

lack of presumption regarding what he knows, and so a desire to find out more and more. This desire eventually gets snuffed out, not only when we think we know enough, but also when we come to believe that knowledge is impossible, or that, even if it were possible, it would be pointless. But this belief, however much it may masquerade, especially in our day, as modesty, is in fact the height of presumption. Genuine intellectual simplicity, being truly poor in spirit, manifests itself not in the *a priori* rejection of all knowledge or its possibility, but in the recognition that there is always more to know, that one's knowledge can always grow and deepen. In other words, true simplicity manifests itself precisely in the *love* of wisdom. And so we may say, unless you become a philosopher, you shall not enter the kingdom of heaven.

In a text composed in 1965, Hans Urs von Balthasar made a startling claim, which in fact has become only more astonishing in the intellectual environment of the twenty-first century. He asserted that Christians, more than anyone else, are called to be the "guardians of metaphysics" in our day, and that it is precisely our faith that leads us to pursue philosophy.[2] What he is saying here is not simply, as others have claimed, that Christians are just as capable of philosophizing as anyone else, that their faith commitments do not prevent them from sitting at the table of academic philosophy any more than the inevitable faith commitments of others, be they believers of other religions, or even atheists. Instead, he is claiming that Christians have a special interest in defending metaphysics, and a special duty to do so. But this strange claim ought to make us a little uneasy: as Christians, we might concede that metaphysics is a useful starting point, perhaps, since some of the matter of metaphysics—for example, philosophical proofs for the existence of God—may open one up to faith by giving it a prima facie credibility, but why cling to the *preparatio* once we arrive at faith? If we have come to know God through revelation, what do we have to learn from philosophy?

If believers feel inclined to direct their attention away from metaphysics, this inclination finds broad support not only in the culture at large but even in the contemporary academy. Few today would want to defend metaphysics in the traditional sense as the study of being qua being, an

2. Balthasar, *The Glory of the Lord*, vol. 5: *The Realm of Metaphysics in the Modern Age*, 646–56: "the Christian is called to be the guardian of metaphysics in our time" (ibid., 656). Elsewhere in this section, Balthasar explains: "The Christians of today, living in a night which is deeper than that of the later Middle Ages, are given the task of performing the act of affirming Being, unperturbed by the darkness and the distortion, in a way that is vicarious and representative for all humanity: an act which is at first theological, but which contains within itself the whole dimension of the metaphysical act of the affirmation of Being" (ibid., 648).

investigation of the fundamental meaning and structure of reality that culminates in an investigation of the nature of God insofar as he is knowable by natural reason.[3] In this chapter, I want to complete the arguments of the book by sketching out some reasons for the necessity of philosophy in faith, supporting Balthasar's claim that this duty falls especially to Christians in our day. If we showed the general importance of philosophy in chapter 1 as deep and respectful interest in the "true inwardness of things," our argument in the present chapter is that philosophy retains its central importance even at the highest level of human existence, our relationship with God. If we deny this importance, we not only impoverish that relation, but we undermine the *reality* of the things we encounter in the world, in the sense that we have sought to describe over the course of this book. To make this argument, I will first lay out some of the implications of rejecting a philosophical account of God; then, I will suggest why the God who reveals himself in Christ is also the God who reveals himself in and as being, and that the transcendence of reason in faith must nevertheless include, or at least not directly exclude, the completion of the mind in the natural order. In a nutshell, I will try to show that metaphysics is vital to faith, and is the natural fruit of a serious love of God.

2. Being Poor in Doctrine

Not long ago, the sociologists Christian Smith and Melinda Lundquist Denton undertook an extensive survey of the religious views of American teenagers across the country, and discovered a remarkable consistency in spite of the diversity of backgrounds, education, and so forth.[4] According to these scholars, the phrase that best describes the generic content of the religious belief of the American Youth is "moralistic therapeutic deism," the belief that there is a god of some sort, or in any event a "higher power," the role of whom, or which, is principally to inspire kindness and to provide emotional support in times of anguish. This god has more of a *function* than a *nature*, and, subsequently, religious institutions, and the practices they

3. The word "metaphysics" has returned in contemporary Continental philosophy, but in a radically anti-humanist sense that bears little connection to the traditional understanding of the science (see, e.g., "speculative metaphysics"). In analytic philosophy, the name is no longer connected with an inquiry into the First Cause—i.e., a search for God—but is restricted to the systematic investigation of the ontological status of various things, especially those that are non-physical (e.g., the ontological status of number).

4. Smith and Denton, *Soul Searching: The Religious and Spiritual Lives of American Teenagers.*

enjoin, have the purpose of promoting certain kinds of behavior or fulfill-ing social needs, but are otherwise essentially superfluous and potentially even a hindrance. The specific point we ought to highlight here is that this American religion is *dogmatically poor*, which is to say that the sole doctrine allowed to be absolute is the doctrine that doctrine does not ultimately mat-ter. In this respect, it is the specifically religious expression of the misology we discussed in chapter 1. Though, as adherents of this particular religion, we may even be passionate about our faith, we are reluctant to think that religious matters have anything to do with objective truth, that is, at some level with propositions that articulate a content-rich claim, a claim that im-poses itself on us—and therefore on anyone and everyone—to the extent that we are creatures of reason. We say "it is true *for me*," and not simply "it is true," in spite of the fact that insisting on this qualification betrays what it means to call something true.[5]

It is important that we recognize the logical connection between the content-poverty of this generic faith and the specific role it ascribes to its god, or higher power. The place wherein one encounters this particular "god" is . . . *in the heart*, we typically say. What we mean by this is rarely the "heart" in the classical sense as the center of the person, the unity of desire and understanding,[6] but far more often in the reduced sense as the seat of feeling. It is the only suitable place for our communion with the therapeutic deity because feeling, whatever significance it may indeed have, is not es-sentially a matter of concepts.[7] Feeling, whether as sentiment or emotion or impulse or sense perception, is subjective in form, and as such cannot be translated into universal terms. To be sure, the very particularity of it, its essential resistance to such translation, is why feeling has the indispensable significance that it does.[8] But if we make a thing exclusively a matter of feeling, or, in other words, if we confine our relationship to some reality

5. As Robert Spaemann has put it, "It may sound like arrogance, but in reality the concept 'absolute truth' is a tautology" (*Philosophical Essays on Nature, God, and the Human Person*, 13).

6. For a more metaphysical interpretation of the heart, in a classically-oriented anthropology, see Siewerth, *Der Mensch und sein Leib*.

7. The point here is not at all to deny the objective significance of feeling, but in fact to *save* that significance: in the end, if there is no *objective* dimension of the world, accessible through concepts, then feeling also loses its specifically *revelatory* character.

8. Heidegger vividly connects the non-conceptual dimension of things—the experience of color, for instance—with a kind of depth dimension of nature, to which he gives the name "earth": "Color shines and wants only to shine. When we analyze it in rational terms by measuring its wavelengths, it is gone. It shows itself only when it remains undisclosed and unexplained. Earth thus shatters every attempt to penetrate it" ("The Origin of the Work of Art," 172).

to the *limits* of the heart, then even if the heart is in some sense infinite, it implies that this reality does not concern anyone or anything else but me. Indeed, it does not even concern me outside of the confines of my heart, which is to say that it does not concern me *specifically as a matter of truth*. A truth is something that makes a universal claim, it establishes a measure to which reason, and indeed all persons with reason, must conform. I cannot deny that a reality makes a claim on others without surrendering its claim on myself, in spite of what may be a sincere and enthusiastic desire otherwise. Such a reality will by its very nature tend to collapse *into* the heart, to become merely a matter of my own sentiment, which means it will tend to take its measure from how I happen, in my particularity, to be feeling at any particular time. It is thus not an accident that the god-without-doctrine of "therapeutic deism" is precisely *therapeutic*, because such a god will bear on me in the form of giving support, a sort of infinite weight, to my momentary "state of mind." This will most often be positive—encouragement, consolation, hope—but it does not in principle exclude the condemnation of an absolute all-seeing judge, when I happen to be feeling bad.

The implications of this collapse of God into feeling go far beyond the quality of my particular relationship with God. Descartes famously sought to prove the existence of God through the strict application of logic in order to provide a foundation for the objectivity of the world, the reality of things beyond the phantasms of the imagination. There are many fundamental criticisms to make regarding the Cartesian project: it turns God into an instrument serving a philosophical purpose, or indeed the primarily psychological purpose of providing certainty; it operates with a radically impoverished sense of reason, which is defined in strict opposition to faith; and it takes for granted a radicalized subjectivity, an isolated consciousness set off against the physical things of the world, as the problematic starting point, which inevitably sets the terms for the resolution. In another context, we could show that these problems are all related. But, here, we may instead highlight something positive in Descartes' reflections, namely, the insight that the objectivity of the world stands or falls with the objectivity of God. The claim I want to make here is not exactly Descartes', namely, that we have to prove the existence of God first in order to be able to affirm the existence of the world, but rather a somewhat more modest contrapositive of his claim: if we *deny* the possibility of a rational proof for the existence of God, or that reason has any business occupying itself with such things, or that God would represent a truth demanding the consideration of reason— in other words, if we insist that the God-question is exclusively a matter of private, personal faith, which does not concern anyone else but me—then we undermine the objective reality of things in general.[9] The world gets emptied of its ontological density at a single stroke, even if the outward shell remains intact for centuries thereafter.

Nietzsche famously observed that the death of God—the disappearance of God's significance—is a "tremendous event" that "has not yet reached the ears of men. Lightning and thunder require time; the light of the stars requires time."[10] It may be that only the appearance of a broad moral controversy brings to light what had in fact been true already for generations: All of a sudden, we come to realize that we do not in fact believe that there is such a thing as "nature," that the physical world, paradigmatically the human body, is meaningful *in itself*, that truth and goodness and beauty have objective weight. As we mentioned in chapter 1, Charles Péguy defined the spirit of modernity as not believing what one believes; perhaps postmodernity arrives when we finally see through this falsehood and shed the pretense. In any event, I wish to suggest that, at the root of the subjectivism and relativism that we regularly encounter in contemporary culture lies the conviction that faith in God is ultimately a personal, *private* affair alone, a matter sealed off from the realm of truth. If the Creator of the world is not in some basic sense an *other*, to whom I must conform, any real otherness that the world may have grows thin, and fails to put up any ontological resistance to human projects—at the moment of crisis, initially, but eventually at any moment of need, however trivial.

Now, it may seem that the most proper response to the doctrine-poverty of "therapeutic deism" would be to affirm the importance of Christian doctrine. While this response is indeed finally the most essential, nevertheless it seems to me that there is a less obvious dimension that is also indispensable, and arguably in the end necessary even for the genuine affirmation of Christian doctrine, and that is the guardianship of metaphysics that Balthasar called us to assume. To put this claim somewhat starkly, I want to suggest that we have to affirm the so-called "God of the Philosophers" if we wish to affirm the truth of Christian revelation precisely *as true*. In other words, the *natural and objective* truth about God that comes to light in metaphysics, as accessible to the light of human reason, is an

9. The reason for putting the claim in this form is that the mind begins and normally operates inside of the assumption of the existence of God. Atheism is essentially a—never fully successfully—acquired opinion.

10. Nietzsche, *The Gay Science*, 182. He concludes this aphorism with the caustic question, "What after all are these churches now if they are not the tombs and sepulchers of God?" The point seems to be that God is not dead in the sense of having been rejected (atheists), but rather most basically as having been rendered effectively meaningless by believers.

essential aspect of the revelation of the Trinitarian God of Jesus Christ that
we receive in faith.

3. God Is Being

A full argument for this claim would require not just a book of its own but a
lifetime of reflection; in the present context we will focus on just one piece,
so to speak, of the larger puzzle. Let us enter into this initial reflection by
taking a basic metaphysical proposition, no doubt *the* metaphysical proposition, regarding God. Rather than explore the question concerning the
precise provenance of the proposition, assess the soundness of the proofs
from which it is derived, seek to justify it in relation to its sources, or even
think through its content in any systematic fashion, I wish instead simply to
reflect on what it means to speak of God in this way, and what implications
it has for us, both as believers and simply as human beings. The proposition is a simple one: "God is being." We recognize it as a statement fairly
common in medieval thought, when metaphysics was in its "golden age,"
no doubt; it may be even more common now in philosophy departments
as an object of criticism, representing, for example, an ungodly god, before
whom one can neither sing nor dance, as Heidegger put it,[11] or the epitome
of idolatry, whereby we adore the highest of human concepts precisely *in
the place of* the God who, as love, never has "to be," as Jean-Luc Marion has
argued.[12] "God is being." What does it mean to say this, and, supposing it is
at least not altogether false, what might we gain by attempting to *think* it, to
sound out its meaning? Is this attempt an act of impiety, an endeavor to lay
hold, by intellectual force, of what St. Paul reminds us is necessarily beyond
our natural ken?[13]

Let us begin a first response to such questions by comparing this proposition to one that more directly concerns the specific content of Christian
doctrine: "God is incarnate in Jesus of Nazareth." There is, to be sure, an
infinite mystery indicated in this statement of faith, but what stands out
most immediately about it when compared to the other, namely, "God is being," is that it does not represent a general statement. Instead, the statement
indicates a particular reality or event that comes to light specifically in history. For this reason, it bears the luminosity of intelligibility only to one who
has had contact, at some level and to some degree, with Christian revelation.

11. Heidegger, *Identity and Difference*, 72.

12. Marion, *God Without Being*, esp. xx.

13. St. Paul speaks of the "love that surpasses all knowledge"—though of course he
speaks paradoxically of *knowing* this love (Eph 3:19).

The statement, "God is being," by contrast, is a more general claim, which would make sense in principle, for example, even to a pre-Christian Greek philosopher. The reason, of course, is that, whereas one can only know Jesus of Nazareth through some historical encounter, whether direct or mediated by witnesses, *being* is universal. In fact, according to Aquinas, being is what is *most* familiar to all of us, to any rational creature whatever, since, as we discussed last chapter, it is the very first notion to enter into the mind's conception and that to which all other notions are reduced.[14] We do not think of *anything at all* except in some relation to being; it is, as it were, the very medium of our intelligence. To say that it is the most familiar to us, however, does not mean that we ever fully know what being is, that we can come to definitive knowledge about it.[15] As the great philosophers have always intuited, being is and will remain, even in its commonness, an unfathomable mystery; in Heidegger's words, it is both nearest to us and furthest away.[16] Nevertheless, this very mystery is one whose presence we *never* escape, even if we rarely take cognizance of it. The point, in any event, is that being is a notion that is universally accessible; it is universal accessibility itself, and does not depend for its intelligibility on any particular historical situation or condition.[17]

Now, we said that the statement "God is being" makes some sense, in principle, to anyone. But what sense does it make? Before we begin to consider the content of this claim, it is necessary that we marvel for a moment (at least!) over its form. The statement is a proposition of the simplest sort: S is P. Typically, in such statements, P represents something universal: according to the tradition, there are 5 "predicables," i.e., kinds of terms that can be predicated of a subject, and they are all universals or general categories.[18] When we say "S is P"—for example, "The apple is red"—what we are doing logically is placing the particular subject into a more encompassing class of items: the apple belongs among the things that are red. But the statement

14. See Aquinas, *De ver.* 1.1.

15. William Desmond writes beautifully, and in great depth, of the "intimate strangeness of being," the utter familiarity of what will always remain a mystery: see *The Intimate Strangeness of Being.*

16. See Heidegger, *Being and Time*, 2–3. Cf., Aquinas, *De pot.* 3.7; *ST* 1.105.5.

17. To say this is not to deny that there may be periods in history in which the meaning of being is more evident than others. It is also not to deny that being will *best* be understood in the light of faith insofar as the understanding of being includes an understanding of its causes, and revelation is the *self*-disclosure of the absolute First Cause of being: which means it will in principle offer a *privileged* insight.

18. Porphyry derived the list of "predicables"—species, genus, differentia, propria, and accidentia—from Aristotle's *Organon*. They all represent common terms, though of course of fundamentally different orders.

"God is being" does not fit this form. Being, first of all, is not a class, because classes are defined by their difference from other classes, and there is nothing different from being: it is, as we said, the universal-est of all universalities. As Aristotle put it, being is not a genus, because any specific differentiation would also be in some respect being.[19] (In this respect, we cannot even say that being is *sui generis*, strictly speaking.) Moreover, God, as Creator, as absolute source or principle, who presupposes nothing outside of himself, is even more clearly not a particular subject that can be grouped into a more encompassing category, alongside other things that would equally fall into it. Whatever else *is*, to the extent that it is at all, must ultimately be in some sense reducible back to God, the First Cause of all things *tout court*.

So, where does this leave us? Does it mean that the statement "God is being," which *looks* like other propositions but doesn't *act* like them, is meaningless? No, not at all. It simply means that, rather than attempt to fit its sense into the typical form of our intelligence, we need instead to raise our intelligence towards *it*, to follow its sense as faithfully as we can with our minds. Let us look more closely at this point. To say that "God is being" is to say that, on the one hand, God and being are the same (this is the logical force of "is" here), but at the same time that being is not simply identical with God, or else we would have an empty tautology. We are saying *something* in this claim, which means that "being" articulates something that is not already articulated immediately in the word "God." What does "being" "add" to God? The most immediate thing we can say here is that it "adds" precisely *universal intelligibility*, which is to say that it implies that the name "God" is not only a personal name, but also indicates a nature; it has objective content that speaks to the human mind as such. Let us be clear that it does not *only* speak to reason: God is not *only* being, so that to understand being is to understand all there is to know of God. The claim is not that "being is God," in the sense that the two terms are simply equivalent and so interchangeable, or that we have all we need in the word "being" alone.[20] Instead, God is being, which is to say that being, insofar as we come to know it, *unfolds* something of the meaning of God, without exhausting that meaning. If intelligibility is the meaning of what the notion of being "adds," we can say that this statement implies that God is intelligible to the human mind, without reducing God to that intelligibility.[21]

19. Aristotle, *Posterior Analytics* 92b14; *Metaphysics* 2.3.998b22. Included in Aristotle, *Basic Works*.

20. Alexander Waugh raises this as an objection in the course of a fictional dialogue on the nature of God: "Well if God is Being-itself, let's dispense with the word 'God,' for we already have a word for Being itself, and that's 'being'" (*God*, 299).

21. The path we have sketched here resembles that described by Hegel in paragraphs

To penetrate more deeply into what is being said in this statement, we need to shift from a *logical* to a more directly *ontological* register. According to the classical tradition, represented here by Aquinas, there is an infinite difference between created being, the being of the world, and divine being, the being that God himself is.[22] At the same time, however, created being is not merely "other than" God: it is wholly, from first to last, *from* God, precisely because it is *from nothing* (*ex nihilo*). God is the absolute cause of all that exists, and effects necessarily reveal their cause.[23] Indeed, effects are identical with their cause *in* their cause, which is to say that, at the ontological foundation of the difference between God and created being is a simple unity. This unity entails a likeness to God that is universal, accessible in all created things.[24] To exist, then, is to have a share in being, and that being is given by God, which is to say, it is in a fundamental sense an expression of him, or to use the more common term, it is a revelation of God.[25] Paul claims that all people, believers or not, are able to see both the power and the divinity, that is, the *nature*, of God *in* the things of this world.[26] What all of this means is simply that, as we discussed last chapter, God gives himself in a certain respect in creation; in giving the world being, he is giving what he *is*, even if he is giving it so perfectly generously as to give it *away*, to make something truly *other* than himself. Thinking of the world as created, specifically in terms of gift or indeed of love, brings out both the unity of being and God and the infinite difference between them.

The traditional notion in metaphysics that arises from this simultaneity of unity and difference, immanence and transcendence, in God's relation to the world, is *analogy*. When we speak analogously, we are naming God "from creatures," i.e., on the basis of the knowledge we have derived from things in the world, but signifying principally what lies beyond them,

---

17–23 of the "Preface" to the *Phenomenology of Spirit*, 9–13, but there is a decisive difference: Hegel insists on the absolute reduction of God to intelligibility (which is understood non-analogically as identical to human understanding in its ideal form), and so the absorption of religion into philosophy, or faith into reason.

22. See Aquinas, *SCG* 7.2 ad 4; cf., *ST* 1.3.8.

23. Aquinas: "Every effect in some degree represents its cause, but diversely" (*ST* 1.45.7).

24. Aquinas, *ST* 1.44.3

25. See Aquinas, *ST* 1.44.1.

26. Paul: "For what can be known about God is plain to [all men], because God has shown it to them. Ever since the creation of the world his invisible nature, namely, his eternal power and deity, has been clearly perceived in the things that have been made" (Rom 1:19–20). Note that God's nature is said to be *clearly* visible and *known* (νοούμενα καθορᾶται) in things, and that this evidence in things is not just a fact that is there, but is God's *revealing* of himself (ἐφανέρωσεν).

namely, God himself, who precontains all creaturely perfections as identical with himself.[27] Thus, in the proposition, "God is being," the mind begins, as it were, not only with a natural object but with its most natural and familiar object. In trying to comprehend what is being indicated in the analogous term, however, the mind rises above itself, as it were; it moves beyond the natural evidence, beyond what it sees, and so the meaning of the term undergoes a transformation, we might say, in the course of its act of signifying. The notion of being itself carries the mind up to God, rather than somehow "eclipsing" him. There is clearly paradox, and drama, in this analogical movement, which would itself offer a great deal to the intelligence to try to sort out, if there were space enough and time. But what we need to observe in the present context is simply that, though the metaphysical proposition "God is being" may be in one respect the conclusion of a chain of reasoning, it is hardly an *endpoint* for thinking. The proposition does not bring the mind to a halt in an idolatrous fashion. Instead, it is itself a new beginning of inquiry, of which there would seem to be no definitive end.

Now, we have been speaking of the mind's knowing of God, but we must acknowledge that we do not know the essence of God directly in this life.[28] As the notion of analogy implies, the being that is the natural element of the intellect is never directly the being of God that is identical with God's existence. But this undeniable claim has to be interpreted properly, that is, precisely in the light of the meaning of being as created. The intellect goes astray if we simply separate created being, which we can know in principle, from divine being, which we cannot know, as if these represented, say, isolated spheres. Given such a separation, we would be inclined to deposit our relation to God, as it were, in a place *outside* our reason, which cannot help degenerating into a place *lower* than our reason. This is just the problem in the radical privatizing and subjectivizing of faith we spoke about at the outset. In this reduction, we believe we know God best by raising him above, placing him *beyond* the world he created, and seeking him there with our hearts. The statement "God is being," in this case, even if we allow that it may be true as far as it goes, loses any significance for us.[29] If we cannot know God *directly*, so much the worse for our knowledge. Let us then *feel* him directly—and back we fall into an incipient therapeutic deism.

But the notion of analogy offers an alternative to this simple intellectual surrender. According to Aquinas, we *can* and also *do* have knowledge

27. Aquinas, *ST* 1.4.2.

28. Aquinas, *ST* 1.12.4.

29. As Marion puts it, "God is, exists, and that is the least of things" (*God Without Being*, xix).

of God in this life, and it is indeed genuine knowledge.[30] But it is always *in* creatures. We know causes in their effects; we know God, who is the universal cause, in the world he created, in our knowing of being. Aquinas compares the presence of God in our mind, which is the natural light of our reason, to the light *in* which we see whatever it is we see, though which never becomes the object itself of our vision.[31] Similarly, while God cannot be the object of our intellect, it remains the case that we understand all that we do only in the light of the First Truth that is God himself. But let us attend closely to this metaphor. It is true that we never see light in itself: without an object to reflect light, it is invisible, which is why outer space, filled with light, is black. But it is also true that the colors that we see are nothing but partial reflections of light. In a sense, we never see *anything but* light, even if we never see light *in itself.* Similarly, though we do not naturally know God *in* himself, but only as represented by his creatures, or in other words, as relative participations in the being that God himself is, there is a sense in which we never know anything at all *except* God. The forms that constitute the intelligibility of creatures are all diverse representations of the divine essence,[32] and, moreover, the *being* that is the medium of all intelligence is the "likeness of divine goodness," or in other words, a revelation of the love that God is.[33]

The metaphor of light opens up a further implication regarding God and human knowledge when we ask a simple question. Given that light is something we cannot see *in* itself, what would this entail for a person who loved light and was moved by a passion to seek it? Would he, in the bitterness of disappointment, refuse to look at any particular color, which is to say would he refuse to open his eyes, since there is never light *as such* offered to his vision, but only color? Or would he not, instead, love colors, and spontaneously see them, not just in their distinctiveness as colors, but simultaneously as reflections of light? One who loved light, it seems to me, would celebrate color in all its manifestations, and would be reluctant only to stare into darkness. Similarly, we ought to see that, to love God is to desire to know him, and this desire does not express itself in a lack of interest in knowing anything else, a shutting of the mind's eye. Instead, this love

---

30. Aquinas explains that, as intellectual creatures, we necessarily desire, by our very nature, to know God, and God does not make any desire in vain (*ST* 1.12.1). In this context, he is speaking primarily of man's eschatological state, but the point here is simply that knowing God is not something to which man is indifferent, but represents a fulfillment—however gratuitous—of our nature.

31. Aquinas, *ST* 1.88.3.

32. Aquinas, *ST* 1.44.3.

33. Aquinas, *De ver.* 22.2 ad 2.

becomes manifest precisely as a desire to know all things, as perfectly as one can—to know in the quintessential sense, which is what metaphysics ultimately is.

There is a certain humility in accepting, in our historical condition in the world, to know God not directly in his essence, in an unmediated way, but *first* and at least in some sense most basically through the mediation of the world he created. This acceptance is in fact the proper recognition of God's absolute sovereignty and his nature as perfect love. Self-communication—or to put it in the contemporary idiom, "self-gift"—is the very essence of love.[34] But, generosity is unthinkable except as somehow involving otherness. As we know from experience, we give ourselves best when we give, as it were, *more* than just ourselves, since our generosity thus gets "embodied" in some real thing that is handed over into the free possession of the other. By analogy, we may think of God's creation of the world as the absolute expression of this generosity:[35] God gives himself in giving being, and in a paradoxical way gives "more" than himself, insofar as the being he gives *really does* belong to the world as *definitively* its own, never to be absorbed back into God himself (which is the haunting danger of non-Christian neoplatonism).[36] To think that God might take the gift back is to imagine God as a less-than-perfect giver—indeed as a *false* giver. If we doubt the stability or integrity of the world in its created nature, if we fail to trust that the world has its own substantial being, an ontological density sufficient to render it a reliable object of the mind, we are betraying God's generosity.[37]

But there is a subtler form of the betrayal of God as giver, which bears even more directly on our line of reflection.[38] To set aside the mediation

34. Aquinas: "It belongs to the very essence of goodness to communicate itself to others" (*ST* 3.1).

35. To describe the creation of the world as an "absolute expression" of generosity is not to call it the *ultimate* expression, which is a description fitting for the incarnation alone.

36. To be given being *of one's own* is to be given genuine agency: agency is always ascribed specifically to what subsists in itself (cf., "only that which subsists in itself can have an operation *per se*, for nothing can operate but what is actual" [*ST* 1.75.2]; "anything acts in consequence of its being in act" [*SCG* 2.7], and "every agent acts according as it exists in actuality" [*De pot.* 2.1]). Here we see the reason Aquinas places such emphasis on "secondary causality": God causes all things and their activities, not in *spite* of them or in their stead, but precisely by causing their own causality (*ST* 1.105.5).

37. This is the spirit of Aquinas's observation that our thinking ought not to be based on the power of God in an abstract sense but on the natures of things (cf., *ST* 1.76.5): this is not a denial of God's power, but perhaps paradoxically a more profound affirmation of it.

38. Ferdinand Ulrich is the inspiration for much of what follows, especially his

of being in order to relate to God im-mediately is implicitly, and no doubt generally contrary to one's intentions, to claim that God fails to give *himself* in creation. It is to separate God from what he gives, and so to isolate him from what he gives. This, however, is to render him no longer a *giver*, but now only one who *might possibly* give at some point, but who has not yet given. In other words, to such a mind, God becomes willy nilly one who hesitates, who holds himself back from generosity; he is not an actual giver, but a mere *power* to give, which may or may not realize itself. God ceases in this respect to be perfect goodness, and becomes instead perfect power, . . . and then eventually only power, since "perfection" implies actual completeness. Such a power, as *mere* power, over against any actual realization, however, is in fact coincident with a radical impotence, an inability to give himself in a genuine, definitive way in what he gives. (Absolute power is absolute potentiality, and absolute potentiality is in fact nothing at all. It is totally unreal.) This point sheds a new light on one of the most traditional metaphysical notions concerning the nature of God, namely, that God is pure *act*. This notion is apt to describe the God who reveals himself as love, because, as we argued last chapter, the God who is love is a God who has always-already definitively—*actually*—given himself "away" in giving being to the world.[39]

Now, to say that God gives himself definitively, and even in a certain sense perfectly, in creation does not at all mean that the created world, even taken as a whole and in all of its mysterious depth, *exhausts* the meaning of God. God infinitely transcends the world, and so the world in its natural reality falls radically short as a revelation of God. There is therefore something profoundly new in the more directly personal self-revelation of God in the covenant he forms with Israel, the people he prepared over the course of generations, indeed from the beginning of time, and the meaning of which is disclosed in even greater depth through the drama of its history. The supreme gift of self, the most complete personal self-gift, occurs of course in God's emptying of himself to take on human nature, even in its sinful state, by means of his incarnation in the person of Jesus Christ,[40] access to whom we receive through the *additional* gift of the Holy Spirit.[41] Because it is the inspired account of this personal self-revelation and self-gift, Sacred Scrip-

---

reflections in *Gabe und Vergebung.*

39. We see here the need to recognize the *Trinitarian* nature of God, who is perfectly given and received love already *in himself*, "prior" to creation, as the ground for its freedom. There is an *analogy* between the creation of the world and the begetting of the Son, but—*pace* Hegel—they are also infinitely different.

40. See Phil 2:6–8.

41. See John 14:26; 14:15–17; 16:12–15; Acts 2:38; Rom 5:5.

ture is the very foundation of the Christian faith. But what I am proposing here is that if we affirm the centrality of Scripture in a way that positively *excludes* the philosophical reflection on God's nature as revealed in the being of creatures, we jeopardize that very centrality, because we undermine the principle that would allow God's self-revelation in Christ to be for us something meaningful, ultimately, in an objective sense. This is one of the implications of the argument just made a moment ago. If God cannot give himself in his creation, his presence in Christ will be in a mode other than that of self-gift, i.e., the communication of his being or nature.[42] To dismiss the proposition "God is being" as trivial or non-essential is by necessary implication to make the incarnation a simple historical fact that we may perhaps accept with our whole heart, but which has to remain opaque to our minds. Christ is then the truth only in a positivistic sense, and not as an infinitely meaningful reality into which we may thoughtfully and contemplatively enter, and to which we are called to conform also our thinking.[43] In this case, revelation does not unfold into substantial doctrine that abides, but reduces instead to a sheer *event*, a kind of lightning bolt, that arrives in total discontinuity and *seems* to change everything all at once, but in fact leaves little but a different subjective attitude once the smoke clears. Moreover, only if "God is being," that is, only if the God of Jesus Christ has also revealed himself in creation, does the extraordinary event of the incarnation bear not just on my feelings or on my moral intentions but also on the meaning of reality as a whole. It is, in other words, only in this way that Christianity provides an objective form that has more than merely moral significance for the political order, that gives shape to culture, that organizes existence as a whole and not just in those aspects that directly implicate the way we treat each other. If we deny the importance of philosophy in faith, we cannot but lose our faith in philosophy more generally, which means we lose an intrinsic interest in the intrinsic meaning of things.

We, as Christians, speak often about the importance of a personal relationship with God, indeed, with our Lord Jesus, and it is of course right that we do: it is an unfathomable grace to have received the direct revelation

42. Obviously, there are many steps here: The Father gives himself, his nature, to the Son, and the Son returns himself to the Father in the Spirit; because self-gift is thus the very nature of God, we may conceive of the Son's becoming incarnate as the gift of the divine nature, so perfectly given as to become one with the human nature of Jesus. The point, in any event, is that all of these mysteries turn on the meaning of goodness as the communication of one's own *being*.

43. Paul speaks of the renewal not of the *heart* but of the *mind* (τὸ νοός), in the conformity to Christ (Rom 12:2; cf., 1 Cor 2:16).

of God "in person," in contrast to the prophets of old[44] and in even greater contrast to the pagans who speculated about the "unknown God."[45] But we must also recognize that there is an indispensable *impersonal* dimension, or perhaps "supra-personal," in the relationship. We must recognize, in other words, that there is a "what is . . . ?" question embedded in our faith, which orients our minds to God's reality in himself. God is not only a person,[46] but a *nature*, which is to say that it means *some real objective thing* to say "God." In one respect, what it means is an objective content that can be, not exactly abstracted from, but in any event considered as distinct within God's absolute simplicity. This is the *TRUTH* of God, which has a compellingness that would impose itself ineluctably on any rational creature who remains, in freedom, faithful to his reason. We can neither separate, in God, nature from person, nor person from nature.

4. Seeking God in Thought

This has two implications for the intellectual life, which I will mention in conclusion. First, the "supra-personal" dimension of God, which renders itself to a certain extent and in a certain respect in the concepts by which our minds think, is not opposed or indeed even simply extrinsic to the personal dimension of relationship. Concepts are not "mere abstractions," fabricated instruments that are somehow outside of being and which we subsequently "apply" to the things we think, but, as we saw in chapter 4, are instead the form that the mind takes in its participation in, and communion with, being; and being is not some *thing* juxtaposed to God, to which God would be related again somehow only subsequently, or somehow from outside. Instead, as we have been arguing, being is God's gift of himself to creatures, a gift in which, precisely in giving it away, he remains ever present. It follows that God is present to us *in* our very concepts. When we attempt, for example, to think, in all of its logical and ontological demands, the claim that "God is being," we are not just spinning mental machinery for the sake of some intellectual puzzle or curiosity, but are *encountering the real God in a distinctive way*. Thinking about God is therefore not idolatry of its essence, even if we can turn it into such through abuse. Metaphysics, undertaken in

---

44. Heb 1:1–2.

45. Acts 17:23. Note that the very God the Greeks have worshiped as unknown is the God of Jesus, whom Paul reveals to them.

46. More precisely, God is personal, not "a person," or we might say, God is Three Persons.

the manner proper to it, is the "piety of thought."[47] To engage it properly is to recognize it as a ground we must remove the intellectual equivalent of our sandals to tread, and in doing so we ought to expect to discover our God, who is indeed a "consuming fire" (Heb 12:29), but a fire that miraculously burns without consuming, without destroying, the natural objects of our mind. And the deeper our expectation, the ever-greater our surprise in this discovery.[48]

The second point is that the deepening of a personal relationship entails an increase in our desire to know not just God himself but, because of God, all other things. In Mark's Gospel, Jesus criticizes the Pharisees for allowing one to withhold the honor due to one's parents if one gives that honor instead to God (Mark 7: 9–13). To honor God in this exclusive way is, paradoxically, to dishonor him. By analogy, we might say that to reject the honor due to the supremely human activity of philosophy in order to glorify God is to betray God, in spite of our intentions. As we pointed out earlier, the desire to know God, if it is true, expresses itself in the desire to know all things as fully as we can. The more we learn of God in Scripture, the more we wish to know him in all things, therefore, philosophically. Our faith, precisely because it is a faith in the God who, as First Cause, brought all things into being, opens up the entire world to our minds, and draws us intellectually into that world with a vital interest. It is for this reason that the guardianship of metaphysics is the special duty of Christians.[49]

To return to our observation at the start of the chapter: the gospel praises above all the *simple*, not those who have amassed intellectual

47. This is obviously an allusion to Heidegger, who famously closes his essay "The Question Concerning Technology" with the sentence, "For questioning is the piety of thought" (See *Basic Writings*, 341). But Heidegger allows precisely *questioning* alone (though elsewhere he refers to *thanking* as a kind of religious form of *thinking*) to be pious, and thus seems to concede conceptual knowledge to the realm of the impious. For this reason, he is supremely reluctant to allow God to be an "object of knowledge" (See Gadamer: "[Heidegger] never found an answer to his original and constantly advancing question; namely, How can one speak of God without reducing him to an object of our knowledge?" ["Being Spirit God," 194–95]. Note that this effort, in spite of its aim at "piety," simply *removes* God from our minds.) We, by contrast, wish to affirm knowledge, *itself* and in its most *essential* form, as pious, i.e., as open in wonder and awe to God.

48. Heraclitus in Diels and Kranz, *Fragmente der Vorsokratiker* B18.

49. For a contrasting view, see Merold Westphal (*Overcoming Ontotheology*), who takes metaphysics to be a temptation rather than a positive contribution to our faith. According to Westphal, the desire to know is a kind of *libido dominandi*, a lust for power. But this judgment takes for granted that knowledge is of its essence a form of domination. There is in this contempt for reason, this misology, a contempt for human nature simply, since it implies an identification of human nature with its sinful condition, which ought to be condemned.

treasures, but the poor in spirit. We have suggested that there is a temptation to interpret this as warning us away from philosophy, as if to seek insight through the often-ascetical rigors of careful thought is to abandon this poverty of spirit and substitute for it a puffed up presumption. But just as one can be poor in spirit even in the midst of one's possessions, or, conversely, can betray this spirit even if one has not a penny to one's name, so too is it possible to learn and to remain simple. Indeed, at the deepest level, we discover that these are inseparable: only the one who remains simple learns, and the very nature of the truth that one learns inspires deeper simplicity. To reject philosophy, deliberately and explicitly, is no longer to be childlike in the gospel sense; rather, this rejection is more like the intellectual version of a loss of innocence. It is a per-version of what Socrates identified as the highest human wisdom: no longer a "knowing that I don't know," but now a knowing avoidance of knowledge, knowingly rejecting not only all actual knowledge but even its possibility. The gospel category for us who betray this wisdom—and all of us do to some extent—is not the simple or the poor in spirit, but the hypocrite and the fool. And the proper response is a recovery of the wonder, the open and unselfprotective desire to know, the "respect for the true inwardness of things," that belongs natively to the child: unless you become lovers of wisdom, you will not be lovers of God.

Glossary of Latin Terms

Accidentia	accidents
actus essendi	the act of being
adhaerare deo	adhering, or clinging, to God
admiratio	wonder
aliquid	something
amare	to love
amari	to be loved
amor	love
amor amicitiae	love as friendship
amor benevolentiae	love as benevolence
amor concupiscentiae	love as desire
amor complacentiae	love as complacency, i.e., being-pleased-with
amor rationalis	rational love
caritas	charity
causa finalis	final cause
causa sui	cause of oneself
claritas	clarity, i.e., luminosity
coaptatio	being adapted to each other
coincidentia oppositorum	coincidence of opposites
communissimum	most common or universal
complacentia	the state of being-pleased-with
conatus	internal impulse drive (typically for existence)
connaturalitas	co-naturality
conversio	turning back
convertuntur	are interchangeable

creatio continua	creation as an ongoing actuality
de gustibus non est disputandum	one cannot argue about taste
differentia	difference
ecstasis	a state of being beyond oneself
ens	being (as entity or existing thing)
esse	to be
esse commune	the common act of being
esse est similitudo divinae bonitatis	being is the likeness of divine goodness
ex aliquo amore	from some love
ex nihilo	from nothing
forma partis	form of the parts
forma totius	form of the whole
formatio	formation
gratia praesupponit naturam	grace presupposes nature
immutatio	a change that is introduced into a thing
in re	in the thing
in se	in oneself
informare	to introduce form into something
inquantum res de non esse in esse mutatur	insofar as a thing is changed from non being into being
intus-legere	to read the inner reality of a thing
liberum arbitrium	free choice or free judgment
libido dominandi	the desire to dominate
pace	peace
partes extra partes	parts outside of parts
placet	pleases
per se unum	a thing that is unified in itself
preparatio	preparation
principium motus	the principle of motion
principium motus appetitus	the principle of the movement of appetite
prius	prior, the quality of preceding what follows

privatio boni	the absence of a due good
propria	those qualities that belong to the essence of a thing
quoad nos	in relation to us
quod visum placet	that which, when seen, pleases
quodamodo omnia	in a certain sense all things
ratio misericordiae	the meaning or logic of mercy
res	thing
sed contra	"but in contrast": the phrase is used to indicate an opposing position
simplex et completum	simple and complete
simul creatur et creatum est	is being created and has already been created at the same time
superficies	the surface
sui generis	a genus unto itself
terminus ad quem	the end point of a movement or relation
unum	unity, oneness, undividedness
vivere	to live
voluntas	will

Bibliography

Adller, Mortimer. *The Idea of Freedom: A Dialectical Examination of the Conceptions of Freedom*. Garden City, NY: Doubleday, 1958.

Aertsen, Jan. *Medieval Philosophy and the Transcendentals: The Case of Thomas Aquinas*. Leiden: Brill, 1996.

Aeschylus. *Oresteia*. Translated by Richard Lattimore. Chicago: University of Chicago Press, 1969.

Anderson, James, ed. *An Introduction to the Metaphysics of St. Thomas Aquinas*. Washington, DC: Gateway, 1997.

Aquinas, Thomas. *Exposito Libri Boetii De hebdomadibus* (*In Boeth. de Hebdom.*). Volume 1 of *Opuscula*. Edited by P. Madnonnet. Paris: Letheilleux, 1927.

————. *Quaestiones disputate De malo* (*De malo*). Edited by P. Mandonnet. Paris: Letheilleux, 1925.

————. *Quaestiones disputatae De potentia* (*De pot.*). Edited by P. Mandonnet. Paris: Letheileux, 1925.

————. *Quaestiones disputate De veritate* (*De ver.*). Volume 22, parts 1–3 of *Sancti Thomae Aquinatis opera omnia*. Leonine edition. Rome: Editori di San Tommaso, 1975–76.

————. *Quaestiones disputatae De virtutibus* (*De caritate*). Volume 3. Edited by P. Mandonnet. Paris: Letheilleux, 1925.

————. *Summa Contra Gentiles* (*SCG*). Volumes 13–15 of *Sancti Thomae Aquinatis opera omnia*. Leonine Edition. Rome: Editori di San Tommaso, 1918, 1926, 1930.

————. *Scriptum super Sententiis*. Volume 1 (*I Sent.*). Edited by P. Mandonnet. Paris: Letheilleux, 1929.

————. *Scriptum super Sententiis*. Volume 3 (*III Sent.*). Edited by M. F. Moos. Paris: Lethielleux, 1933.

————. *Summa theologiae* (*ST*). Volumes 4–12 of *Sancti Thomae Aquinatis opera omnia*. Leonine Edition. Rome: Editori di San Tommaso, 1888–1906.

————. *Super Librum Dionysii De divinis nominibus* (*In. div. nom.*). Volume 2 of *Opuscula*. Edited by P. Mandonnet. Paris: Letheilleux, 1927.

Arendt, Hannah. *The Human Condition*. 2nd ed. Chicago: Chicago University Press, 1998.

Aristotle. *The Basic Works of Aristotle*. Edited by Richard McKeon. Reprint ed. New York: Modern Library, 2001.

————. *Nichomachean Ethics* (*NE*). Volume XIX. Loeb Classical Library. Cambridge: Harvard University Press, 1926.

Augustine. *Confessions*. Translated by F. J. Sheed. 2nd ed. Indianapolis: Hackett, 2006.

Bacon, Francis. *The Essays*. New York: Pauper, n.d.

Balthasar, Hans Urs von. *The Glory of the Lord*. Volume I: *Seeing the Form*. San Francisco: Ignatius, 1982.

———. *The Glory of the Lord*. Volume 5: *The Realm of Metaphysics in the Modern Age*. San Francisco: Ignatius, 1991.

———. *The Grain of Wheat*. San Francisco: Ignatius, 1995.

———. *Herrlichkeit*, Volume III/1. 3rd ed. Freiburg: Verlag-Einsiedeln, 2009.

———. "The Mass, A Sacrifice of the Church?" In *Explorations in Theology*. Vol. III: *Creator Spirit*, 185–244. San Francisco: Ignatius, 1993.

———. "On the Tasks of Catholic Philosophy in Our Time." *Communio* 20.1 (1993) 147–87.

———. *Theologic I: The Truth of the World*. San Francisco: Ignatius, 2000.

———. *Theologic III*. San Francisco: Ignatius, 2005.

Baumgarten, Alexander Gottlieb. *Aesthetica*. Hildesheim, Germany: Impens. I.C. Kleyb, 1750.

Benedict XVI (Joseph Ratzinger). *Called to Communion: Understanding the Church Today*. 3rd ed. San Francisco: Ignatius, 1996.

———. "Faith, Reason and the University: Memories and Reflections." 12 September 2006. Available at https://w2.vatican.va/content/benedict-xvi/en/speeches/2006/september/documents/hf_ben-xvi_spe_20060912_university-regensburg.html.

———. *God Is Love: Deus Caritas Est, Encyclical Letter*. Washington, DC: United States Conference of Catholic Bishops, 2006.

Benjamin, Walter. *The Work of Art in the Age of Mechanical Reproduction*. New York: Penguin, 2008.

Berry, Wendell. *Jayber Crow*. Washington, DC: Counterpoint, 2000.

Borgmann, Albert. *Holding onto Reality: The Nature of Information at the Turn of the Millennium*. Chicago: University of Chicago Press, 1999.

———. *Technology and the Character of Contemporary Life: A Philosophical Inquiry*. Chicago: University of Chicago Press, 1984.

Carr, Nicholas. *The Glass Cage: How Our Computers Are Changing Us*. New York: Norton, 2014.

Chesterton, G. K. *Heretics*. 6th ed. Norwood, MA: Plimpton, 1905.

Clarke, W. Norris. "Forward." In *An Introduction to the Metaphysics of St. Thomas Aquinas*, edited by James Anderson. Washington, D.C.: Regnery Gateway, 1997.

Claudel, Paul. *La Ville*. Paris: Librairie de l'Art indépendent, 1893.

Congar, Yves Marie-Joseph, O.P. *Lay People in the Church*. Translated by Donald Attwater. Rev. ed. Westminster, MD: Newman, 1965.

Cory, Therese. "Knowing as Being? A Metaphysical Reading of the Identity of Intellect and Intelligible in Aquinas." *American Catholic Philosophical Quarterly* 91 (2017) 333–51.

Dawkins, Richard. *The Selfish Gene*. Oxford: Oxford University Press, 2006.

Descartes, René. *Passions of the Soul*. Translated by S. Voss. Indianapolis: Hackett, 1989.

Desmond, William. *The Intimate Strangeness of Being*. Washington, DC: Catholic University of America Press, 2012.

Diels, Hermann, and Walter Kranz. *Die Fragmente der Vorsokratiker*. 5th ed. Berlin: Weidmann, 1935.

Dionsyius. *The Divine Names and the Mystical Theology*. Translated by C. E. Rolt. Mineola, NY: Dover, 2004.

Eliot, T. S. *The Rock: A Pageant Play*. New York: Harcourt and Brace, 1934.

Floridi, Luciano. "The Informational Nature of Personal Identity." *Minds and Machines* 21.4 (2011) 549–66.

———. "Is Information Meaningful Data?" *Philosophy and Phenomenological Research* 70.2 (2005) 351–70.

Franzen, Jonathan. *Freedom*. New York: Picador, 2011.

———. "Pain Won't Kill You." In *Farther Away: Essays*, 5–14. New York: Picador, 2013. (Originally published as "Liking Is for Cowards: Go for What Hurts." *New York Times*, May 29, 2011, page WK10.)

Gadamer, Hans Georg. "Being Spirit God." In *Heidegger's Ways*, 181–95. Albany, NY: SUNY Press, 1994.

———. *Truth and Method*. 2nd ed. New York: Continuum, 2002.

Gleick, James. *The Information: A History, a Theory, a Flood*. New York: Vintage, 2012.

Grant, George. *Technology and Justice*. Concord, ON: Anansi, 1986.

Grene, Marjorie. "Hobbes and the Modern Mind: An Introduction." In *The Anatomy of Knowledge: Papers Presented to the Study Group on Foundations of Cultural Unity*, edited by Marjorie Grene, 4–12. Amherst, MA: University of Massachusetts Press, 1969.

Hanby, Michael. *No God, No Science? Theology, Cosmology, Biology*. Oxford: Wiley-Blackwell, 2013.

Hegel, Georg Wilhelm Friedrich. *On Art, Religion, and the History of Philosophy: Introductory Lectures*. Edited by J. G. Gray. Indianapolis: Hackett, 1997.

———. *Phenomenology of Spirit*. Translated by A. V. Miller. Oxford: Oxford University Press, 1977.

Heidegger, Martin. *Being and Time*. Translated by Joan Stambaugh. Revised by Dennis Schmidt. Albany, NY: SUNY Press, 2010.

———. *Identity and Difference*. Translated by Joan Stambaugh. Chicago: University of Chicago Press, 2002.

———. "The Origin of the Work of Art." In *Basic Writings*, 139–211. New York: Harper, 2008.

———. "The Question Concerning Technology." In *Basic Writings*, 307–41. New York: Harper, 2008.

———. "What Is That—Philosophy?" Translated by Eva T. H. Braun. Annapolis, MD: St. John's College, 1991.

Hildebrand, Dietrich von. "Beauty in the Light of the Redemption." *Logos: A Journal of Catholic Thought and Culture* 4.2 (2001) 78–92.

Hobbes, Thomas. *Leviathan*. New York: Penguin, 1985.

Hume, David. *An Enquiry concerning Human Understanding*. Indianapolis: Hackett, 1997.

———. "Of the Standard of Taste." In *Moral Philosophy*, edited by G. Sayre-McCord, 345–60. Indianapolis: Hackett, 2006.

———. *A Treatise of Human Nature*. 2nd ed. Edited by P. H. Nidditch. Oxford: Clarendon, 1978.

Hutcheson, Frances. *An Inquiry into the Original of Our Ideas of Beauty and Virtue*. Indianapolis: Liberty Fund, 2004.

Jefferson, Thomas. *The Writings of Thomas Jefferson*. Edited by Paul Leicester Ford. New York: Putnam's Sons, 1892–90.

John Paul II (Karol Wojtyła). *Address to the Roman Rota*, 1 February 2001. Available at https://w2.vatican.va/content/john-paul-ii/en/speeches/2001/february/documents/hf_jp-ii_spe_20010201_rota-romana.html.

————. *Love and Responsibility*. Boston: Daughters of St. Paul, 2013.

————. *Man and Woman He Created Them*. Boston: Pauline Books, 2006.

————. "A Meditation on Givenness." *Communio* 41.4 (2014) 871–83.

Kant, Immanuel. *Critique of Judgment*. Translated by Werner Pluhar. Indianapolis: Hackett, 1987.

————. *Critique of Pure Reason*. Translated by Paul Guyer and Allen Wood. Cambridge: Cambridge University Press, 1999.

————. *Metaphysics of Morals*. Cambridge: Cambridge University Press, 1996.

Kierkegaard, Søren. *Works of Love*. Translated by Howard Hong. New York: Harper Torchbooks, 1962.

Kimbriel, Samuel. *Friendship as Sacred Knowing: Overcoming Isolation*. Oxford: Oxford University Press, 2014.

Kovach, Francis. *Die Ästhetik des Thomas von Aquin: Eine genetische und systematische Analyse*. Berlin: de Gruyter, 1964.

Leo XIII. *Arcanum Divina*. Papal Encyclical Letter, 1880. Available at http://w2.vatican.va/content/leo-xiii/en/encyclicals/documents/hf_l-xiii_enc_10021880_arcanum.html

Lewis, C. S. *Till We Have Faces*. New York: Harcourt, 1956.

Locke, John. *An Essay concerning Human Understanding*. Edited by Alexander Fraser. New York: Dover, 1959.

Lopez, Fr. Antonio. *Gift and the Unity of Being*. Veritas. Eugene, OR: Cascade, 2014.

Lyotard, Jean-François. *Lessons on the Analytic of the Sublime*. Stanford, CA: Stanford University Press, 1994.

Marion, Jean-Luc. *The Erotic Phenomenon*. Chicago: University of Chicago Press, 2007.

————. *God without Being*. Chicago: University of Chicago Press, 1991.

Maurer, Armand. *The Philosophy of William of Ockham in the Light of Its Principles*. Toronto: Pontifical Institute of Medieval Studies, 1999.

Meek, Esther Lightcap. *Contact with Reality: Michael Polanyi's Realism and Why It Matters*. Eugene, OR: Cascade, 2017.

————. *Loving to Know: Introducing Covenant Epistemology*. Eugene, OR: Cascade, 2011.

Montaigne, Michel de. *Essays*. Philadelphia: Amies, 1879.

Montessori, Maria. *The Child in the Family*. New York: Discus, 1970.

————. *Spontaneous Activity in Education*. New York: Schocken, 1965.

Murdoch, Iris. "The Sublime and the Good." In *Existentialists and Mystics*, 205–20. New York: Penguin, 1997.

Nietzsche, Friedrich. *The Gay Science*. Translated by W. Kaufmann. New York: Vintage, 1974.

Nygren, Anders. *Agape and Eros*. Philadelphia: Westminster, 1953.

Oster, Stefan. "Thinking Love at the Heart of Things: The Metaphysics of Being as Love in the Work of Ferdinand Ulrich." *Communio* 37.4 (2010) 660–700.

Ouellet, Marc. "Paradox and/or Supernatural Existential." *Communio* 18.2 (1991) 259–80.

Péguy, Charles. "L'Argent." In *Oeuvres en proses complètes*. Vol. III. Paris: Gallimard, 1992.

———. *The Portal of the Mystery of Hope*. Grand Rapids: Eerdmans, 1996.

Pieper, Josef. *Faith–Hope–Love*. San Francisco: Ignatius, 1997.

Plato. *The Complete Works of Plato*. Edited by John Cooper. Indianapolis: Hackett, 1997.

Plotinus. *Enneads*. 7 vols. Loeb Classical Library. Cambridge: Harvard University Press, 1966, 1967, 1968, 1984, 1988.

Polanyi, Michael. "Faith and Reason." *Journal of Religion* 41.4 (1961) 237–47.

———. *Personal Knowledge: Toward a Post-Critical Philosophy*. Chicago: University of Chicago Press, 1974.

———. *Tacit Dimension*. Rev. ed. Chicago: University of Chicago Press, 2009.

Pollan, Michael. *The Omnivore's Dilemma*. New York: Penguin, 2006.

———. "Unhappy Meals." *New York Times Magazine*, 28 January 2007.

Portmann, Adolph. *Animal Forms and Patterns: A Study of the Appearance of Animals*. New York: Schocken, 1967.

Rilke, Rainer Maria. *Letters to a Young Poet*. In *Selected Letters 1902–1926*. New York: Quartet, 1988.

Rousseau, Jean-Jacques. *Confessions*. New York: Penguin, 1953.

———. *La Nouvelle Héloïse*. Translated by Judith McDowell. University Park, PA: Penn State University Press, 1990.

Scheler, Max. "Love and Knowledge." In *On Feeling, Knowing, and Valuing*, 147–65. Chicago: University of Chicago Press, 1992.

———. *Ressentiment*. Milwaukee, MI: Marquette University Press, 2010.

Schelling, Friedrich Wilhelm Joseph. *Philosophical Inquiries into the Nature of Human Freedom*. La Salle, IL: Open Court, 1936.

———. *System of Transcendental Idealism (1800)*. Translated by P. Heath. Charlottesville, VA: University of Virginia Press, 1978.

Schiller, Friedrich. "Kallias or Concerning Beauty: Letters to Gottfried Körner." In *Classic and Romantic German Aesthetics*, edited by J. M. Bernstein, 145–83. Cambridge: Cambridge University Press, 2003.

———. *On the Aesthetic Education of Man*. Translated by R. Snell. Mineola, NY: Dover, 2004.

Schindler, D. C. "Beauty and the Holiness of Mind." In *Being Holy in the World: Theology and Culture in the Thought of David L. Schindler*, edited by Nicholas J. Healy and D. C. Schindler, 2–29. Grand Rapids: Eerdmans, 2011.

———. *The Catholicity of Reason*. Grand Rapids: Eerdmans, 2013.

———. "The Crisis of Marriage as a Crisis of Meaning: On the Sterility of the Modern Will." *Communio* 41.2 (2014) 331–71.

———. "Disclosing Beauty: On Order and Disorder in Plato's *Symposium*." In *Beauty and Goodness in Ancient and Medieval Philosophy*, edited by Alice Ramos. Washington, DC: Catholic University of America Press, forthcoming.

———. *Freedom from Reality: On the Diabolical Character of Modern Liberty*. Notre Dame, IN: University of Notre Dame Press, 2017.

———. "The Loss of Beauty and the De-Naturing of Faith." In *The Beauty of God's House: Essays in Honor of Stratford Caldecott*, edited by Francesca Murphy, 36–62. Eugene, OR: Cascade, 2014.

———. *Plato's Critique of Impure Reason: On Goodness and Truth in the* Republic. Washington, DC: Catholic University of America Press, 2008.

Schindler, David L. "America's Technological Ontology and the Gift of the Given: Benedict XVI on the Cultural Significance of the *Quaerere Deum.*" *Communio* 38.2 (2011) 237–78.

———. "Being, Gift, Self-Gift: Reply to Waldstein on Relationality and John Paul II's Theology of the Body." Parts 1 and 2. *Communio* 42.2 (2015) 221–51 and 42.4 (2015) 409–83.

———. *Ordering Love: Liberal Societies and the Memory of God.* Grand Rapids: Eerdmans, 2011.

Schmitz, Kenneth. *The Gift: Creation.* Milwaukee, WI: Marquette University Press, 1982.

Scruton, Roger. *The Soul of the World.* Princeton, NJ: Princeton University Press, 2014.

Sherwin, Fr. Michael, OP. *By Knowledge and By Love: Charity and Knowledge in the Moral Theology of St. Thomas Aquinas.* Washington, DC: The Catholic University of America Press, 2011.

Shipley, Joseph T. *The Origins of English Words.* Baltimore, MD: Johns Hopkins University Press, 1984.

Siewerth, Gustav. *Der Mensch und sein Leib.* Einsiedeln, Switzerland: Johannes Verlag, 1954.

Smith, Christian, and Melinda Lundquist Denton. *Soul Searching: The Religious and Spiritual Lives of American Teenagers.* Oxford: Oxford University Press, 2005.

Sokolowski, Robert. *God of Faith and Reason: Foundations of Christian Theology.* Washington, DC: Catholic University of America Press, 1995.

———. *An Introduction to Phenomenology.* Cambridge: Cambridge University Press, 2001.

Spaemann, Robert. *Happiness and Benevolence.* Notre Dame, IN: University of Notre Dame Press, 2000.

———. "Nature." In *Philosophical Essays on Nature, God, and the Human Person: A Robert Spaemann Reader,* edited by Jeanne Heffernan Schindler and D. C. Schindler, 22–36. Oxford: Oxford University Press, 2015.

———. "In Defense of Anthropomorphism." In *Philosophical Essays on Nature, God, and the Human Person: A Robert Spaemann Reader,* edited by Jeanne Heffernan Schindler and D. C. Schindler, 77–96. Oxford: Oxford University Press, 2015.

———. *Philosophical Essays on Nature, God, and the Human Person: A Robert Spaemann Reader.* Edited by Jeanne Heffernan Schindler and D. C. Schindler. Oxford: Oxford University Press, 2015.

———. "What Does It Mean to Say That 'Art Imitates Nature'?" In *Philosophical Essays on Nature, God, and the Human Person: A Robert Spaemann Reader,* edited by Jeanne Heffernan Schindler and D. C. Schindler, 192–210. Oxford: Oxford University Press, 2015.

Steiner, Steiner. *Real Presences.* Chicago: University of Chicago Press, 1989.

Strauss, Leo. "Reason and Revelation." In *Leo Strauss and the Theologico-Political Problem,* edited by Heinrich Meier, 141–80. Cambridge: Cambridge University Press, 2006.

Taylor, Charles. *A Secular Age.* Cambridge: Harvard University Press, 2007.

Ulrich, Ferdinand. *Gabe und Vergebung: Ein Beitrag zur biblischen Ontologie.* Freiburg: Johannes Verlag Einsiedeln, 2006.

———. *Homo Abyssus: Das Wagnis der Seinsfrage.* 2nd ed. Freiburg: Johannes Verlag Einsiedeln, 1998.

————. *Der Tod in Erkenntnis und Liebe (Ein Fragment)*. In *Leben in der Einheit von Leben und Tod*, 147–99. Freiburg: Johannes Verlag Einsiedeln, 1999.

Vattimo, Gianni. *Nihilism and Emancipation: Ethics, Politics, and Law*. New York: Columbia, 2004.

Veatch, Henry. *Two Logics: The Conflict between Classical and Neo-Analytic Philosophy*. Evanston, IL: Northwestern University Press, 1969.

Vonnegut, Kurt. *Mother Night*. New York: Dial, 2009.

Walker, Adrian. "Personal Singularity and the Communio Personarum: A Creative Development of Thomas Aquinas's Doctrine of *Esse Commune*." *Communio* 31.3 (2004) 457–79.

Wallace, David Foster. *Infinite Jest*. New York: Back Bay, 2006.

————. *This is Water*. New York: Little, Brown and Company, 2009.

Waugh, Alexander. *God*. New York: St. Martin's, 2002.

Webster, Gerry, and Brian Goodwin. *Form and Transformation*. Cambridge: Cambridge University Press, 1996.

Westphal, Merold. *Overcoming Ontotheology: Toward a Postmodern Christian Faith*. New York: Fordham University Press, 2001.

Wirzba, Norman. *From Nature to Creation: A Christian Vision for Understanding and Loving Our World*. Grand Rapids: Baker Academic, 2015.

Wittgenstein, Ludwig. *Tractatus Logico-Philosophicus*. Mineola, NY: Dover, 1998.

Index

CPSIA information can be obtained
at www.ICGtesting.com
Printed in the USA
BVHW031135080519
547716BV00008B/146/P

9 781532 648748